PATTERN FOR LIFE
THE TEN COMMANDMENTS

Pattern
for
Life

Norman Shields

 EVANGELICAL PRESS

EVANGELICAL PRESS

16/18 High Street, Welwyn, Hertfordshire, AL6 9EQ, England

© Evangelical Press 1983

First published 1983

ISBN 0 85234 166 0

Unless otherwise stated, Bible quotations are from the
New International Version.

Typeset in Great Britain by Inset, Hertford Heath

Printed in the U.S.A.

Contents

Preface

Some twenty years ago I produced a series of teaching sermons on the ten commandments. The purpose was to show the relevance of God's law to life in West Africa, where I was then working as a missionary.

More recently, in the 1970s, I was privileged to write a series of articles on the commandments for the *Irish Baptist,* the monthly magazine of Baptists in Ireland. That series ran for five years and, though completely rewritten and considerably pruned, it forms the basis of the material now made available in this book.

The ten commandments wonderfully cover the whole range of human activity. They have been terribly neglected by Christendom and often, alas, by those who claim complete commitment to the authority of the Scriptures. In the early part of this century many apparently well-intentioned evangelicals were guilty of this neglect. Happily, however, Bible teachers have become aware of this defect and are now seeking to give God's law a stronger emphasis in their preaching and writing.

Without knowledge of God's law, without vision of God's requirements, people cast off restraint. Now, in the late twentieth century, we are reaping in many parts of the world the fruit — the overripe fruit of lawlessness and anarchy that result. My prayer is that this book, despite its many inadequacies, will in some measure help readers to have a truly biblical view of the ten commandments and a truly Christian submission to them.

I must acknowledge my gratitude to the readers of the *Irish Baptist* for their patience and encouragement while the original series of articles was being published. It was some of them who urged me very strongly to try to have the material

1

put into more permanent form. I must also thank my wife, Joan, and our family for their patience when, over a number of years, the writing of the articles, and more recently of the book, kept me for many hours away from them ensconced in what they call 'the crow's nest' — my roofspace study!

This is not intended as a work of scholarship, and so the sources on which I have drawn are not acknowledged by appropriate references. Nevertheless, there were undoubtedly sources and little, if any, of the material is really original. To identify those whose ideas have become my own would now be impossible. Certainly my tutors at London Bible College had a formative influence on my thinking and I am greatly indebted to them for the tuition I received. During the writing of the articles for the *Irish Baptist* I made frequent use of Anthony Philipps' book, *Ancient Israel's Criminal Law* (Oxford, 1970) and I am sure that some of his insights come through in the succeeding pages.

My warmest thanks go to Miss Gretta Totten who painstakingly typed and retyped the manuscript. She often had to decipher handwriting that bordered on the illegible, but was always helpful as well as efficient.

For those who may wish to engage in additional reading on the ten commandments the following titles may be noted. All except that by Rushdoony are written in a popular style and are available as paperbacks.

Rushdoony, R. J., *The Institutes of Biblical Law,* Presbyterian and Reformed Publishing Company, U.S.A., 890 pp. hardback.
Watson, T., *The Ten Commandments,* Banner of Truth Trust.
Eddison, J., *God's Frontiers,* Scripture Union.
Prime, D., *Bible Guidelines,* Hodder and Stoughton.
Catherwood, F., *First Things First,* Lion Publishing.

1. To set the scene — I
Old Testament background

There was a time, and that not so long ago, when one could assume that almost everyone who attended church would know the ten commandments off by heart. They would also, it could be assumed, understand the application of those commandments to everyday life. But this is not the case today and the commandments are, in fact, terribly neglected. Before looking at each in some detail it seems necessary to look at some aspects of the background to, and significance of the commandments in order to set the scene for what is to follow.

The decalogue, as the ten commandments are sometimes called, was given to ancient Israel on an occasion of great solemnity. Israel had come to Mount Sinai, where God spoke to Moses and told him that he would meet with him three days afterwards. Meantime, Moses was to sanctify the people so that they would be ready for the special visitation. The whole mountain was declared sacred and no one was to be permitted to come within special bounds that were to be set around it.

On the third day there were thunders and lightnings and a thick cloud descended on the mountain. There were trumpetings so loud that the people in the camp below trembled. The mountain was encompassed in fire and quaked greatly. After a long period during which the trumpeting grew louder and louder, Moses spoke with the Lord, who answered by calling him up to the top of the mountain.

At this point Moses was charged to go back down to the people and to warn them that they must not break through the bounds which had been set lest 'the Lord break out against them'. At the same time Moses was told to bring his brother Aaron up the mountain with him. Then came the giving of the law in ten maxims which could easily be remembered and which were so simple, so crystal clear, that none could avoid their import.

'You shall have no other gods before me.'
'You shall not make for yourself an idol . . .'
'You shall not misuse the name of the Lord your God . . .'
'Remember the Sabbath day by keeping it holy . . .'
'Honour your father and your mother . . .'
'You shall not murder.'
'You shall not commit adultery.'
'You shall not steal.'
'You shall not give false testimony . . .'
'You shall not covet . . .'

A code for the redeemed
The Israelites were God's chosen people. They were the inheritors of a special covenant relationship granted to Abraham and his descendants. Under the terms of this covenant God pledged himself to give them the land of Canaan and to be himself their God (Genesis 17:8). For many years, however, they had lived in Egypt, where they were under alien control and were unable to enjoy the land promised to them.

Now at Sinai the bondage of Egypt was over. God had brought them through the Red Sea and into freedom. They had been redeemed and were on the way to Canaan to repossess the land, to enter into the inheritance covenanted to them through Abraham.

Before the commandments were given Moses was told to remind Israel of the position in which they now stood as God's redeemed people. He had brought them out of Egypt so that they might be in his presence, separated to, and in fellowship with himself. In this covenant relationship they had an obligation to observe the conditions of the covenant and only by doing so would they enjoy its privileges: 'If you obey me fully and keep my covenant, then out of all nations you will be my treasured possession . . . you will be for me a kingdom of priests and a holy nation' (Exodus 19:5–6).

The point was that now, able by redemption to enjoy

anew the blessing of the inheritance covenanted to them, God's people must accept and fulfil the obligations resting on them. They were to live according to the stipulations of the covenant, being loyal to the Lord in every way possible. Clearly the people knew that this loyalty involved a way of life appropriate to, and distinctive of God's people, because they responded with a firm and unequivocal, 'We will do everything the Lord has said' (Exodus 19:8).

When this general acceptance of God's way was given, the solemn ceremony of lawgiving went ahead. Thunder and lightning, trumpet and smoke marked the occasion and symbolized God's presence. Then came the decalogue, or ten words, as the commandments are sometimes called, and again a reminder of God's redeeming act: 'I am the Lord your God, who brought you out of Egypt, out of the land of slavery' (Exodus 20:2). This made God's redemptive act the basis of the spiritual and moral demands in the commands that follow. Those commands were thus given as a code of conduct for a redeemed people and show how those who belong to God, who have been purchased as his own, must live. No lower standard was, or ever could be, appropriate.

The preamble just quoted, 'I am the Lord your God, who brought you out of Egypt, out of the land of slavery,' takes Israel's relationship to the Lord back even further – to the covenant with Abraham and to God's pledge to be the God not just of the patriarch, but also of his descendants. It was not by a stranger, not by a god hitherto unknown to Israel, but by the Maker of the covenant, Israel's very own and only God, that the ten words were given.

In ancient covenant records the covenanting party or parties began with self-identification. So here Israel's God, reaffirming his covenant and introducing a new phase in its administration, identifies himself by affirming his name: 'I am the Lord.' Unfortunately we cannot be precise about the pronunciation of this name because Jewish reverence for it became so exaggerated that the vowels of a somewhat synonymous word meaning 'Lord' were uniformly substituted for its own vowels. There are four consonants which can be written JHVH or YHWH. The traditional 'Jehovah' is JHVH with the vowels 'e', 'o' and 'a' substituted for the

original ones by later Judaism. It is now generally thought
that *Yahweh* is nearer to the original, but to avoid confusion
it is proposed in these studies to use as far as possible the
translation 'the Lord' as in most English Bibles.

What is much more important is the significance of the
name. It means something like 'I am who I am' or 'I will be
what I will be' (cf. Exodus 3:14) and stresses God's real
and abiding existence and life. He is the living, the eternal
God and, as such, he had come into covenant with Abraham
and now imposed the stipulations of that covenant on his
people. He did so in a thoroughly authoritative stance that
would allow of no argument. He was Lord in every sense
of the word, while his people now redeemed were his vassals
and must keep his commands. Because he was the God of
covenant and because he was their Redeemer, Israel was
obligated to worship him alone, to honour his day, to respect
parents and to love their neighbours as themselves.

Spiritual and moral obligations

It should be clear to all that the commandments are concerned with things spiritual and moral, with man's relationship to God and with his behaviour towards his fellows.
The first three obviously concern themselves with the
spiritual side of life, with the priority of worship and with
its methods. The fourth enjoins a religious observance as an
expression of devotion to the Lord — 'Remember the
Sabbath day by keeping it holy' — and so fits in with those
that precede. But the fourth is expanded and provides for
rest for our fellow men and so also has a manward reference.
The fifth is concerned with parents, and so on the face of it
is manward, but some scholars see parents as mediators of
life and so in direct line between the individual and God.
Such sometimes argue that this command belongs with
those having a God-ward reference, but it can be suspected
that, in some instances at least, the real motive is to make
two equal groups of five. There is no doubt whatever that
the fifth imposes an obligation to other human beings and
that it must therefore be seen as joining with numbers six
to ten, where the thrust is moral and the concern is with
how a man treats his fellows.

Throughout the decalogue, however, the overriding

responsibility is God-ward. Whether it is a matter of worshipping him alone, of honouring parents or of avoiding covetousness, the command is God's and a breach is an offence against him, even where it is primarily an offence against a fellow man. This is made absolutely clear by the prologue, in which God puts the whole authority of his sovereign person behind the commandments: 'I am the Lord your God . . . you shall . . . you shall . . .' etc. Spirituality and morality are not, therefore, to be separated. They belong together. If a man would be right with God, spiritually right, he must also be right with his fellow men. If he is not right with his fellows, morally right, he is not and cannot be right with God because, by the very fact of offending someone else, he offends God.

Relation to civil and ceremonial laws
For much of the Old Testament era Israel was a theocracy, a state ruled by God. Its civil law takes up a great deal of space in the Pentateuch and gives constant expression to the spiritual and moral obligations contained in the decalogue. However, with the exile to Babylon in 586 B.C., the theocratic state came to an end and the Jews who returned in and after 539 B.C. were very much under the control of foreign overlords — Persian, Greek and ultimately Roman. Mostly they had considerable local autonomy and were able to manage their affairs according to their own traditions. No doubt they aimed at a good measure of theocratic rule, or thought they were doing so, but things were inevitably different. In Roman times, for example, they did not have the authority necessary to inflict the death penalty and so could not put our Lord to death but had to persuade the Romans to do so. Thus the civil laws of the Pentateuch could no longer operate and it is important to realize that when our Lord came into that very situation he concentrated on the spiritual and moral aspects of life. The kingdom he came to establish was not of this world, not ethnic and not geographical, and he did not therefore need to enact civil laws. What he did do was to teach a morality which would govern his followers' relationships, not only with each other, but with all their fellows and thus the state or community concerned: 'Give to Caesar what is Caesar's and to God what is God's' (Mark 12:17).

In any study of the ten commandments it must always be remembered that they are spiritual and moral rather than civil laws. This is not to say that there is no relationship between them and civil law. Indeed, there is every reason why a community should follow the example of ancient Israel and base its laws on the principles enshrined in the commandments. In fact, to some degree the laws of many states do just that — something for which we should be profoundly thankful. However, we must see the commandments for what they are: a code of conduct for the redeemed people of God, Israel in the first instance but, as will become evident presently, the members of Christ's kingdom also.

There is in the Old Testament yet another group of laws, the ceremonial, which relate to a worshipper's approach to God in the sanctuary. These laws indicate a variety of conditions which could deprive an Israelite of *ritual* purity and so of the status which entitled him to meet an all-holy God in the fellowship of the sanctuary. The disability so incurred was only removed by following appropriate 'atonement' rituals which, as the Epistle to the Hebrews tells us, illustrate the much greater and much more important atonement made by Christ. They were imposed, the same Epistle makes clear, only for the Old Testament era, 'until the time of the new order' (Hebrews 9:10). With the work of Christ the new covenant was initiated, the time of reformation had come and the laws of ritual purity had fulfilled the purpose for which they were given. They can never again be an essential part of the soul's relationship with God.

In one sense, therefore, we can forget about the ceremonial laws but in another we cannot do so. This is because the Jews of our Lord's day still observed them, or adaptations of them, and used the term 'law' to include everything they regarded as an essential observance. The New Testament records discussions between our Lord and the Jewish teachers of his day, and between the apostle Paul and those who wished to impose Jewish ways on Gentile believers, and in these passages the word 'law' can be used in more than one sense — in the purely spiritual and moral sense, or in the ceremonial, or both. Indeed it can also include Jewish civil law or have the wide general connotation of 'instruction'. This means that when we meet the word we must always seek as best we can to discover precisely what body of law is being mentioned.

We will return to some of the misunderstandings which have arisen presently but it needs to be understood just now that the ceremonial laws of the Old Testament and the adaptations of them in later Judaism are to be distinguished from the ten commandments. The ceremonial laws have had their day and have ceased to have relevance, but the spiritual and moral laws of the decalogue are of a different order. As we shall see, they are endorsed by our Lord and the apostles and are of abiding validity.

Negative format: positive duties

The commandments, with the exception of the fourth and fifth, are presented in a negative form: 'You shall not . . .' This has sometimes been regarded as a weakness by critics who assert that positive injunctions would be much superior.

In actual fact, as we shall see again and again, these commandments are not simple prohibitions, not purely negative. Each carries a clear positive implication which will be discussed in the expositions that follow. In the case of the first three this concerns man's worship of and devotion to God. Firstly, God is to be worshipped with individual devotion. Secondly, God is to be worshipped as spirit (incapable of material representation) and thirdly, his name may be used by his people, but not in an empty way.

In the case of the second five commandments, each prohibition bestows an inalienable right on every human being and in so doing imposes positive duties. The prohibition on killing confers the right to life, that on adultery confers the right to a stable marriage, that on stealing the right to own property. In forbidding false witness the right of the individual to his reputation, and thus to justice, is asserted. The tenth word, 'You shall not covet', gives to each man protection from the schemings that give rise to murder, adultery, theft and false witness.

The idea that the decalogue is weak because of its negative format is thoroughly misleading and must be rejected. It is rather a positive, a wholesome, a superb charter for man in his relationship to God and to his fellow men. 'The law', says Paul, 'is holy, and the commandment is holy, righteous and good' (Romans 7:12; cf 1 Timothy 1:8).

A universally binding standard

Our discussions so far have focused on the ten commandments as a code of conduct for God's covenant people,
Israel. We must enquire, however, if these laws had a wider
application.

The Old Testament clearly shows that in pre-patriarchal
times, that is before God's covenant with Abraham, there
was some knowledge of the spiritual and moral absolutes
enshrined in the decalogue, even if the ten pithy pronouncements had not themselves been formulated. For example, in
yielding to the temptation to eat forbidden fruit, Adam and
Eve gave allegiance to a rival spirit and were thus in some
way recognizing another god and violating the first commandment. The story recording Cain's murder of his brother
Abel (Genesis 4:8–16) reflects the divine disapproval of
murder and anticipates the sixth commandment. The sanctity
of human life is likewise asserted in the injunction given to
Noah and his sons: 'Whoever sheds the blood of man, by man
shall his blood be shed; for in the image of God has God
made man' (Genesis 9:6). The sanctity of marriage and therefore opposition to adultery emerges in the story of the
creation of Eve and particularly in the positive affirmation
that husband and wife become one (Genesis 2:24).

In subsequent Old Testament times the main interest is in
God's covenant people Israel, and references to others are
usually concerned with their relations with Israel. There are
oracles pronouncing judgement on a variety of nations which
have somehow trespassed against Israel, and in a number of
cases offences are named which undoubtedly assume that
the moral law had been violated. Nahum, for example,
denounces the ruthless murderings of the Assyrian armies
(Nahum 2:11–12; 3:1–3) and the unmitigated greed, not
only of the armies, but of the merchants who followed in
their wake, stealing the wealth of the conquered (Nahum
2:9; 3:16). Habakkuk taunts the Babylonians for heaping
up what is not their own, for shedding blood, for making
their neighbours a spectacle of shame and for worshipping
idols that in reality are nonentities, 'no-gods' (Habakkuk
2:6–12). The implication of such passages surely is that
these foreign nations somehow ought to have worshipped
God and God alone and somehow ought to have adhered
to his moral laws.

A study of the wisdom of the ancient world shows that pagan peoples were not without moral values that harmonize with those in the decalogue. From Egypt we find this warning against stealing land: 'Do not be greedy after a cubit of land nor encroach on the boundaries of a widow,' and this one against false balances: 'Do not lean on the scales nor falsify the weights nor damage the fractions of the measure.' From Syria we have a proverb to warn against dishonest speech: 'My son, the words of a liar are like fat sparrows and he that is void of understanding eats them.'

The existence of such ideas in pagan cultures is surely evidence of an awareness, far beyond the confines of Israel, of moral values fully in harmony with those of the decalogue. That God's pronouncements of judgement on those nations are often based on their breaches of this morality would surely suggest that in the Old Testament era he regarded the principles enshrined in the decalogue as being of universal authority.

2. To set the scene — II
New Testament background

Jewish perversions

By the time of the Lord Jesus and of his apostles, the Jews had perverted the whole picture by making law-keeping the way of salvation. It was not just the ten commandments that must be kept, but a whole mass of additional laws known as 'the traditions of the elders'. The scribes and Pharisees gave these traditions the same authority as God's law and, indeed, not long after New Testament times, some of the rabbis said it was a more serious thing to break one of these traditions than to break one of the ten commandments! The one, the only thing that mattered was to keep the exact letter of the law. If a man did not kill his neighbour nor steal his neighbour's bullock, if he kept the rules about ceremonial purity, avoiding certain foods, avoiding contact with Gentiles, indulging in the right ablutions and keeping the required feasts, then all would be well with him. That man would have God's acceptance and would in the end be raised to eternal bliss.

The Jews of the day ought to have known better than to allow themselves to fall into a cold legalism which really had no place for personal communion with God or for personal kindness in human relationships. The Pentateuch, on which they claimed to base their entire philosophy of life, contained the two absolutely fundamental divine requirements: 'Love the Lord your God with all your heart and with all your soul and with all your strength' (Deuteronomy 6:5), and 'Love your neighbour as yourself' (Leviticus 19:18). Somehow this emphasis was lost, and for this and other reasons first-century Judaism had ceased to be the religion of the divine revelation through the Old Testament. Again and again, our Lord had to correct the perversions

12

that had arisen and which very often related to the law and its application.

Jesus and the law

Our Lord most emphatically upheld and endorsed the law. 'Do not think', he said, 'that I have come to abolish the Law or the Prophets; I have not come to abolish them but to fulfil them. I tell you the truth, until heaven and earth disappear, not the smallest letter, not the least stroke of a pen, will by any means disappear from the Law until everything is accomplished' (Matthew 5:17–18). Yet he was no mere legalist, demanding adherence for its own sake and unworried about the quality of a man's inward motivation. Quite the reverse was the case. 'The things that come out of the mouth', he said, 'come from the heart, and these' (that is, the things which come from the heart, which motivate action) 'make a man "unclean"' (Matthew 15:18). For our Lord sinfulness arises not in mere failure to conform to law, but in the underlying urges of the inner man which lead to such failure.

Our Lord's endorsement of the law (Matthew 5:17–18) was clearly in terms of the moral law, in essence the ten commandments. At no point did he attempt to reform civil law or even pronounce upon it. He had come rather to infuse moral qualities into men's hearts. He wanted men to accept the rule of God inwardly and thus to rule their lives by true divine law.

In harmony with this our Lord proceeded to draw out the deep inward application of several of the commandments. He put the angry man on a level with the physical murderer, the lustful man on the same moral plane as the actual adulterer. He was saying that outward conformity to law is never sufficient for the children of God's kingdom, who must have an inward righteousness, a purity of heart and of thought and motive which excels the requirements of the scribe and of the Pharisee. In short he affirmed the absolute demands of the decalogue and at the same time made its application to man's inward thoughts and intentions absolutely clear.

It is generally agreed that our Lord was summarizing the requirements of the decalogue when he enunciated what he called the two greatest commandments. He was answering a Pharisaic teacher, an expert in the Jewish law, who asked, 'Teacher, which is the greatest commandment in the Law?' Our Lord replied, ' "Love the Lord your God with all your heart and with all your soul and with all your mind." This is the first and greatest commandment. And the second is like it: "Love your neighbour as yourself." All the Law and the Prophets hang on these two commandments' (Matthew 22:36—40; cf. Mark 12:28—31). The commandments, as we have seen, fall into two groups, the first of which deals with man's relationship to God - no other gods, no idols, etc. — while the remainder deal with man's relationship to his fellows — no murder, no stealing, etc. Summing up each group in a single sentence, our Lord emphasized the important word 'love': 'Love the Lord your God . . .', 'Love your neighbour . . .' Thus he joined together *'love'* and *'law'*. The fulfilling of the law, he affirmed, is through love, love to God and love to other people.

One of our Lord's main pronouncements on the place of the law, that is to say of the spiritual and moral laws given by God, is rarely recognized for what it is. It is in the words of commission spoken to Peter after his confession at Caesarea Philippi and repeated in the context of instruction about how a disciple should deal with a brother who sins against him. Said our Lord, 'Whatever you shall bind on earth shall be a thing having been bound in heaven and whatever you shall loose on earth shall be a thing having been loosed in heaven' (Matthew 16:19; 18:18).

The translation just given will not be found in any of the English versions, though J. B. Phillips comes very near to it: 'Whatever you forbid on earth will be what is forbidden in heaven and whatever you permit on earth will be what is permitted in heaven.' The traditional Catholic interpretation of our Lord's words has been in terms of Peter and those succeeding him having judicial authority to make decisions and laws for the church, and doing so with the assurance that God in heaven would ratify those decisions. Protestants have been divided, some following the Catholic view and others tending to avoid the statement altogether because it seemed to endorse tenets held by Catholicism. In fact, as the translation given above suggests, the Catholic view rests on a mistranslation and the embarrassment of Protestants is quite unnecessary.

The Greek text involves an unusual but straightforward construction. There are two verbs in the future tense: 'Whatever you *shall bind* (*dēsēs*) on earth *shall be* (*estai*)', and a complement made up of a perfect participle passive, meaning literally '*a thing having been bound*' (*dedemenon*) and '*a thing having been loosed*' (*lelumenon*). At the time Jesus spoke, what Peter and his friends and successors in the faith were to do would be in the future, so he used verbs in the future tense. When, however, the time would come to act they would be using something already promulgated and still in force, namely what had been bound or loosed in heaven, hence the perfect participles used to refer to what they were later to bind and loose.[1]

What our Lord said to Peter was that he and those like him commissioned to teach the church were to bind and loose what God had already bound and loosed in heaven. In fact his words amount to a virtual command that this be done. Binding and loosing were terms in common use among the Jews and meant respectively to forbid and to permit. Thus a rabbi who taught that something was 'bound' was insisting that the practice in question was forbidden, and when he said a practice was loosed he meant that there was no prohibition and people were permitted to do it. So our Lord told Peter and later all the disciples that their job was to proclaim the old rules, the rules made in heaven, and not to make new ones as the Pharisees and scribes were doing. The law of God was to be affirmed as part of the Christian message, the gospel, and there were to be no extra prohibitions of any kind.

Christians have often fallen into the error of Pharisaism, of making laws additional to the spiritual and moral absolutes of the ten commandments. The famous Judaizers who came to Antioch (Acts 15:1), insisting that Gentile believers could not be saved unless they became Jews by circumcision and acceptance of the yoke of the law – ceremonial and traditional, as well as spiritual and moral – were an early example. So, too, were those of similar views who troubled the Galatian Christians and those who were outlawing marriage (1 Timothy 4:3) or insisting on vegetarian habits of eating (Romans 14:2).

Our Lord rejected the Pharisaic system lock, stock and

barrel. His instruction was simply that the rules of heaven for earth be proclaimed, that men be told what God the Lord required of them, what he had bound or forbidden, and what he had left loose, unforbidden or permitted. Our Lord was commanding that in matters of culture and custom, as distinct from spirituality, and ethics, as distinct from the ten commandments, there be no distinctively Christian rules whatsoever. Such matters are for the individual conscience to decide in the light of the absolute requirements of God's law that his people love him with their whole being and love their neighbours as themselves.

Law and love

The relation between 'law' and 'love' can only properly be appreciated when we understand the significance of 'love' in Scripture. The New Testament uses words (*agape* and *agapao*) which are very rare anywhere else in Greek literature. They refer to something which can and which has to be willed and not to the kind of interpersonal attraction which we usually call 'love'. These words refer rather to an active personal concern for the well-being of another, to a love that is not mere sentiment but a motivation of the will which produces positive action.

The great example of such love is in God himself. He loved us when our hearts were at enmity against him. He so loved us that 'he gave his one and only Son' (John 3:16). His love was such that he acted for our well-being by giving his Son for us. The Lord Jesus himself was equally motivated by love: 'Greater love', he could say, 'has no one than this, that one lay down his life for his friends' (John 15:13). His love moved him to sacrificial action for our salvation.

Because 'love' in the Bible is a matter of the will, it is something which can be commanded and which can be related to 'law'. 'Love' and 'law' are not, as many have thought, contradictory principles. In the Bible they are complementary; the one completes the other. The absolutes of God's moral law stand unshaken, but they are not to be construed in terms that are external and legalistic. They are to be espoused by the heart and observed through the will as expressions — as *the* expression — of love.

We live in an age which has revolted against law in any

shape or form. The champions of what in the 1960s was called 'the new morality' imbibed this antagonism and, rejecting the whole idea of absolute laws, argued that 'love' is the only absolute. They say that there are no rules which can always be relied upon to direct men as to how they should behave. This is what John A. T. Robinson calls 'a radical "ethic of the situation" with nothing prescribed except love'.[2] For these teachers each person must weigh up the situation in which he or she is and seek to react in a way which demonstrates 'love'. If 'love' dictates adultery or theft, murder or false witness, then those actions would be right in that situation.

There is, of course, value in the emphasis on love as against legalism, but there is also great danger and gross error in the denial of moral absolutes. The 'situation ethic' is, as it says, without rules that can always be relied upon. Its only absolute rule is the rule of love. But if there are no absolute moral values, indeed, as many would say, no transcendent God who sets standards for his creatures, how can anyone, adherent of situation ethics or not, ever know whether or not an attitude or an action is really motivated by love? Behaviour, on this view, becomes in the end a matter of a man's own, or in some cases of society's view of what love is and thus of what is right or wrong, virtuous or sinful. This is simply, as has often been said, a recipe for anarchy, a return to the old immorality with every man doing what is right in his own eyes.

The fact is that human beings need more definite guidance than this. We need a moral law given on the supreme authority of the Almighty to tell us what love really demands. This is indeed what the ten commandments, the basic moral laws of the Bible, provide. They show how a truly loving person will live, how love works. There may not be, indeed there are not, specific commands to cover every conceivable situation, but there are principles in the decalogue which the conscience of one who truly loves God and his neighbour can use to ensure that he acts lovingly in every relationship.

In the Bible, law and love belong together. He who would love God, he who would love his neighbour, will keep God's laws. The Lord Jesus said, 'If you love me, you will obey what I command' (John 14:15). Similarly, the apostle Paul writing to Galatia and arguing for Christian freedom, as against a movement that tried to get Gentile converts to accept law-keeping as essential to salvation, joins love and law together. He urges his readers to serve one another through love and adds, 'The entire law is summed up in a single command, "Love your neighbour as yourself"' (Galatians 5:14). Like Jesus, he used the obligation to love our neighbours as a summary of the ethical or moral section of the decalogue. Love does not neglect those commands. Rather it keeps them, it fulfils them. Love and law belong together.

Law and grace

The Judaism of the first century was, as we have seen already, a very different religion from that of the Old Testament. It had turned from the principle of salvation by faith to one of salvation by works. This was not fully appreciated by some of the early Jewish Christians and as a result controversy arose in the churches at Antioch and in Galatia, where teachers who had come from Jerusalem were saying that faith in Christ was not sufficient to effect salvation. The extra which they wanted from Gentile converts was circumcision, which meant, of course, that those converts would have to become Jews and accept the whole body of Jewish law, traditional as well as biblical.

This was an attempt to mix grace and works, but to the apostle Paul it was a complete negation of the principle of salvation by grace to those who believe. Salvation is either God's free gift, or it is a reward for work or works done, but it cannot be both at the same time. For him a religion of works was a denial of the promises God had made to Abraham, a denial of the Old Testament principle that the just live by faith and a denial of the atoning work of Christ: 'If justification could be gained through the law, Christ died for nothing!' (Galatians 2:21.) The issue was fought out at the council of church leaders held in Jerusalem and described in Acts 15. Paul and his friends won the day and an agreed statement was sent to Antioch apologizing for the disturbance caused by those who had come without authorization to insist on circumcision.

Paul dealt with the matter in more detail in his letter to the Galatians, where he sometimes used the term 'law' to refer to the Jewish idea of meriting salvation by law-keeping; sometimes to refer to the principle of God's rule over Israel in the period between Moses and Christ; and sometimes to the whole Old Testament revelation including the moral law. It is often difficult to be sure which sense is used in a particular instance and this has led to an unfortunate misunderstanding in that some Bible teachers thought Paul was declaring that the ten commandments were no longer binding on God's people. This became a cardinal point with many 'Dispensationalists'. The argument was that the Christian, being under grace rather than law, can in no way be regarded as obligated to keep the commandments. Happily, these views are now very largely abandoned, but their effect in the nineteenth and twentieth centuries has been to produce in many quarters a considerable neglect of a proper teaching of the moral law.

Another cause of antinomianism (rejection of law-observance) has been an unbalanced piety of a mystical hue. Every generation produces its mystics and we owe a great deal to them and to their very direct and immediate sense of fellowship with God. The trouble is that they sometimes become so taken up with their spiritual or mystical experiences that they lose concern for the ordinary business of day-to-day life on earth. They can very easily assume then that rules like the commandments do not really matter very much. Sometimes, alas, good people, highly spiritual people, have been taken off guard and have fallen into serious moral breakdown. Had the law of God been given its proper place, their consciences would have been better educated and better able to apply the brakes that were needed in the moment of crisis.

Paul himself will not in fact allow his readers to think that the true law of God is in any way in opposition to grace. His battle was not to have the decalogue rejected, or even relegated, but to overthrow the influence of a false gospel, a teaching which insisted on adherence to the traditions of the elders as well as to the Old Testament as the way to earn salvation. To safeguard the moral law he asked a rhetorical question: 'Is the law, therefore, opposed to the promises of

God? (Galatians 3:21.) His answer was unequivocal
'Absolutely not!' (Greek, *mē genoito*, 'Let it not be so',
AV, 'God forbid'.) The law, the true law of God, is not
contrary to, or in any way in opposition to grace. It was
rather the current Jewish concept of law-keeping as a way
of meriting God's salvation which was, and is, totally incompatible with the true biblical doctrine of salvation by grace
alone.

Law and the gospel

Since law-observance is not a way of earning salvation, as the
Jews thought it was, we must seek to discover what relation
the ten commandments have to the unconverted world around
us and what place, if any, they can be given in gospel
preaching.

In the first instance we have the fact that our Lord used
the law in his evangelistic preaching. The sermon on the
mount sets out the way in which the law judges men's inner
thoughts and motivation. It requires an inward righteousness,
far more valuable in God's eyes than the outward observances
of the Pharisees, and it applies this evangelistically. The man
who hears and heeds this teaching is the one who builds
safely on solid rock, while the one who hears but fails to
heed builds foolishly on sand. The implication is that anyone
who wants to be a disciple of the Lord Jesus and a citizen
of God's kingdom must commit himself to the kind of life
he had portrayed, a life purified and renewed by an application of the true law of God to his inward thoughts and
motives.

On another occasion Jesus used the commandments more
directly. The Gospels tell us that a young man came asking
what he needed to do in order to inherit eternal life. The
very question reflected, no doubt, the current Jewish belief
that salvation was earned by observance of the whole body
of Jewish law. Our Lord's response was 'Do not murder, do
not commit adultery, do not steal, do not give false testimony, do not defraud, honour your father and mother'
(Mark 10:19; cf. Matthew 19:16–30; Luke 18:18–30).
This cited six of the ten and should, presumably have
brought a confession of failure from the man. In fact it
provoked the opposite reaction: 'All these I have kept since

I was a boy. What do I still lack?' He felt he had kept those laws well enough and wanted some extra thing which would guarantee his position. Our Lord took him up and in a more oblique way brought home to him the fact that, despite his own belief, he was not really living up to God's standard – he was putting his great wealth in the position of supreme importance in his life. That possessions had become a god before the true God is evident from his reluctance to give them up. 'Go, sell everything you have and give to the poor, and you will have treasure in heaven. Then come, follow me.' The things of God must be given first place; he must commit himself to discipleship, whatever the cost, or forego eternal life. Tragically he chose treasure on earth rather than treasure in heaven, but by a clear application of God's law the issues of life and death were brought home to him. Our Lord was using the commandments as an evangelistic tool.

In both of these instances our Lord spoke in a Jewish context to people who would know the ten commandments backwards. Later on, the apostles were sent to areas where they preached to audiences containing both Jew and Gentile. Paul's Epistles were in the main addressed to Christians who came from both backgrounds, and in the one in which he gives his fullest exposition of the doctrines of salvation, the Epistle to the Romans, he shows that while men normally fail to honour God and his truth, the Gentiles can do what God's law requires. In doing so without actually having the law, they show that what the law requires is written on their hearts and is used by their consciences (Romans 2:14–16). This surely testifies to the role of God's law (however received) as a restraining and a convicting agent in human life. If it has such a beneficial effect even where the formulated law is not known, it must surely be of even greater value to those privileged to know it.

At a slightly later stage in his argument Paul shows that though the law cannot effect salvation, it does do two very important things. First of all, he affirms that it pronounces 'the whole world' guilty before God. Thus Gentile as well as Jew come within its scope and will be held accountable for breaking it (Romans 3:10). The judgements pronounced in the Old Testament on Israelite sinners (e.g. those cited in vv. 10–18) apply to Gentiles as well because all men, both

Jews and Greeks, are under the power of sin. Secondly, he tells us that it is through the law that men have the know-ledge of sin (Romans 3:20). He himself would not have known that covetousness was sin had not the law said, 'Do not covet' (Romans 7:7, 8). The law then makes men aware of their sin and is used by the conscience to produce the self-accusation we now call 'conviction of sin'. Without such conviction no true conversion would seem possible, for it is only when we become aware that we have broken God's law, and so offended him, that we have the inclination to repent and with a new mind seek to please him.

It should now be clear that the ten commandments have a continuing, an abiding relevance. They stand as a transcript of God's character telling all his creatures what he is like and what he wants them to be like. Christians, like the Israelites, need them as a prophylactic, a restraining influence, against the inroads of sin. Non-Christians need them to be aware of God's requirements and of their own shortcomings and of their inability to please him. It is only as men wrestle with the law of God till, as Paul says, the commandment kills the proud self that is within every one of us, that we give up the struggle and yield heart and life to the Lord Jesus, the one who alone can deliver from the body of this death, that is, from the hopelessness of con-viction brought about by the due application of law.

The ten commandments are then an essential part of evangelism. Young people need to be instructed in them; older folk need to be reminded of them. As Professor Hallesby says, 'We can never persuade anyone to believe in the Gospel before we, by the grace of God, have helped him to believe in the law of God.'[3] If they are not taught, and taught persistently and widely, the number of true conver-sions to Christ will drop and the future of Christianity will be in jeopardy.

It is the purpose of these studies to focus on the meaning and the application of the commandments in the hope that God's law, given so long ago through Moses, will be more clearly seen and more loyally kept as his Word for today.

[1] See J. B. Phillips, the *New Testament in Modern English,* Note 3; Nigel Turner, *Grammatical Insights into the New Testament,* pp. 80–82.
[2] Robinson, J. A. T., *Honest to God,* p. 116.
[3] Hallesby, O., *Conscience,* London, 1939, p. 94.

3. No other gods
The First Commandment

'You shall have no other gods before me.'

An exclusive relationship is demanded

In making his covenant, God had promised Abraham and his descendants a unique relationship with himself. He would be their God and would give them the land of Canaan for a possession (Genesis 17:7—8). While not specifically denying the existence of other gods, this covenant did require that its Giver be acknowledged and served as God, and as God alone.

When the ten commandments were given some centuries later, Israel had just emerged from a long period of residence in Egypt, where many gods were worshipped. In their more distant background was the fact that Abraham had been called from Mesopotamia, where again there was the worship of many gods. Now they were bound for the land of Canaan whose people also had a multiplicity of gods. As a new phase of the covenant began, God's first stipulation was that his people worship no god other than himself: 'You shall have no other gods before me.'

There is general agreement among scholars that this commandment does not specifically assert that there is only one God. It says simply that Israel was to put no other god or gods before the Lord. In strict theological language it is monolatrous, allowing the worship of only one God, rather than monotheistic, insisting on the existence of only one God. As we examine the command more closely in its context, we find that while the existence of other gods is not denied, the emphasis is such that they cannot be regarded as in any way sharing the glory, the ultimacy, of the Lord.

Men might worship and serve them as 'gods', but they are not and cannot be 'God'.

The phrase 'other gods' (Hebrew, *'elohim 'aherim*) must be understood in relationship with the words of the divine introduction to the entire decalogue, which immediately precede the commandment: 'I am the Lord your God . . .' (Exodus 20:2). The plural Hebrew noun, *'elohim,* translated 'God' in the introduction, is exactly the same as that translated 'gods' in the commandment. Its basic ideas are of power, authority and strength. It could be applied to spirit beings, good or bad, and even to human leaders. Here it is used with two distinct shades of meaning. In the first instance, the introduction of verse 2, it is a plural of intensity stressing ultimacy of power, while in the second, the command of verse 3, it is a normal plural stressing a number above one. In the introduction the Lord asserts that he is Israel's *God*, the one who is thoroughly, intensely, perfectly *God*. He is the ultimate in all that the word *'elohim* stands for, absolutely perfect in every aspect of his being. In the commandment, however, *'elohim* is not used to refer to the Ultimate Reality but to beings which, if they exist at all, must be lesser than he is. If one such existed that shared his perfection, he would have ceased to be ultimate and would be less than worthy of the intensive use of *'elohim*; he would have ceased to be *'God'* and would have become one of many powerful beings or 'gods'.

Men, of course, believed in 'gods and lords many' and we can be quite sure that in Moses' day there were many in Israel who did so. Whatever the degree of reality in these deities, they were conceived as powerful beings and this is why the word *'elohim* was applied to them. Some, like Satan and his minions, were real spirit powers, others may have been figments of the human mind, but that distinction is not made here. Real or imagined, the command required that they be ignored and rejected completely. The covenant people were forbidden to have any other god than the Lord. He required them to have an exclusive relationship with himself. No other deity could legitimately have a place in their affections.

The words 'before me' also call for some comment. The Hebrew is *'al-pani'* which means literally 'before my face'.

Scholars have put a variety of interpretations on it, like 'in addition to', 'in preference to' or 'in opposition to' but the plain implication is surely in terms of 'God's presence'. What is 'before his face' is in his presence. The thought seems to be that God would not tolerate any other deity among people with whom he deigned to dwell. For them to worship or serve another god would be to put that god in front of his face and thus to put their covenant relationship at risk. This is why Joshua presented the issue very clearly after the conquest of Canaan: 'Now fear the Lord and serve him with all faithfulness. Throw away the gods your fathers worshipped beyond the River and in Egypt, and serve the Lord. But if serving the Lord seems undesirable to you, then choose for yourselves this day whom you will serve . . . As for me and my household, we will serve the Lord' (Joshua 24:14—15). It was the Lord or other gods; it could not be both. To choose other gods would be to break covenant. The Israelites were the Lord's people and he was to be exclusively their God. His honour he would not, he could not, share with another.

The exclusive covenant relationship God demanded of his people has close parallels to the marriage covenant which in ancient Israel also required complete and exclusive fidelity, certainly on the part of a wife, who must never form an adulterous relationship with another man. When during the course of history Israel turned to other gods, this in the Lord's eyes was spiritual whoredom, a violation of the covenant, the marriage covenant, that joined him to them. Hosea among the prophets had an unfaithful wife and out of the depths of his own feelings portrays the disappointment of a God let down by those whose loyalty should have been given exclusively to him. Says the Lord, 'I will punish her [Israel] for the days she burned incense to the Baals [Canaanite gods]; she decked herself with rings and jewellery, and went after her lovers, but me she forgot' (Hosea 2:13) and again, 'They are unfaithful to the Lord; they give birth to illegitimate children' (Hosea 5:7).

The same prophet also portrays the restoration of a penitent people to an exclusive relationship with God and for this also used the analogy with marriage: ' "In that day," declares the Lord, "you will call me 'My husband'; . . . I will betroth you to me for ever" ' (Hosea 2:16—19).

The infidelity of Israel
The history of Israel up to the exile in Babylon (586—539
B.C.) was marked by repeated breaches of this commandment. Before his death Joshua elicited the declaration: 'We
will serve the Lord' from a solemn assembly at Shechem.
Before long, however, things went wrong and we read that
the people 'forsook the Lord . . . and served Baal and the
Ashtoreths' (Judges 2:12—13). This happened repeatedly
throughout the period of the judges and was not stamped
out in the days of Samuel (1 Samuel 12:10). Even Solomon
fell into this sin as a result of the influence of his foreign
wives (1 Kings 11:1—8).

In the days of King Ahab and his infamous wife Jezebel,
Syrian and Canaanite Baal worship was very strong in Israel.
At one point the prophet Elijah felt that he alone remained
faithful. He was wrong, of course, for the Lord still had
seven thousand faithful people. The southern kingdom of
Judah was marked by the same delinquency. High places
were built for the worship of Baal and even the reforming
zeal of good kings like Hezekiah and Josiah could not stamp
it out. Ahaz, father of Hezekiah, descended to the point of
sacrificing his sons in the fire to Molech, a Canaanite deity.

The great prophets constantly denounced the unfaithfulness of the covenant people in turning to the Baal cults of
Canaan and Syria. As time went on they had to condemn
another form of worship which came from Mesopotamia.
This was the worship of Ishtar, or Astarte, who was variously
regarded as the goddess of love, of sex, of fertility and of
war. In some places she was regarded as 'queen of heaven',
spouse and consort of the god of heaven. In Jeremiah's time,
around 600 B.C. and just before the exile, she was actually
worshipped in Judah. Jeremiah says, 'The women knead the
dough and make cakes for the Queen of Heaven' (Jeremiah
7:18). Later on, when Jeremiah had been dragged to Egypt
by Jews who had not been taken into exile, his prophecies
were defiantly answered by a group of men and women
who said, 'We will not listen to the message you have spoken
to us . . . We will certainly do everything we said we would:
we will burn incense to the Queen of Heaven and will pour
out drink offerings to her just as we and our fathers, our
kings and our officials did in the towns of Judah and in the

streets of Jerusalem' (Jeremiah 44:16–19; cf. v. 25). The implication is surely that this pagan worship had been very widespread in Judah.

There is good reason to believe that in many cases those concerned added Baal or Molech or Astarte to the worship of the Lord. They did not believe that they were actually abandoning their proper God by the fact of adding another! However, he, like a jealous husband, would not share his glory with another. He would have no other gods before his face.

There is also evidence that sometimes pagan ideas were attached to the worship of the Lord and that for some he was Israel's particular Baal. Even Jonathan named his son Meribaal (1 Chronicles 8:34; 9:40). This in effect degraded the Lord by bringing him down to the level of the gods of the heathen.

It was the intrusion of these cults, together with a great deal of gross social injustice in Israelite life, which lay behind the exile of the Jews in Babylon. The Lord warned his people again and again through the prophets that their country would be overrun and that they would be led away as captives. The northern kingdom, Israel, had fallen to Assyria in 722 B.C. but in Judah reforms by Hezekiah and Josiah and, indeed, that of Manasseh staved off the débâcle for a time. Eventually, however, in 586 B.C. the Jews went to Nebuchadnezzar's Babylon. Not long before this happened Jeremiah put the impending judgement of God in clear perspective:

'Therefore this is what the Lord says . . .
"My people have forgotten me;
    they burn incense to worthless idols,
which made them stumble in their ways
    and in the ancient paths.
They made them walk in bypaths,
    and on roads not built up . . .
Like a wind from the east, I will scatter them
    before their enemies
I will show them my back and not my face
    in the day of their disaster"'
(Jeremiah 18:13–17).

The outward loyalty of Judaism

It has traditionally been believed that the exile purified the
Jews of the sin of apostasy. After the return there was never
again Baal worship or involvement with the cults of the East.
However, this is disputed by those scholars who regard
Isaiah chapters 56—66 as coming from an anonymous
prophet living some seventy to a hundred years after the
return from exile or, as is now more common, in the period
between the return of the first party and the rebuilding of
the temple (539—516 B.C.). Since those chapters refer to
idolatry (e.g. Isaiah 57:7—10; 65:7) they are taken as implying its existence at the time when they were written and
therefore, in the view of the scholars concerned, after the
exile. This, however, is far from proved and it is better to
regard these chapters as coming from the later period in
Isaiah's life when the wicked Manasseh ruled in Judah and
was actively fostering the worship of Baal. Isaiah apart, post-
exilic Old Testament writings like Haggai, Zechariah,
Nehemiah and Malachi condemn many failings in the returning exiles but they do not charge them with worshipping
other gods. Later Judaism fiercely maintained its integrity
on this point and there is no suggestion in the teaching of
our Lord or of the other New Testament writers that the
Jews of the day were engaging in the worship of other gods.
Indeed, the outbreak of the Maccabean revolt in 168 B.C.
was sparked off by Syrian officials attempting to force
Jewish leaders to make sacrifices to Baal-shammayim. One
of the factors in Jewish dislike of Herod the Great was that
he had built a temple at Caesarea for the worship of Caesar.

This is not, of course, to imply that post-exilic Judaism
achieved anything approaching perfect obedience to the
first commandment. The tragedy was that much of the
richness of a personal relationship with the Lord was lost
to a hard legalism which almost put 'the law' in the place
rightly belonging to the Lord. This is one reason why Jesus
found the religion of his day so distasteful, a matter of
keeping the outside of the cup clean and of neglecting the
inner life and its needs for living fellowship with a loving
Father in heaven. It was a religion which claimed to worship
the Lord alone, which excluded other gods and their images,
but which somehow failed to know and therefore to worship

God. It is epitomized in the Pharisee who went to the temple to pray. He addressed his prayers to God but Jesus says, 'he prayed about (literally "to" or "with") himself' (Luke 18:11). His prayers went no higher than the roof; he was talking to himself, inflating his ego and knowing nothing of the essentials of true faith. Another god, self, was before the Lord and despite the outward conformity the commandment was being broken.

New Testament endorsement

Full monotheism
There is no precise citation of the first commandment in the New Testament but this does not for one moment mean that it had ceased to be mandatory. The fact is that our Lord and the apostles thoroughly endorse its spirit and present the one God in such ultimate terms that the worship of every rival is excluded. In the Jewish environment of much of the New Testament the principle of worshipping the one God was accepted and needed no particular affirmation. Where the gospel preachers came in contact with non-Jews the supremacy of God, the Lord, was unequivocally asserted. He is the only true God and he alone should be worshipped.

In the first instance we have our Lord's response to Satan's third temptation: 'Worship the Lord your God, and serve him only.' This cites a passage in Deuteronomy which is really an expansion of our commandment, 'Fear the Lord your God, serve him only, and take your oaths in his name. Do not follow other gods, the gods of the peoples around you; for the Lord your God, who is among you, is a jealous God . . .' (Deuteronomy 6:13–15). By himself refusing to bow down before Satan, our Lord clearly endorsed the first commandment, requiring that the Lord, and the Lord alone, was to be worshipped. The same is true of his answer later on to the lawyer who asked, 'Which is the greatest commandment in the Law?' Again he quoted words from Deuteronomy 6 which also focus on the requirement for single-minded devotion: 'Love the Lord your God with all your heart and with all your soul and with all your mind' (Matthew 22:37; cf. Mark 12:30; Luke 10:27; Deuteronomy

6:5). Obedience to that demand would certainly require an exclusive relationship, one that would admit reverence for no other deity.

The apostle Paul has several passages in which the ultimacy of God, the Lord, is proclaimed. He is the ultimate source of all that exists: 'From him and through him and to him are all things. To him be the glory for ever!' (Romans 11:36); 'Everything comes from God' (1 Corinthians 11:12); 'There is . . . one God and Father of all, who is over all and through all and in all' (Ephesians 4:6).

Clearly Paul's view of God is thoroughly monotheistic. The Lord is uniquely God and has no rival. The issue of other gods comes to the fore through a question raised by the Corinthian church about whether or not a Christian was free to eat meat which had just been consecrated to, and offered as a sacrifice to an idol. Paul stated the Christian position: 'We know that an idol is nothing at all in the world and that there is no God but one. For even if there are so-called gods, whether in heaven or on earth (as indeed there are many "gods" and many "lords"), yet for us there is but one God, the Father, from whom all things came and for whom we live . . .' (1 Corinthians 8:4–6).

This is indeed a full-blooded monotheism which asserts that there is only one real *God* and that every other object of men's worship, real or unreal, is something less than ultimate and less than *God*. That there are objects of worship, many gods and lords, both in heaven and on earth, is recognized. Men may give them loyalty, worship and service. But for the Christian such deities are not to be put on a level with the one God whose supremacy is complete, whose being is unique and whose glory cannot, in the nature of things, be shared.

Anti-materialist theology
The New Testament underlines the demands of our commandment in another way by the strong contrast it draws between God and material wealth. In the sermon on the mount our Lord taught that true discipleship involves a choice to have treasure in heaven rather than in the material things of earth. He told his hearers that wherever their treasure lay, there their heart would be also (Matthew 6:21).

The implication of this, surely, is that the heart devoted to earthly possessions will not be devoted to the things of God, that possessions can take first place in a man's life and in effect become his 'god' or one of his 'gods'. When that happens he worships another god rather than the Lord. It was, no doubt, because of dominance by riches that Jesus challenged one young man to sell all that he had, give the proceeds to the poor and thus have treasure in heaven (Matthew 19:21). That the man concerned had made a god of his possessions is shown by his sorrowful rejection of the demand of Jesus, and by our Lord's comment to the disciples: 'I tell you the truth, it is hard for a rich man to enter the kingdom of heaven . . . it is easier for a camel to go through the eye of a needle than for a rich man to enter the kingdom of God' (Matthew 19:23–24). The point quite simply is that those who put earthly riches before God find themselves barred from entry to God's kingdom. A man can serve God or he can serve money, but he cannot serve both at once. 'You cannot serve both God and money' (Matthew 6:24) is then a specific application of the first commandment, a particular way of saying, 'You shall have no other gods before me.'

The rest of the New Testament maintains this anti-materialist stance. Covetousness, which is usually a desire to get possession of earthly treasure, is called 'idolatry' (Colossians 3:5), showing that when an object of strong desire takes over our affections it takes on the role of an idol, a god, in our lives. Ultimately, of course, the pursuit of possessions, like the pursuit of pleasure, is a kind of deification of the self. Man is worshipping and serving the creature rather than the Creator (Rom. 1:25); he is putting other gods before the Lord.

The trinitarian revelation
In the Old Testament there is a very strong emphasis on the oneness or unity of God. The key passage is one we have quoted already: 'Hear, O Israel: The Lord our God, the Lord is one' (Deuteronomy 6:4). This became the primary dogma in the creed of the Jews and their understanding of it certainly played a major part in their rejection of the claims of Jesus. 'We are . . . stoning you,' some of them said to

him, 'because you, a mere man, claim to be God' (John 10:
33). For them there was but one God, the Lord Jehovah or
Yahweh, one in nature, one in power and one in person.

The New Testament presents Jesus as born of a virgin by
the work of God's Spirit, without human paternity and
uniquely the Son of God. His true identity was voiced by
Peter at Caesarea Philippi: 'You are the Christ, the Son of
the living God' (Matthew 16:16). This, said Jesus, was an
insight Peter had gained not by the normal processes of
discovery or learning but by special revelation from God:
'This was not revealed to you by man, but by my Father
in heaven' (Matthew 16:17). As time went on, the knowledge of Christ was deepened and his full deity became a
firm conviction for his disciples and those who followed
them. Paul, writing to Titus, anticipates our Lord's return
as the glorious appearing of our great God and Saviour,
Jesus Christ. The one to come again is God and Saviour.

The New Testament also brings the revelation that the
Holy Spirit is not only the Spirit of God, divine by nature,
but has distinct personality. Jesus used masculine pronouns
when speaking of the Spirit: 'He will testify about me'
(John 15:26). 'I will send him . . . When he comes, he will
convict the world of guilt in regard to sin . . . he will guide
you into all truth' (John 16:7, 8, 13).

Again and again, both our Lord and the apostles conjoin
Father, Son and Spirit as three Persons active together in
the work of salvation. Jesus actually commanded the baptism
of disciples in the name (one name) of the Father and of the
Son and of the Holy Spirit (Matthew 28:19). A full list of
the passages or a full consideration of the doctrine of the
Trinity is impossible in this context. What is important is
that the acceptance of the existence within the Godhead of
three distinct Persons, the Father, the Son and the Holy
Spirit, did not in any way involve a denial of monotheism.
Trinitarianism is not belief in three gods but in *one God* who
subsists as three Persons. To give worship to Christ or to the
Holy Spirit is to worship that *one* God and not to put
another god before him.

Further implications

Divine consorts excluded
Human life is bisexual, male and female. So, too, is the animal kingdom. It was natural, therefore, for men to project a bisexual image on to their deities, who were thus thought of as having wives or husbands. The first commandment clearly excluded from the religion of Israel, and therefore from the Christian religion which followed, any such bisexual ideas of God. He, and he *alone,* is God. There is no consort in his presence nor will he tolerate such an idea.

It is now realized that Canaanite Baal-worship was thoroughly bisexual in its belief and practice. At the shrines, known disparagingly in the Bible as 'high places', were two symbolic objects. The first, called in Hebrew the *mazzebah* (AV 'image', 'standing image' or 'pillar'), seems to have represented the male god, the Baal, while the second, the *asherah* (AV 'grove'), represented the female consort. The *mazzebah* was evidently made of stone, because when it was being destroyed it had to be broken rather than cut down. The *asherah* was apparently made of wood and could be cut down. There may have been a plurality of Asherah poles at each shrine indicating belief in polygamous Baals. Both symbols are mentioned in 2 Kings 18:4, where we read that as part of his reformation Hezekiah 'removed the high places, smashed the sacred stones (plural of *mazzebah*) and cut down the Asherah poles.'

Outside Palestine gods of both sexes were also very common. The Graeco-Roman world of New Testament times had a pantheon headed by Zeus, known to the Romans as Jupiter or Jove. His wife was Hera, or Juno, the queen of the heavens. Similarly, Pluto, lord of the underworld, had a wife called Persephone or Proserpina, and Hermes or Mercury, god of science and trade, was married to Aphrodite, the goddess of beauty and love. These gods were presented as producing offspring to whom various roles in the control of human life were assigned.

The exclusion of the female consort from the Jewish and Christian view of God is sometimes said to make both religions cold and lacking in emotional warmth. The veneration of Mary in Roman Catholicism is sometimes said to

meet the need of humans for this warmth because it brings
in the mother image so essential in childhood and so precious
throughout life.

Now it must be said at once that Roman Catholicism
officially repudiates any suggestion that Mary was or is a
divine being. She is rather thought of as supreme among
God's creatures, but this supremacy has often been interpreted in a way that allows ordinary Catholics to think of
her and to venerate her as a virtual divine consort. We see
this, for example, in the following extract from an essay
entitled 'Mary' by Gabriel Roschini: 'Mary transcends all
other creatures . . . She is not at the base or centre of the
universe but at its summit, and she is there as its apex . . .
Above her there is only One: God . . . She immerses herself
in the infinite luminous sphere of the Most Holy Trinity.
She was and will always be the beloved Daughter of the
Father, the affectionate Mother of the Son, and the faithful
Spouse of the Holy Ghost. She is related to the three divine
persons and belongs to their divine family, a family which
transcends all human families, that is, all that is created.'[1]

To suggest that Mary belongs to the divine family of the
Trinity, even if it is also said that she is a creature, surely
makes her in some way the female 'consort' of deity. That
she was officially designated 'Queen of Heaven' by Pope
Pius XII suggests that ancient Mesopotamian beliefs about
Ishtar have been taken over. It is hard to avoid the conclusion
that, whatever the official position, such veneration of Mary
violates the first commandment: 'You shall have no other
gods before me.'

What we must realize, however, is that somehow God is
not simply male and masculine, but a total person, whose
image man, male and female together, bears. He is neither
male nor female, even if the masculine pronouns 'he, him
and his' are the ones used of him. He gathers up within
himself, in the perfection of his fatherhood, all the qualities
of uprightness, love and goodness which we see but partially
in every true father and mother. The exclusion of a female
consort from his throne in no way robs his people and
their religion of maternal warmth. We come in worship, we
commit ourselves in service, to a loving heavenly Father who
cares as could no earthly parent, male or female.

Occultism excluded

There are numerous references in both Testaments to practices of the type now generally designated 'occult'. Divination, magic and personal involvement with spirits, or the
mediums essential to communication with such spirits, all
found a place in Israelite and Gentile life. Their presence
in Israel does not mean, however, that they were an essential or proper part of religion. Indeed, the reverse is the case,
for whenever they appeared, and even when certain kings
gave them official and religious status, they were condemned
and the kings concerned were branded as evil.

Where occultism involves spirit beings of any kind,
questions of reverence, of devotion and of loyalty arise and
religious acts follow. This is why there is such strong divine
disapproval of the mediums who claim to link men with the
spirits. 'Do not turn', we read, 'to mediums (Hebrew
'obhoth) or seek out spiritists (Hebrew *yiddeonim*), for you
will be defiled by them: I am the Lord your God' (Leviticus
19:31). The implication is that involvement with these
people and the spirits with which they were supposed to
communicate was inconsistent with Israel's exclusive relationship with the Lord their God.

Baal worship, which, as we have seen, was very common
through much of Israel's history, was in fact the worship of
nature spirits. It was believed that each area of land was the
domain of a local spirit or Baal, who controlled the fertility
of the land and of its animal and human occupants. At the
high places bands of consecrated women were maintained
for ritual prostitution, which was thought to be the proper
way to stimulate the spirits to give the fertility their devotees
so much desired. The whole business was so abhorrent to
God, and so detested by the faithful men to whom he
entrusted the writing of Scripture, that little information
has been preserved. The details are so degraded as to be
better forgotten.

Another common form of spiritism in the ancient world
was necromancy, that is, romancing after the dead, the contacting or apparent contacting of the spirits of deceased
human beings. How far there was real contact with the dead
is difficult to say, but three passages in Scripture show that
it is possible, if God so permits, for the dead to speak to the

living. They are the appearance of Samuel to Saul (1 Samuel 28), the presence of Moses and Elijah in conversation with our Lord at the transfiguration (Mark 9:2–8 etc.), and the story of the rich man and Lazarus, in which Abraham said it would be useless, but not therefore impossible, for Lazarus to return and speak to the rich man's five brothers (Luke 16:27–31).

This is not, however, to admit that the dead do actually speak to the living in necromancy or its modern equivalent, 'spiritualism'. Indeed the possibilities of conscious or unconscious fraud by the mediums is very great. They may be able by telepathy to learn something from the living about the deceased, and then with some element of ventriloquism produce a voice which is believed to be that of a departed relative even if it does not sound very much like him or her. What is clear in Scripture is that necromancy is totally alien to the worship of God, the Lord. Says Isaiah, 'When men tell you to consult mediums and spiritists, who whisper and mutter, should not a people enquire of their God? Why *consult the dead* on behalf of the living?' (Isaiah 8:19.) The issue was clearly that spiritism in general, and the attempted consultation with the spirits of dead humans in particular, had taken over and was taking the place of a proper reliance on the Lord. For Isaiah this was spiritual apostasy, spiritual adultery, a rejection of the sole sovereign rule of the one God. It was a breach of the first commandment, a putting of other gods, other strong powers, before the Lord.

In the ministry of Jesus there were a number of cases of people under the power of spirits, possessed by spirits. The exact nature of such possession is difficult to define, but it would seem in some way to involve spirits as 'powers' operating in opposition to the Lord and thus challenging his unique sovereignty. At any event, Jesus consistently dealt with them in a summary fashion. He would not and did not discuss or debate with them, but always rebuked or commanded with sovereign authority.

The temptations of our Lord show that Satan is the ultimate challenger for the worship due alone to God. At the third attempt to seduce the Lord, Satan offered him the kingdoms of the world if he would but fall down and worship him. Our Lord flatly refused, again speaking with sovereign authoritative command: 'Away from me, Satan! For it is written: "Worship the Lord your God, and serve him only"' (Matthew 4:10; cf. Deuteronomy 6:13). He was quoting words which expand the first commandment and showing that to give worship to Satan would involve putting another god before the Lord.

The apostles followed our Lord's example and never involved themselves in any association with spirits. Thus Paul, confronted by a girl with a spirit of divination at Philippi, commanded the spirit in the name of Jesus Christ to come out of her (Acts 16:18). Luke tells us that it (the spirit) came out at that moment.

In concluding his argument about meats offered to idols, Paul warned the Corinthians that behind the idol was a demon spirit: 'The sacrifices of pagans are offered to demons, not to God, and I do not want you to be participants with demons. You cannot drink the cup of the Lord and the cup of the demons too; you cannot have a part in both the Lord's table and the table of demons' (1 Corinthians 10: 20–21).

While a believer could feel free to eat such meat as food because he knew it was not in any way changed by conse-cration to a pagan deity, he dare not get caught up in the worship of idols, a worship which involved giving honour to, and having communion with spirits. This, like the Baal worship of Old Testament times, would be a violation of an exclusive covenant relationship with the Lord, an act of spiritual adultery provocative of his jealousy as truly as would be the case when a wife forms an illicit relationship with another man.

There is no evidence of a specific cult of Satan worship in the Bible but this has, of course, developed in the Western world in recent times. It is in fact the terrible end of the occult road, the ultimate degradation to which spiritism can lead. It is the nemesis of all spiritual and moral values, turning good into evil and evil into good. Those actively caught up in the cult may be relatively few, but we need to remember that Satan gets the allegiance of multitudes by less obvious means. He entices men to sin just as he put it into the heart of Judas to betray our Lord (John 13:2).

He masquerades as an angel of light and deceives men through messengers who disguise themselves as servants of righteousness (2 Corinthians 11:12—15). Those who yield to his machinations, who doubt, as Eve was made to doubt, that God will punish sin, do in fact hand their lives over to his control. As John put it, 'He who commits sin is of the devil' (1 John 3:8). So it is not just those who openly worship Satan in a cult, but those who follow his deceits, those who commit sin, who are in his clutches and yielding allegiance to a power other than the Lord. All such to some degree break this first and most fundamental command: 'You shall have no other gods before me.'

No other gods today

People who regard themselves as Christians may tend to feel that, whatever may be the case with other commands, this is one that hardly needs to be applied to them. They would not for one moment think of bowing to an idol and they have no images in their homes. Whether they are keenly religious or not, they recognize one God, the Lord; they do not break the commandment, they have no other gods!

Perhaps, however, as some of the implications of the command have been examined, there have been qualms of conscience. Indeed if the Word of God is being given its rightful place that should be the case. It may be that, as areas of modern life where the command is broken are mentioned, even the more committed Christian will become aware of shortcomings. This is not to be feared, not a sign to stop reading, but rather to press on prayerfully, looking to the Lord to draw one's heart closer to himself and away from every illegitimate affection. With the hymn writer we can pray,

> The dearest idol I have known,
> Whate'er that idol be,
> Help me to tear it from thy throne
> and worship only thee.

Not earthly possessions

The twentieth century has been very much marked by materialism. The Western world has largely lost its faith in God and lives for the enjoyment of possessions and of pleasure. The dominant philosophy at the popular level has been that of the Epicureans: 'Eat, drink and be merry for tomorrow we die.' Christians may not subscribe to that, but all too often they, too, are highly materialistic in their behaviour patterns. Somehow belief in God and experience of his salvation do not always deliver us from the appetite for possessions. Most of us find it hard to be content with our lot and very often the more we possess, the more we want.

There are, of course, exceptions — rich men who are not enslaved by their riches and who use them carefully and wisely for the benefit of others and the glory of God. Equally, there are poor men who have little of this world's wealth but have the great gain of godliness with contentment. Yet there are many who simply fall into the pattern of the world, who live for, who constantly talk about possessions.

To list the trends would take up too much space and might in any case be misleading because it might unfairly attack some or unwittingly neglect others. The principle of putting possessions in their proper place is what matters. Money is to be used and not worshipped. It is to be low on the list of our affections and never a matter of priority or indispensability. When we covet possessions, when we are so attached to them that we will not let them go, they have too large a place in life and either threaten to be, or actually are other gods than the Lord.

On one occasion a man asked Jesus to intervene in a quarrel between himself and his brother over the division of their father's estate. Jesus declined to intrude into a matter of civil law but, knowing that within this particular man there was an inordinate attachment to possessions, he sought to show that it is of prime importance to get rid of such worship of wealth. He first warned against covetousness and asserted, 'A man's life does not consist in the abundance of his possessions.' Then he told a story about a rich man whose land produced a great harvest, who built

new barns and who delighted himself in the prospect of
affluent ease without thought of God or of his fellow men.
It concluded thus: 'But God said to him, "You fool! This
very night your life will be demanded from you. Then who
will get what you have prepared for yourself?" ' Riches
cannot be taken into the next world and the man who puts
them in first place in this life is a fool. 'This is how it will
be' (like the man in the story) 'with anyone who stores up
things for himself but is not rich towards God' (Luke 12:
21).

Our Lord did not say, and Scripture never says, that
riches, wealth, possessions are wrong. What is affirmed again
and again is that attachment to them, domination by them
and worship of them are wrong. The love of money, but not
money itself 'is a root of all kinds of evil' (1 Timothy 6:10).
It is the serving of wealth as another god alongside the Lord
which is sin.

Each of us must submit his or her own life to the micro-
scope and seek to discover and eradicate every trace of the
worship of money. The command is clear: 'You shall have
no other gods before me.'

Not pleasurable experiences

Pleasure is a notoriously difficult thing to define. Usually
the word points to experiences which are enjoyed through
the senses — sight, hearing, smell, taste or touch. Often
pleasure is very much a thing of the moment and passes as
soon as the enjoyable sensations cease. Thus understood it
can be distinguished from happiness which is a more settled
emotional condition of contentment, which is often sus-
tained even when unpleasant sensations have to be endured.

The pursuit of pleasure, or more precisely of pleasures, is
perhaps basic to the lust for wealth which we have just discussed. We seek, and we hold on to possessions because we
enjoy doing these things and because we enjoy the pleasant
experiences the possessions bring to us.

Pleasure is not, of course, an unworthy experience. Indeed,
God intends us to have it, for he has richly provided us with
everything for our enjoyment (1 Timothy 6:17). The world,
the universe indeed, is ours for enjoyment, for pleasure, but
not in a selfish way which has no interest in the glory of God

the Creator or in the well-being of our fellow men. The Epicurean maxim, 'Eat, drink and be merry, for tomorrow we die,' whatever its original intention, became and remains the slogan of the selfish and the irresponsible and is quite unworthy of the Christian. It epitomizes a way of life tried and found 'empty' by the writer of Ecclesiastes, whose advice to a young man was to enjoy his youth, to 'do his own thing' and avoid the things that are without pleasure, but to do so as one responsible before God: 'But know that for all these things God will bring you to judgement' (Ecclesiastes 11:9—10).

Christianity is not, and must not be made, a killjoy religion. The Pharisees did just that with Judaism and imposed on their followers pettifogging regulations which made life burdensome and drained it of any true pleasure. Some Christians fall into the same trap and add all sorts of cultural extras to the requirements of divine revelation. They pervert the gospel and must take their due share of blame for the fact that many of those who come under their influence turn away from Christianity. They make some little ones stumble — a serious sin indeed.

The danger these days seems, however, to be very much in the other direction, and more and more the pleasure-seeking practices of the world have become part and parcel of the ways of God's people. The tragedy is that what God gives for our enjoyment as his gift becomes more important than the Giver and at that point takes on the role of 'another god'. Thus pleasure all too often has such a high place in our affections that it stands between us and God; it is another god before his face.

The spectrum of pleasures which nowadays clamour for the affections is beyond description in the space available here, but one or two elements do need special mention because of the way in which they have got out of hand and have unquestionably become 'gods' for this generation. Gambling is one which links in very closely with the laying up of treasure on earth. The amount spent each year is staggering, the time and money spent in bingo halls, mainly by women, is equally amazing. Lotteries are becoming very common and gaming machines abound in amusement centres and clubs. Gambling is 'another god'.

Then there is sex, something which can and does bring out
the highest and best in men and women as they relate to each
other in marriage, but something which can also be debased
to levels below the behaviour patterns of the animal world.
And nowadays the debasements and perversions are openly
portrayed and discussed in the press and on radio and television. Under the guise of 'good drama' or of 'reflecting life'
we are constantly exposed to sex in one form or another. It
is 'the god' of multitudes, most of whom are only concerned
with the pleasures of the moment and have little or no
serious concern for a responsible use of their God-given
powers as men or women.

Not demagogue heroes
On one occasion the apostles, Paul and Barnabas, were taken
for the gods Hermes and Zeus. The priest of Zeus in Lystra
proceeded to bring oxen and garlands and wanted to offer
sacrifice! (Acts 14:11–13.) The two apostles were horrified
and ran out, asserting that they were but men whose calling
in life was to bear witness to the living God, the Creator of
all and therefore, by implication, the one and only true God.

The cult of personality worship may not take the same
form today but, no doubt about it, the garlands come out
and the offerings are made. It may be a favourite entertainer
or a sporting personality whose talent makes him the idol of
a generation. The incredible earnings of those who become
'stars' is evidence of the reverence in which they can be held.
It may be a political demagogue who strides on to the scene
with the aura of a messiah and who is honoured as if he were
the incarnation of a god. It may even be a loved one, a child,
a parent or a good friend, who is elevated to a position where
he or she is supreme in one's thinking and in effect takes the
place of God.

There is also a considerable danger of personality worship
within Christendom. The biblical example is the church at
Corinth where attraction to different 'stars' was a grave
threat to the unity of the church. Some were saying, 'I follow
Paul', some, 'I follow Apollos', some, 'I follow Cephas' and
still others, 'I follow Christ' (1 Corinthians 1:12). At first
sight it might seem that the fourth group was the only one
on the right lines, but there is general agreement that they

were using the words, 'I follow Christ', as a kind of party
slogan, which was far from ideal. They may even have been
proudly scoring points over the other parties. At any event,
the whole business was indicative of low spirituality, serious
immaturity and a total misunderstanding of the role of
Christian ministers.

Paul's correction of this misunderstanding stands as a
permanent warning against any elevation of ministers to
stardom. He writes, 'So then, men ought to regard us'
(i.e. the ministers), 'as servants of Christ and as those
entrusted with the secret things of God . . . Therefore judge
nothing' (i.e. about the ministers) 'before the appointed
time; wait till the Lord comes . . . At that time each will
receive his praise from God' (1 Corinthians 4:1–5).

This passage makes clear that a minister of the gospel is
first a servant of Christ. The word used is *hupēretēs* meaning
primarily an under-rower in a ship, a slave consigned to row
in the low headroom of the under deck and below a rank of
more privileged upper-rowers. While this word is usually
translated 'servant' or 'minister', it suggests lowliness and
the very opposite of stardom. The minister of Christ is an
underling slave with no entitlement to adulation or praise.
He is the last person on earth to be the object of veneration
in a personality cult.

Paul goes on to say that ministers are also stewards or
house managers to whom valuable possessions are trusted.
In the ancient world such would generally be slaves, so that
no high status is suggested in the title. The point of its use
is simply to illustrate the fact that a minister, like a steward,
operates not on his own account, not to secure a following
for himself, but for the good and the glory of his master.
The ministers have been trusted with the priceless treasure
of gospel truth, but this does not justify others in judging
them and making them their party leaders. Evaluation of
their worth is the Lord's business and must await his return.

The other side of the coin is, of course, that there is a
proper respect due to those who serve the Lord, a respect
that Paul himself does a great deal to foster, but honour,
even double honour to those who labour in preaching and
teaching (1 Timothy 5:17) is not a prescription for large
offerings of money or for a veneration that borders on, or

becomes worship. We must remember that it is not our place
to pass judgement on others, but we need to see to it that
we do not allow ourselves to give to pastors or evangelists
even a little of the glory that is due to the Lord. Those who
are in the ministry and who have gifts for preaching and
influencing people must beware of any attitude or practice
that would draw people's emotions towards themselves and
lead to the minister becoming a virtual substitute for God,
another god before God's face.

Not occult spirits
There is widespread interest and considerable personal
involvement in spiritism today. There are witches' covens,
which involve not a few people of intellectual and material
substance. There is the spiritualist movement, with its claim
to be in contact with the dead. There are the extreme
Satanist cults which demand outright commitment to the
devil and whose devotees will sometimes engage in the most
outrageous acts of murder for ritual or religious reasons.

Then there is what appears to be a simpler occultism
in the use of ouija, the tinkling of glasses and the daily
horoscope. Often folks with no conscious intention of
worship get involved in these things almost accidentally,
perhaps just for a laugh. Unfortunately, some become
hooked and begin to walk the occult road. Interest in divination and spirits grows, fear of offending the spirits develops
and then measures have to be taken to keep on the right side
of them. At this point the whole thing has taken on a
religious character and the personality becomes dominated
by it. One thing that is certain then is that God the Lord is
not being given his due place. Other gods are before him and
the first commandment is being broken.

The firm 'no' to the occult which runs right through
Scripture is something we breach at our peril. Anyone who
is in any way involved, even on the fringe, will have to make
a complete break. He should burn the entire paraphernalia
of the occult — books, charms, the lot — as did certain
young Christians at Ephesus whose story is recorded in
Acts 19. He must claim the victory of Christ over the powers
of darkness and live by faith in sole dependence on the
Lord.

But whole-hearted devotion

The first commandment excluded all other gods from the life and from the religion of God's covenant people. In the very doing of this it demanded whole-hearted devotion to the Lord. There would have been no point in excluding other gods without insisting on proper honour for the one true God.

In a very real sense this is the most vital of all the commandments because it sets man's attitude right by calling him to a single-minded vertical relationship. This is why, after reiterating the commands as Israel approached the land of promise, Moses developed the positive implications of the basic God-ward command: 'Hear, O Israel: The Lord our God, the Lord is one. Love the Lord your God with all your heart and with all your soul and with all your strength . . . Fear the Lord your God, serve him only and take your oaths in his name. Do not follow other gods, the gods of the peoples around you; for the Lord your God, who is among you, is a jealous God and his anger will burn against you, and he will destroy you from the face of the land' (Deuteronomy 6:4–5, 13–15).

As we have seen, the Lord Jesus thoroughly endorsed the positive requirement and taught that the great, the most important, command is this: 'Love the Lord your God with all your heart and with all your soul and with all your mind and with all your strength' (Mark 12:30).

The kind of devotion required of God's people, now as then, is exemplified in the response of Daniel's three friends at the time when everyone in Babylon was commanded to worship Nebuchadnezzar's image. They defied the command with a tremendous assertion of their total devotion to the Lord: 'If we are thrown into the blazing furnace, the God we serve is able to save us from it, and he will rescue us from your hand, O king. But even if he does not, we want you to know, O king, that we will not serve your gods or worship the image of gold you have set up' (Daniel 3:17–18). Those three young men put God first. They would allow no other gods to have a place in their lives. They gave the Lord their whole-hearted, their undivided devotion.

The first commandment has deep implications for us all. It requires that we avoid allowing some lesser love, some lesser object of reverence or affection, to stand before the Lord's face and to have in our lives the priority that is due to the Lord. It requires that in a most positive way we give him the devotion of our hearts. Half-heartedness just will not do.

'You shall have no other gods before me.'

---

[1] *The Marian Era*, vol. III, p. 34.

4. No idols
The Second Commandment

'You shall not make for yourself an idol in the form of anything in heaven above or on the earth beneath or in the waters below. You shall not bow down to them or worship them; for I, the Lord your God, am a jealous God, punishing the children for the sin of the fathers to the third and fourth generation of those who hate me, but showing love to thousands who love me and keep my commandments.'

It is generally agreed that this commandment assumes and builds on the observance of the first, and seeks to guide those who do in fact worship the Lord alone. Such are now told that they are not to worship him by means of images. The command is concerned not so much with whom or what men worship, that being already fixed, but with *how* they worship the Lord, the one true God.

Images of the Lord proscribed

When the animist of ancient times made an image or an idol, he believed that the spirit it was designed to represent was brought nearer to him and, indeed, became somehow present with him in tangible form. He performed rituals at or before the image, not to venerate the image itself, but with the idea of moving the spirit to act in a way favourable to himself.

The second commandment forbids the introduction of such practices into the religion of Israel. God could not be represented by or contained in an image of any kind. He would not allow his people to think of him in such terms. Hence this commandment: 'You shall not make for yourself an idol . . .'

The Hebrew word *pesel* translated 'idol' (AV 'graven image') undoubtedly refers to any figure carved out of wood or sculptured from stone or metal. It is generally agreed, however, that its meaning was extended to include other images that might be used as objects of worship, as for example, the cast idols prohibited in Exodus 34:17: 'Do not make cast idols.' In an inspired commentary on this issue Moses makes the point that when God spoke to Israel at Horeb no visible form of Deity had been seen, and uses that fact as the basis of the prohibition on the use of images in worship (Deuteronomy 4:15–24). To introduce images in any form, male or female, animal or bird, insect, reptile or fish, and even if supposed to represent the Lord himself, would be an act of treacherous apostasy, a violation of the covenant made at Sinai without the use of a material image of any kind.

The second part of the commandment is, of course, a further imperative: 'You shall not bow down to them or worship them . . .' It focuses on what is the really crucial thrust of the command and tells us that it is not sculpture as such, not visual and pictorial representations as means of communication or as works of art, which are prohibited. It is rather the products of the sculptor or the carver when designed for, or used in acts of religious worship. The people of God were not to make any images of their God, and if such images ever were made, they were not to bow before them in veneration or prayer, and they were not to engage in acts of sacrificial ritual or services of praise before them.

God did not intend totally to prohibit the making of 'images' or their use in religion for very soon after the command was given Moses was commissioned to have various figures made in brass and gold for use in the tabernacle. There were, for example, the 'two cherubim . . . of hammered gold' to sit at each end of the mercy-seat (Exodus 25:18–20). Had God meant that the Israelites should never make any likeness of things in heaven or earth, he would not have given such instructions. The prohibition was on images made to be worshipped as images of 'the Lord'.

In forbidding material representations of God, the commandment asserted something of his essential nature as a spiritual Being. He was not, and he could not be confined to a material object or to one particular location. Rather he was constantly and everywhere in overriding control of, and available to his people, the High and Lofty One who inhabits eternity and who yet also dwells 'with him who is contrite and lowly in spirit' (Isaiah 57:15). He did, of course, meet with his people in the Holy Place and in a special way made himself present between the cherubim on the sacred ark, but his presence on earth was never restricted to that spot, and he would not allow the ark or any other object, however sacred, to be venerated by his people. Their devotion was to be to him as God the Lord, as the living, the eternal God, and not to objects made by human hands.

Breaches of the law in Israelite history

Throughout the Old Testament there is scathing condemnation of the use of images and, indeed, of idols in general. In some instances the worship of other gods prohibited by the first commandment may be in view, but in others it seems very probable that the polemic is against the use of such images by Israelites who regarded them as representing the Lord. The words of Isaiah 40:18–20 would indeed suggest this: 'To whom, then *will you compare God?* What image will you compare him to? As for an idol, a craftsman casts it, and a goldsmith overlays it with gold and fashions silver chains for it. A man too poor to present such an offering selects wood that will not rot. He looks for a skilled craftsman to set up an idol that will not topple.' The point is that an image overlaid with expensive gold, or cut for the less wealthy from durable hardwood, cannot ever be an adequate representation of God, who sits above the circle of the earth, who stretches out the heavens and reigns sovereignly over all the rulers of earth.

There were, in fact, a number of specific occasions on which Israelites did attempt to worship the Lord by means of images. The best known was soon after the giving of the decalogue when Moses was delayed on Mount Sinai. The people clamoured for a visible representation of God that would go before them and readily provided Aaron with a

supply of ornaments to be smelted and moulded and
sculptured into an image. When in due course Aaron produced the golden calf or bull the people acclaimed the
appearance of their god: 'These are your gods,' (your
'Elohim', God), 'O Israel, who brought you up out of Egypt'
(Exodus 32:4). They knew quite clearly that God, the Lord,
had delivered them from Egypt and accepted this image as
representative of him. Aaron evidently shared their belief,
for when he saw the enthusiastic reception given to the image
he proceeded to build an altar and proclaim a festival 'to the
Lord'. In so doing he was asserting that the calf-image represented the Lord and was in no way the introduction of
another god. The subsequent paragraphs (Exodus 32:7—35)
record God's intense displeasure at a blatant breach of the
second commandment.

The image made by Micah, an Ephraimite, in the time of
the judges seems to have been very much of the same order.
His mother, after some financial dispute with him, dedicated
a sum of money *'to the Lord'* and proceeded to give two
hundred shekels of it to a silversmith to make what is termed
'a carved image and a cast idol'. Subsequently Micah's images
were captured by the tribe of Dan and set up in a sanctuary
of their own in the far north of the land. The sacred record
(Judges 17—18) makes it clear that both Micah and the
Danites acted illegitimately. They were being lawless in a
time when there was no king and no discipline in the land,
a time when every man did what was right in his own eyes.
At no point, however, is it suggested that either party was
turning to the worship of another god and it is therefore
reasonably certain that both thought of the images as representing Israel's God, the Lord.

A little later on there developed, at least in a section of the
people, the idea that the presence of God was somehow tied
to the sacred ark with its cherubim figures. It was for this
reason that at a time of military defeat by the Philistines they
called for the ark to be brought to the field of battle. 'Let
us', they said, 'bring the ark of the Lord's covenant from
Shiloh, so that it (or 'he' — the Lord) may go with us and
save us from the hand of our enemies' (1 Samuel 4:3).
Clearly their hope was not centred simply in the wooden box
and the cherubim figures which constituted the ark, but in

the God they thought to be present in it. Indeed, they were to some considerable degree reflecting ancient Near-Eastern ideas of gods localized in images and shrines.

Still later in history, Jeroboam, the founder and first king of the northern kingdom, made calf or bull images and placed them in shrines at Bethel and Dan. The reason was to prevent his subjects making regular religious pilgrimages to Jerusalem, where he feared they might become disaffected and renew their loyalty to the kings of David's line. Again the shrines and the images at them were not intended to introduce new gods but to concentrate the worship of the Lord by the northern people within their own borders. Because of the breaking of the second commandment which this entailed, Jeroboam has gone down in history as one who caused Israel to commit sin (1 Kings 14:16; 2 Kings 3:3 etc.).

Observance of the law among the Israelites

Despite the frequent aberrations led by renegade kings, and the equally frequent attachment of the people to images, there was considerable obedience to the command. The great leaders, whose names are so well known to us as heroes of faith, were men of consistent monotheism whose devotion to the Lord rose far above the use of material images. King David and, for a time, Solomon his son were shining examples. So, too, were prophets like Samuel, Elijah, Elisha, Isaiah, Jeremiah and Ezekiel, who stood firm against every intrusion of pagan ideas into Israel. Then there were reforming kings like Hezekiah and Josiah, who at times when the worship of the Lord seemed to be virtually in eclipse sought at the official level to purge out the paganism which had arisen. That their efforts were not marked with complete success at the popular level in no way detracts from the genuineness of their devotion to the Lord and to his commandments.

At the time when the threat of exile hung heavily over Judah, Jeremiah had to deal with an unhealthy attachment to the temple and to its most sacred object, the ark of the covenant. It would seem that those around him regarded the temple as a kind of charm guaranteeing God's presence and protection, irrespective of how they behaved. The words, 'the ark of the covenant of the Lord' (Jeremiah 3:16) and 'This is the temple of the Lord, the temple of the Lord, the temple of the Lord' (Jeremiah 7:4) were being used more or less as magical formulae asserting that, come what may, God was with Judah. Jeremiah declared these phrases 'deceptive words' and called for an amendment of the people's ways. It was only then that they would be assured of God's presence (Jeremiah 7:5—7). The point was that God's presence among his people did not depend on material objects of any kind, but on moral and spiritual qualities which he required them to display. The temple and the ark of the covenant were not images, but Israelites seem to have been giving them a similar significance and the way in which Jeremiah rejects trust in them would certainly also exclude the use of an image as a means of worshipping God.

A little later on, when the first group of exiles in Babylon were feeling the desolation of captivity in a foreign land, Jeremiah wrote assuring them that God had not forgotten them but was in fact working out his plans for their welfare and for their future. They were urged to settle down, build houses, engage in farming and trade and arrange marriages for their children. They were to pray for the welfare of Babylon and to seek the Lord for themselves. God's promise was 'You will seek me and find me when you seek me with all your heart' (Jeremiah 29:13). This meant that in Babylon, without the temple, without the ark, without the rituals of the sanctuary, God's presence could be enjoyed by those who sought him in the right way — inwardly, single-mindedly and with the whole heart.

Again Jeremiah was not, of course, dealing with images specifically carved as representations of the Lord, but with abuses which tended to attribute to symbolic objects a localization of God's presence like that associated with images. His insistence that God was not tied to any locality, object or land, would also argue strongly against any use of images in worship.

The lesson, like that of cutting out the worship of foreign gods, seems to have been well and truly learned by the exiles and there is no indication that there was ever again any inclination among the Jews to worship God by means of images. When they came to the erection of synagogues, about the time of our Lord and subsequently, they often avoided the inclusion of sculptures, mosaics or paintings because they feared that even if not representing God, such objects might be a breach of the second commandment. Thus in going beyond the requirements of the command they showed their strict adherence to it. This would, of course, explain the fact that we have no record of our Lord directly quoting the second commandment. To the Jewish audiences to whom he spoke it was just not necessary to put emphasis on this prohibition.

The threat and the promise

To the imperatives of the commandment there is added a further statement basing them on the character of God and strengthening their force by what appears as a threat and a promise. The text reads, 'For I, the Lord your God, am a jealous God, punishing the children for the sin of the fathers to the third and fourth generation of those who hate me, but showing love to thousands who love me and keep my commandments.'

The reference to the Lord as a jealous God has occasioned some difficulty, largely because the English word 'jealous' rather suggests pettiness or some similar and unworthy motivation. The Hebrew, however is *qanna*[1] ', an adjective denoting strong feelings of envy or anger, and confined in the Old Testament to affirmations of God's opposition to idols or images. A closely related word, *qana'* is used similarly but also to refer to a husband's reaction to his wife's infidelity. The clear inference is that God is likened to a husband, who desires the total allegiance of his wife and who reacts with some vehemence when she forsakes him for another man. There is no suggestion of pettiness or of overbearing pride, but rather an affirmation of the legitimate rights of one on whom Israel was wholly dependent, and to whom she had solemn covenant obligations.

The threat and the promise which follow have also given rise to a good deal of discussion. Many people see them and other similar statements (Exodus 34:7; Numbers 14:18; Deuteronomy 5:9; Jeremiah 32:18) as presenting an unacceptable, perhaps even an immoral picture of God. They think that for anyone other than an actual offender to be punished is contrary to the view of God as a loving heavenly

Father which is found in the teaching of Jesus. The extent to which there is any real moral problem here is very much a matter of the exact meaning of the text and of its theological and historical context.

As to the text, a number of points emerge.

1. The phrase 'to the third and fourth generation' was apparently a concise way of referring to a whole family, in which there would normally be a span of three or four generations alive at any one time. It need not be regarded as implying the deliberate carrying forward of divine punishment to subsequent generations, but rather the limitation of God's wrath to an immediately definable family circle.

2. The contrast between bane and blessing may be rather different from what appears at first sight. The Hebrew word *'elephim* translated 'thousands' is used for the ordinal 'thousandth' as well as for the cardinal 'thousand(s)'. It would therefore be feasible to translate differently and read, 'showing love to the thousandth generation of those who love me and keep my commandments'. In this event the point is that while the visitation of iniquity is of short duration, limited to three or four generations at most, the covenant loyalty of God to those who are faithful is unlimited and goes on for ever. Deuteronomy 7:9–10 actually puts the contrast in these terms, but without mentioning any punishment of children for the sins of the fathers: 'The Lord . . . keeping his covenant of love to a thousand generations of those who love him and keep his commands. But those who hate him he will repay to their face . . .'

3. There is no suggestion that the sinning fathers, for whose sins up to three or four generations would be punished, would not themselves suffer punishment. That such would get off 'scot free' is contrary to the whole drift of the divine revelation, in which personal accountability and family involvement go hand in hand.

4. Those whom God punishes for their fathers' sins are almost certainly to be understood as somehow themselves involved in these sins. They are generations which hate God as did their fathers and which therefore participate in or repeat their fathers' sins.

With reference to the theological and historical context several comments can be made. Even if these do not fully satisfy everyone they may help to ease the difficulty for some.

1. Divine revelation was progressive. By this we mean that God took men up where he found them, with the beliefs and practices of their times, and disclosed to them bit by bit, as they were able to receive it, more truth and new moral standards. We should, therefore, expect some new and higher emphases in the later parts of Scripture.

2. In ancient Israel, as still in many societies, 'individualism' was not as marked as in our Western world. The family, the tribe, the nation were the significant units and it was expected that a man's family or even his whole community would suffer with him the results and penalties of his misdeeds. Thus it seems it was accepted without question that Achan's family would share his fate at Ai (Joshua 7:24–25).

3. Individual accountability was also evident. Thus Moses did not enter the promised land because of an act of rebellion against God's Word (Numbers 27:12–14; Deuteronomy 3:23–27). He had to bear the penalty of his sin himself. Later on, individual accountability was given greater stress, notably through the prophets Jeremiah and Ezekiel. See Jeremiah 31:27–34, especially verses 29–30, and Ezekiel 18:1–4.

4. Individual and family or community liability to divine punishment belong together and need not be regarded as contradictory. A man's actions, good or bad, often affect, and sometimes drastically affect, his family, the members of which have to live with the after-effects and may have to do so for quite some time.

5. The laws of Israel expressly forbade the imposition of civil penalty on anyone other than an offender. A man's children or other relatives could not be touched. 'Each is to die for his own sin' (Deuteronomy 24:16). Where a murder was unsolved a community had to take responsibility and perform the appropriate acts of atonement, but the execution or punishment of anyone other than the offender was not contemplated (Deuteronomy 21:1–9). These laws give expression to the justice of God and surely show that he is in no way capricious or to be understood as dealing with men in an unjust or immoral way.

In the end we will be well advised to avoid dogmatism.

There may well be factors which we do not and cannot appreciate after the passage of more than three thousand years. The threat and the promise of this commandment bring together two aspects of God's character — his justice and his love — which can all too easily be made to appear opposed to each other. In fact, they belong together and complement each other. God is just, but not harshly or arbitrarily so. He is loving and gracious, but not weakly or sentimentally so.

The psalmist puts the same truth, the same contrast as occurs in the commandment, in different words: 'For his anger lasts only a moment, but his favour lasts a lifetime' (Ps. 30:5). Anger and favour, justice and mercy are divine prerogatives and belong together, but the balance is tipped on the side of favour and mercy. God is love, holy love. He cannot ignore sin. His holy nature in its entirety reacts against evil. His love reacts against evil and must chide and punish the sinner, but he will not always chide. His anger is necessary but temporary; his love, his favour, his mercy are without limit.

New Testament endorsement

While our Lord did not quote, or need to quote this commandment to his Jewish hearers, he did endorse its implications in a number of ways. He was himself in the closest possible relationship with God, but at no point do the inspired records of his life indicate that he used an image. In fact, the reverse is the case, for he could commune with his father at any time and was not even dependent on the temple or any other shrine. He taught his disciples to pray to God not in a public shrine, but in the seclusion of an inner room in the home, where God would hear and so be directly and immediately accessible to them. Indeed, it is this essential inwardness of a disciple's relationship to, and worship of God which excludes the use of material images.

Again, when the woman of Samaria began to talk about the right place in which to worship God, in Jerusalem or 'on this mountain' as she called Gerizim, where for some centuries the Samaritans had maintained a rival temple to that at Jerusalem, he dismissed the implication that God was localized. 'A time is coming and has now come', he said, 'when the true worshippers will worship the Father in spirit and truth, for they are the kind of worshippers the Father seeks. God is spirit, and his worshippers must worship in spirit and in truth' (John 4:23–24). In the context our Lord was asserting that God was not localized in any shrine, but could be worshipped anywhere by those whose inward attitude to him was one of genuine devotion. God is spirit and is ever and always accessible to those who worship him in spirit and in truth. This surely endorses the spirituality of God, which is the primary concern of the second commandment, and which makes the use of images as aids to worshipping him both superfluous and offensive.

We must, of course, be careful not to get things out of balance and conclude that there can be no place at all for works of art in pictures, stained windows, plaques or even buildings in Christian worship. When Jesus said that God has to be worshipped in spirit and in truth he was calling for inward and genuine communion with God in contrast to a worship that is merely outward and formal. He was not totally rejecting the use of buildings or of symbolic objects, but asserting that a religion dependent on such things is not acceptable to God. He himself visited the temple and sought to make it a better place for the worship of God by purging it of abuses. He did not, however, criticize the fact that the building existed or imply that because it was most ornately decorated it violated the second commandment. Such violation would only arise when an object was given veneration and when men bowed down before it and transferred to it the loyalty rightly due to God. It is the fact of bowing down in worship before, and of giving devotion or service to an object which makes it an idol and an offence to God.

In the writings of the apostles there are frequent warnings against the use of idols. These occur in the context of discussion of problems arising from the conversion of Gentiles and their incorporation into the church. It is therefore very probable that in the passages concerned (Acts 15:20, 29; 1 Corinthians 5:10, 11; 6:9; 8:1–13; 10:7, 14–22; 1 John 5:21 etc.) the emphasis is not specifically on images thought to represent the Lord, but on images of other gods. Yet

Gentile converts accustomed to the use of such images would very easily think that they needed an image of their new God and so could openly or secretly introduce the use of images into Christian worship. In teaching them to keep themselves from idols the apostles would have such images as well as those of foreign gods in mind. Their warnings do, therefore, further endorse our commandment.

Continuing relevance

To worship an image is to substitute a material object for a non-material God. In the eyes of the Lord it is in fact to turn one's back on him and worship another god. It is spiritual adultery and arouses the jealousy of him who demands man's sole and whole-hearted devotion. The warning is still applicable: 'Be careful not to forget the covenant of the Lord your God . . .; do not make for yourselves an idol in the form of anything the Lord your God has forbidden. For the Lord your God is a consuming fire, a jealous God' (Deuteronomy 4:23–24).

Protestants in general, and evangelicals in particular, will no doubt feel that since they do not have images in their homes or in their churches they are in no danger of breaking the second commandment. They tend to feel that Roman Catholics, with their crucifixes, their statues of Mary, their representations of the saints and their veneration of church buildings and of the bread and wine in the eucharist, are, or in the past have been guilty of breaking it. Equally they would think of the icons of the Eastern Orthodox churches as images which, though painted rather than carved, violate the spirit of the command. And in so far as worship has been, or is given to these things, even if it is thought that the worship is directed God-ward, there would seem to be some violation of the law.

But let us not cast stones at others, or boast that our imageless worship fully satisfies God. Our responsibility is to ensure that we truly worship him in spirit and in truth, that from our hearts we give to him the adoration, the thanksgiving, the glory due to him, and not a mere aesthetic response to works of art, whether in images, ornate buildings or pleasant music. God has, of course, given some people wonderful artistic powers, through which they can produce pictures or symphonies which reflect something of the glory of creation and so bear a witness to him, but the feelings of awe or sense of pleasure which we enjoy through them is not, and of itself cannot be, true spiritual worship. Whether we have elaborate church buildings or simple ones, whether we have beautiful windows and expensive mosaics or plain walls and floors, whether we have elaborate music or the rough strains of rustic voices, we can and we must see to it that without trust in any of those things we get through to him in spiritual worship.

Some Christians have been guilty, or nearly guilty of making an idol of the Bible. The Eastern Orthodox think indeed that Protestants as a whole materialize God in the letter of Scripture. The Bible is the Word of God, an authoritative and final revelation coming from God to man. But we worship, we must worship, the God of the book and not the book itself. If we objectify God in, and confine him to a written document, or if we give the document, rather than the Lord, our devotion, we have made an image of the book and have fallen into idolatry.

The second commandment, then, teaches not only the spirituality of God but the essentially spiritual nature of worship. It is not material images of God, but worshipping hearts which matter, and it is those who give themselves to God and who do his will who render true spiritual worship. 'I urge you', writes the apostle Paul, 'to offer your bodies as living sacrifices, holy and pleasing to God — which is *your spiritual worship*' (Romans 12:1).

'You shall not make for yourself an idol . . .'

5. No misuse of God's name
The Third Commandment

'You shall not misuse the name of the Lord your God, for the Lord will not hold anyone guiltless who misuses his name.'

The first commandment teaches us that there is but one God and that he alone is to be worshipped. The second tells us that God is spiritual and must not be worshipped by means of any material form or image. The third is concerned to guard the name of this one sovereign and spiritual God from misuse by men.

Requiring reverence for God's name

The command itself does not precisely say how God's name is misused. The Hebrew word translated 'misused', or 'taken in vain' *(shave')* is rather vague, suggesting something false, without meaning or value, or lacking in worthwhile purpose. It could imply deliberately insulting and guilt-incurring behaviour of the type we would call blasphemy, or the careless indifference which amounts to an insult even if not deliberately intended to be one. As we shall see, the commandment has wide ramifications and must be seen as inculcating the deepest reverence for God's name. The very vagueness of the prohibition means that every deliberate and every unintentional insult to, or empty use of God's name is to be avoided. It further means that his name is only to be used in contexts and with intentions that are consistent with his character.

In the ancient world, names indicated some aspect of a

person's birth or character and had really important significance for the person himself. A man's name stood for and represented the man himself and to honour or defame it was to honour or defame its owner. So, too, the name of God has great importance. It stands for all that he is, for the glory of his person, the living, the eternal, the almighty, the all-holy God, and for the glories of his character — all-wise, all-good, ever-loving and merciful Father.

The exact pronunciation of the name of God has not, as we have already noticed, been preserved, but scholars nowadays generally favour Yahveh or Yahweh rather than Jehovah. It was by this name, sometimes written without vowels as YHWH, that God identified himself when he gave the decalogue: 'I am YHWH, the Lord, your God . . .' The significance of this name has already been discussed (above pp. 5—6) and need not be re-examined here. Its revelation was an especial token of the covenant relationship binding God and his people and it was therefore very important that it be given due and proper reverence. By prohibiting irreverent use of the name the third commandment seeks to preserve and inculcate this due and proper reverence.

Stipulation reinforced by threat

The words, 'for the Lord will not hold anyone guiltless who misuses his name', attached to the basic injunction of this commandment, clearly give added weight to its prohibition. It was no light thing to break this commandment, and anyone who did so could look forward to incurring the divine penalty appropriate to his guilt. The nature of the penalty is not stated, nor is it affirmed that the offender would never be forgiven. The point seems to be that God could not and would not ignore the misuse of his name.

The threat attached to this commandment is not unlike that of punishment to the third and fourth generation which is attached to the second. That nothing comparable occurs in any of the other commandments would suggest that these two have some common element which required the addition of words of threat. This would seem to be the fact that both commands prohibit abuses which implied or involved a paganizing debasement of worship. Breach of the remaining commandments (four to ten) could take place and could be put right within the framework of covenant faith. An adulterer, a thief or even a murderer would be dealt with on the assumption of reverence for and faith in God. But the use of images or the misuse of God's name affected the basic structure of the covenant relationship and would put in jeopardy the covenant standing and privileges of the offender.

The threats in both commandments may present us today with exegetical problems because we do not know exactly how to interpret them, but there can be no misunderstanding of the way in which they reinforce the commands. The threats were 'for real' and the requirement to reverence God's name was a vital element in covenant life.

Safeguarding covenant privileges

Possession of the divine name was a token of the privileges the Israelites enjoyed in covenant. They had fellowship with God and access to him. They had an assurance of his presence and of his care for them. These privileges were not, however, automatic but depended on and could only be maintained by a proper reverence for 'the name'.

In prohibiting the misuse of God's name, the third commandment is insisting on this reverence. In the process it seeks to safeguard the covenant privileges of God's people by preventing them from incurring the guilt which would accrue to them if the covenant were broken. This safeguarding of covenant privilege can be seen in two areas which involve the name of God, the marking out or identification of his people and their worship.

Covenant identity

In a promise of blessing on his people God said that all the peoples on the earth would see that they were called by the name of the Lord (Deuteronomy 28:10). Two passages in the book of Isaiah show that in later times this was still the ideal. In the first (43:7) God promised to call from afar all who were called by his name, and in the second (63:19) the prophet bemoaned the fact that his people had become like those who were not called by his name. Their behaviour patterns were such as belied their covenant identity, but nevertheless that identity still obtained — God had not yet cast off his people.

It was probably by extension of this provision that the Israelites freely incorporated the sacred name into the names they gave to their children. It was, of course, common ancient practice to incorporate the name of a god in that of a child, and the Israelites did just that, using several abbreviated forms of the name JHWH or YHVH. So we get names like 'Elijah', which means 'My God is "Jah" (or "Yah")', or 'Jonathan' meaning 'gift of "Jo" (or "Yo")'. We have 'Isaiah' or 'Isa'yahu' meaning 'Jah (or Yahu) is my helper' and 'Jeremiah' meaning 'Jah (or Yah) is high'. The list is long but the procedure of naming children in this way was clearly legitimate and indeed gave outward, and in a sense tangible, expression to the fact that Israel was in covenant with the Lord.

The sins of the Israelites belied the fact that they were identified by God's name. Indeed, their behaviour polluted or profaned that sacred name which was, as we would say, dragged in the gutter. Amos showed this profanation with devastating frankness:

'This is what the Lord says:
"For three sins of Israel,
even for four, I will not turn back [my wrath].
They sell the righteous for silver,
and the needy for a pair of sandals.
They trample on the heads of the poor
as upon the dust of the ground
and deny justice to the oppressed.
Father and son use the same girl
and so profane my holy name "' (Amos 2:6—7).

To be called by God's name and to behave immorally was to profane, and thus in some way to misuse that name. The exile in Babylon, which came as punishment for sins of idolatry and immorality, was a defeat for God's people and in the very process a profaning of the name of God which they were privileged to bear. 'They *profaned my holy name,* for it was said of them, "These are the Lord's people,

and yet they had to leave his land."' God was clearly grieved
over the profanation of his name and said, 'I had concern
for my holy name, which the house of Israel *profaned*
among the nations where they had gone' (Ezekiel 36:20—21).

Israel, then, was privileged to know God's name and to use
it to identify themselves. They were a people 'called by the
name of the Lord'. But this privilege carried with it responsibility so to live and so to order their affairs that the God
whose name they bore, and to whom they professed
devotion, was honoured. Any life-style or behaviour pattern
that was out of tune with that goal meant automatically
that their use of his name became worthless, empty and vain.
They misused and profaned his name.

Covenant worship
In the restatement of Israel's covenant obligations in the
book of Deuteronomy, 'the name of the Lord' known in
Israel is a token of his presence among his people. Again
and again Moses speaks of a place to be chosen as a central
sanctuary and in which God would put his name and (in
consequence) manifest his presence: 'You are to seek the
place the Lord your God will choose . . . to put his name
there for his dwelling' (Deuteronomy 12:5; cf. 12:11, 21;
14:23, 24; 16:2, 6, 11; 26:2). The plain implication of these
passages is that the putting of God's name in, and the habitation of God in the place to be chosen were synonymous.
Where his name was, he was, and to be the possessors of
that sacred name was to have inestimable privilege — in short,
to be his chosen and his covenant people. In prohibiting the
misuse of his name God was undoubtedly requiring behaviour
essential to the continuance of that privilege.

One aspect of Israel's covenant privilege was its worship of
the Lord. In the place marked by the presence of God's
name the people were to engage in acts of worship. There
they would bring their tithes to God and there they would
rejoice in his blessings. There they would eat the passover,
enjoying it as a joyous celebration of redemption.

The name YHWH was used in addressing God. Moses himself so used it: 'O *Lord,* why should your anger burn?'
(Exodus 32:11), and we read of Samuel calling *on the name
of the Lord.* To call on God's name was clearly to address

oneself to him in an attitude of dependence and worship. The supreme blessing of salvation was promised in Joel's prophecy to those who would 'call on the name of the Lord' (Joel 2:32).

At the same time the name of God is so identified with the reality of his person that it is itself sometimes virtually the object of worship. Thus the psalmists call on men to ascribe to the Lord the glory due to his name (Psalm 29:2) and to praise the name of the Lord, because his name alone is exalted (Psalm 148:13). In so doing they mean, of course, that glory and praise are elements essential to true worship and should be given to God, the bearer of the name. For them his name is greatly to be revered: 'Holy and awesome is his name' (Ps. 111:9). Any profanity or carelessness in the use of the name in worship would thus be a direct insult to God, whose name it was, and an instance of taking that name in vain. The privilege of worship was for those who honoured the name and was therefore safeguarded by the prohibition in the command: 'You shall not misuse the name of the Lord your God.'

Focusing on the invocation of divine power

Swearing by his name

There is one clear instance in the Old Testament of God permitting, indeed requiring, the invocation of his name. This is in the making of oaths: 'Fear the Lord your God, serve him only and take your oaths in his name. Do not follow other gods . . . ' (Deuteronomy 6:13–14; cf. 10:20).

This passage is in a context which demands the exclusion of other gods from Israelite life and so would clearly prohibit, for the purpose of swearing oaths, the use of the name of any other god. At the same time the fact that the Lord's name was to be used would mean that such oaths as were made had to be of a type that conformed to his will. It is inconceivable that God would condone the use of his name in an oath which was detrimental to a neighbour, whom his law required to be loved as a man loves himself.

It is not at all clear on what occasions oaths could legitimately be made in Israel. The laws which insist on fair play

and proper justice for accused persons require the confirma-
tion of an accusation by two or three witnesses, but they do
not specify that accused, accuser or witness be put on oath.
It may, of course, have been common practice to take court
evidence on oath, but we cannot prove that this was so.

It does seem, however, that in the time of Solomon oaths
in the name of the Lord were taken when civil disputes were
brought to court. Thus, addressing God in his prayer at the
dedication of the temple, Solomon said, 'When a man wrongs
his neighbour and is required to take an oath and he comes
and swears the oath before your altar in this temple, then
hear from heaven and act. Judge between your servants,
condemning the guilty . . . Declare the innocent not
guilty . . .' (1 Kings 8:31–32; cf. 2 Chron. 6:22). If a civil
action involved or could involve solemn oath-taking before
God's altar, and therefore involving God as witness, it is
certainly possible that the judges could call for, or a witness
could volunteer to give evidence on oath.

At any event, the oath was a means of affirming that a
statement was true or that an intention to do something was
genuine. To swear in the name of the Lord was to invoke his
power to attest truth or affirm fidelity and was a solemn
exercise indeed — one which, as the words of Solomon's
prayer indicate, called for divine judgement to be applied to
the parties concerned. To so use God's name in a careless,
a false, an empty or vain way would be an indignity to him,
a profaning of his name and an invitation to his wrath.

This is why perjury, the affirmation on oath that something is true when in fact it is false, was a serious crime in
Israel. The Lord said, 'Do not swear falsely by my name and
so profane the name of your God' (Leviticus 19:12). To
swear falsely, using or involving the name of the Lord, was
another way of dragging his name and thus his character in
the gutter. It was a misuse of his name.

In the well-known story of David's friendship with
Jonathan we have a fine illustration of the way in which an
oath in the name of the Lord was regarded as absolutely
binding. Jonathan had come to recognize that David, and
not himself, was God's choice to succeed Saul as King of
Israel. He persuaded David to swear to him, calling on the
Lord as witness, that when he, David, became king, he would

spare both Jonathan and his descendants and show them the unfailing kindness of the Lord (1 Samuel 20:12–17). David made the oath and years later kept his solemn undertaking by preserving alive Jonathan's son, Mephibosheth, 'because of the oath before' (or 'of') 'the Lord between David and Jonathan' (2 Samuel 21:7). Clearly the divine involvement arising from the fact that God's name had been invoked was so strong that the oath between the two men could be called 'the oath of the Lord' (Hebrew – cf. AV and RSV). Clearly, too, for David to have failed to keep it would have been to call upon himself some expression of divine wrath.

An oath is in one sense a curse calling down some form of divine penalty on oneself if one fails to meet the conditions of the oath. 'May God deal with me, be it ever so severely, if . . .' (1 Kings 2:23) was a form used by Solomon in a burst of anger. It was of doubtful validity because it did not use the name of the Lord and was in fact very similar to the more pagan oaths of Jezebel or Benhadad: 'May the gods deal with me, be it ever so severely, if . . .' Valid or not, this form of oath illustrates the principle of calling wrath upon oneself if one's words are proved untrue or one's intentions are unfulfilled. As long as the intention was that God should hold a man to his word, and not that damage be done to someone else, it seems to have been legitimate for an Israelite to swear an oath using or invoking the name of the Lord.

The illegitimate oath
In the ancient world curses were usually spoken in order to discredit or disadvantage or eliminate someone else, and the invocation of the name of a god would be an attempt to secure the power of that god for the accomplishment of the desired end. In Israel, however, such curses seem to have been completely outside legitimacy, at least for the individual. Rulers or judges could include them in pronouncements of judgement on criminals or enemies, but the private or personal curse in which one person tried to manipulate divine power for his own ends had no place. Thus Job, defending his integrity, could say that he had not caused the death of someone who hated him by uttering a curse: 'I have not allowed my mouth to sin by invoking a curse against his life' (Job 31:30).

In Ezekiel Jewish women involved in magic were accused
by God of profaning his name among his people because
they 'have killed those who should not have died and have
spared those who should not live' (Ezekiel 13:19). Clearly
the women concerned had intruded into a realm from which
humans are precluded. They were manipulating the powers
of life and death by magic, and since they are charged with
profaning God's name, they had possibly invoked that name
for their nefarious ends and were thus breakers of the third
commandment.

There is a rather enigmatic instance recorded in Leviticus
24:10—16 of a man, half-Israelite, half-Egyptian and
evidently a sojourner in Israel, who blasphemed the name
of the Lord with a curse. It is agreed by scholars that he
broke the third commandment by misusing God's name in
an oath, resorting no doubt to a magic style use of the divine
name in an attempt to secure the death of his opponent. The
verdict that the man himself should die suggests that the
offence was absolutely intolerable to the Lord and equivalent to the ultimate blasphemy of cursing him.

General exclusion of magic

In a more general way the third commandment excludes the
use of God's name from any magical practice. The spells,
curses or charms of sorcerers and charmers would normally
invoke the name of deity and in Israel would thus involve
the use of God's name for what was a false, a worthless, a
vain end. In Deuteronomy 18:10—11 sorcerers and charmers
were described as detestable to the Lord and were to be
excluded from Israel. At a later date, when they were
apparently present in some numbers, God threatened to
remove from Jerusalem 'the skilled craftsman and clever
enchanter' (Isaiah 3:3).

Magic in all its forms is the negation of any true faith in
God. It seeks not to rest in God's ordering of events but to
manipulate them for selfish ends. Whereas in prayer man
takes the place of a dependent and asks for help, in magic
man commands the god he thinks he can use to achieve his
goals. And if that god happens to be the Lord and his name
is used, as could have been the case when magic appeared in
Israel, then that name is misused, the third commandment
is broken and guilt is incurred.

New Testament endorsement

Confirmed by Jesus and the apostles

In a very special way Jesus was the representation of God on earth. He therefore presented himself as working on behalf of, or in the name of his Father in heaven. 'I have come', he said, *'in my Father's name'* (John 5:43) and again, 'The miracles I do *in my Father's name* speak for me' (John 10:25). Twice in the great high-priestly prayer recorded in John 17 he affirmed that he had revealed or made known God's name among men (vv. 6, 26). He also prayed that the disciples God had given him would be kept in or through God's name ('by the power of your name' v. 11) and then declared that while he had been with them he had kept them by that name (v. 12).

Clearly he attached great importance to the name of God and gave due reverence to it. He regarded the publication of that name as a major element in his mission and prayed earnestly that it would be glorified: 'Father', he said, 'glorify your name!' (John 12:28.)

In the pattern prayer our Lord's care for the honour of God's name comes out in the very first petition: 'Our Father in heaven, hallowed be your name.' This recognizes the sovereign majesty of the Lord as Father in heaven and asks that his name be hallowed, that is, sanctified, kept separate from other names as one that is alone worthy of God. In so praying the disciple further asks for grace that God's name will be hallowed rather than profaned in his own life, that he will so live that those with whom he comes into contact will be compelled to respect and honour, to glorify the name of the Lord.

The apostles likewise respected and honoured God's name. They quoted the Old Testament freely and carried forward its ethos of reverence for the Lord, King of kings and Lord of lords, the Lord God Almighty, to whom glory and honour and power are due. The last thing these men would have done, the last thing they would condone, would have been a misuse of the name of the Lord. It may well be that Peter had done this when with oaths and curses he denied the Lord Jesus at the time of his trial, but it was a new, a strengthened Peter who emerged at Pentecost and who quoted Joel's

prophecy about salvation for those who call on the name of
the Lord.

Paul confessed that prior to his conversion he had been
guilty of causing others to blaspheme or speak ill of God's
name (Acts 26:11). Later on he shared the concern of the
other apostles and instructed Timothy to teach those
believers who were slaves to give proper honour to their
masters, so that the name of God and the Christian teaching
associated with it be not slandered (1 Timothy 6:1). James
shows the same reverence when he warns his readers against
showing partiality to rich men, who were in fact blasphemers
of 'the noble name' of the one to whom they, his Christian
readers, belonged (James 2:7).

Peter, Paul and James unite then with the evangelists and
with our Lord himself in giving reverence to the name of God
and in eschewing everything, whether spoken word or inconsistent act, that could profane or devalue it. Whatever else
this respect may involve, it certainly means that the third
commandment was recognized and observed. The new gospel
does not cancel, but rather endorses the command: 'You
shall not misuse the name of the Lord your God.'

Extended with trinitarian significance

Inclusion of Jesus as Lord
When the birth of a unique child was announced to Joseph
and Mary a name was given for him. He was to be called
Jesus, a Greek form of the Hebrew name Joshua, and meaning 'The Lord is Saviour'.

Though this name had been used in Old Testament times
of those who were purely human, the angelic announce-
ments pointed to one who was to be somehow more than a
human deliverer: 'You are to give him the name Jesus,
because he will save his people from their sins' (Matthew
1:21). 'You are to give him the name Jesus. He will be great
and will be called the Son of the Most High . . .' (Luke
1:31–32). Certainly Matthew so understood the message,
for he immediately applied to it a prophecy from Isaiah:
'All this took place to fulfil what the Lord had said through
the prophet: "The virgin will be with child and will give

birth to a son, and they will call him Immanuel," – which means, "God with us"' (Matthew 1:22–23). Here was one in whom God had come among men and the name he bore clearly betokened not just his mission to save, but also the divine involvement in that mission. This was no more an ordinary name but the name of the incarnate Son of God.

The way in which our Lord referred to his own name is wholly consistent with this. He told his disciples that they would incur human hatred for his name's sake, that is, because of their association with his name and, of course, with himself as the bearer of that name (Matthew 10:22 etc.). He told them that he expected them to forsake everything for his sake (Matthew 19:29), saying, 'for my name's sake' (Greek, AV, RSV etc.). Similarly, the disciples were told that he would be present with those who would gather in his name (Matthew 18:20). Clearly, his name was to be the focal point for the devotion of his followers and was being invested with significance like that possessed by the name of God in Old Testament times.

On a number of occasions Jesus was addressed as 'Lord'. The seventy-two disciples returning from mission said to him, '*Lord,* even the demons submit to us in your name' (Luke 10:17). When he asked where Lazarus had been buried, the reply was 'Come and see, *Lord,*' (John 11:34). Earlier a man whom he had invited to become his disciple had replied, '*Lord,* first let me go and bury my father' (Luke 9:59). These and similar passages do not, however, indicate that those who so addressed him recognized his divine identity. This is because the Greek word *kurios,* which is translated as 'Lord', often meant something like 'sir' in English.

However, when we turn to the preaching and the writing of the apostles, where under the inspiration of the Holy Spirit we have a more fully developed understanding of the person of Jesus, we discover that this same word is used of him with the full Old Testament significance of YHWH. He is indeed *the Lord* and is frequently spoken of as such, or as the *Lord* Jesus Christ. As Jesus appeared to the confused group of disciples fishing in Galilee, John said to Peter, 'It is *the Lord*!' (John 21:7.) In his sermon on the day of Pentecost Peter said, 'God has made this Jesus,

whom you crucified, both *Lord* and Christ' (Acts 2:36).
Greeting his readers in Rome and Corinth, Paul prayed for
them: 'Grace and peace to you from God our Father and
from the *Lord* Jesus Christ' (Romans 1:7; 1 Corinthians
1:3).

As a matter of background it should be mentioned that
before the coming of Christ the Old Testament had been
translated into Greek and that the sacred name of God, the
vowelless YHWH, was rendered by this very word *kurios*. So
for those with a Greek Old Testament *kurios* was YHWH.
This meant that when the apostles moved out of Palestine
and into the Greek-speaking world of Asia Minor, Egypt
and Greece itself, they had to use *kurios* when they meant
to refer to God, YHWH. But, in addition, on a number of
occasions they used Old Testament prophecies about YHWH
with reference to Christ, thus calling him not only *kurios*
but YHWH.

A well-known example of this occurs in Paul's Epistle
to the Philippians, where he says of the risen Christ,

'God exalted him to the highest place
and gave him the name that is above every name,
that at the name of Jesus every knee should bow,
in heaven and on earth and under the earth,
and every tongue confess that Jesus Christ is *Lord*,
to the glory of God the Father' (Philippians 2:9–11).

This passage clearly cites the words of Isaiah 45:22–24
where God, YHWH, speaks affirming that every knee would
one day bow to him and every tongue swear that righteousness and strength are only found in him. Paul is saying that
what was predicted there had now been fulfilled in Christ,
who had been given *the name above every name,* the name
that signifies true deity, the name YHWH. That name was
properly applicable to him and one day every knee would
bow before him as its bearer acknowledged him to be *Lord,
kurios,* YHWH. The fact that in Romans 14:11 Paul cites
the same passage from Isaiah with reference to the day
when all men will give account to God shows that for him
the name above all names, the name borne by the ascended

Saviour, is the name of God. That name, YHWH, rightly belonged to, and belongs to Jesus.

Inclusion of the Holy Spirit

In the Old Testament the divine Spirit appears as God in action and without any clear indication of distinct personality. In the New Testament the Spirit becomes the third Person of the divine Trinity, a 'he' distinct from, but yet one with both Father and Son. He can be lied to and grieved; he is the Spirit of God and the Spirit of Christ.

There is an intriguing parallel between our Lord's teaching on the sin of blasphemy against the Holy Spirit and the third commandment. This lies in the threat that such a sin would never be forgiven and in that attached to the command: 'The Lord will not hold anyone guiltless who misuses his name.' The words of Jesus were even stronger and introduced the idea of a sin which would never be forgiven (Matthew 12:31–32; Mark 3:28–29). Exegesis of the saying is notoriously difficult but if it echoes the threat of the third commandment it would seem at least to suggest that our Lord was somehow investing the name of the Holy Spirit with the full sanctity of the divine name.

When our Lord gave his great missionary commission to the disciples he commanded that converts be baptized '*in the name* of the Father and of the Son and of the Holy Spirit' (Matthew 28:19). He spoke of three Persons, but only one name, and must surely have meant that all three Persons of the Godhead are rightly known by YHWH, the one supreme and sacred name of God. The Holy Spirit is thus brought, with the Lord Jesus Christ himself, into the connotation of the name YHWH and therefore within the scope of the third commandment. We can misuse the name of the Lord in relation to the Spirit.

Further consideration of these matters would involve a far fuller discussion of the doctrine of the Trinity than could be justified here. The point of what we have been saying is simply that the third commandment now has to be interpreted in a trinitarian frame of reference. To misuse God's name can relate to the Father, the Son or the Holy Spirit, as well as to the overall name YHWH by which the Godhead is rightly known.

Applied to Christian discipleship

False professions

The identification of Israel as the people of the Lord in Old Testament times has a parallel in the way in which New Testament believers became known as Christians or 'Christ's ones'. The term first arose at Antioch (Acts 11:26) and epitomized the fact that they belonged to Christ and had indeed been baptized into his name. At this early stage the converts were mainly Jewish and had a background of belief in the one God, YHWH. As such the new elements in their lives were the recognition of Jesus as God the Son and the acceptance of his teachings as the basis of their new lifestyle. They were therefore, it seems, baptized into the name of Jesus rather than into the triune name, as commanded by our Lord in the Great Commission, where his concern was with the proclamation of the gospel to nations which did not worship God and for whom conversion would mean the acceptance, not just of Jesus, but of YHWH as Father, Son and Spirit.

In any event, the convert, Jewish or Gentile, is clearly marked out as belonging to Christ. He receives and is privileged to use Christ's name, legitimately calling himself a Christian or 'Christ's one'. This being so, a great responsibility lies on him to behave in a way consistent with the significance of this identity. If he is Christ's one he must live in Christ's way and so bring honour to Christ's name.

The great danger which arises is that men profess Christ's name in baptism or in testimony and live so inconsistently that their profession becomes empty or vain. Our Lord himself depicted very forcefully the fate of those who even at the final assize will make such a profession: 'Lord, Lord', they will say, 'did we not prophesy in your name, and in your name drive out demons and perform many miracles?' Such will be bitterly disappointed, for he will then say to them, 'I never knew you. Away from me, you evildoers!' (Matthew 7:22–23.) His words show that it is very easy, all too easy, to profess his name, to claim to follow and serve him and yet to be an evildoer. Said our Lord again, 'Not every one who says to me, "Lord, Lord", will enter the kingdom of heaven, but only he who does the will of my Father who is in heaven.' If such is to be the case when at last we stand awaiting entrance to the realms of eternal bliss, how important that now we act as those who do espouse and practise God's will! To profess his name and do otherwise is to misuse, to profane that name and is a violation of the third commandment: 'You shall not misuse the name of the Lord your God.'

Oath-taking

The stipulations of the old covenant between God and Israel required that such oaths as were necessary be in the name of the Lord: 'Serve Him only and take your oaths in his name' (Deuteronomy 6:13). They also required absolute honesty in such oaths: 'Do not swear falsely by my name and so profane the name of the Lord your God' (Leviticus 19:12).

These regulations made swearing an oath a thing of real significance, never to be undertaken carelessly, and made perjury, or affirmation of a falsity under oath, a serious sin. This the Jews of our Lord's day knew full well. Indeed, they were so afraid of breaking the third commandment in this way that they devised oaths of convenience to avoid the use of the divine name. They swore 'by heaven', 'by the earth', 'by Jerusalem' or even by their own heads. Our Lord called a halt to this in the sermon on the mount by showing that God was still being invoked in these oaths: 'I tell you, Do not swear at all, either by heaven, for it is God's throne; or by the earth, for it is his footstool; or by Jerusalem, for it is the city of the Great King. And do not swear by your head, for you cannot make even one hair white or black. Simply let your "Yes" be "Yes", and your "No," "No", anything beyond this comes from the evil one' (Matthew 5:34—37).

James seems to have had this saying in mind when he wrote, 'Do not swear — not by heaven or by earth or by anything else. Let your "Yes" be "Yes", and your "No", "No", or you will be condemned' (James 5:12).

These two passages have led many Christians to the conclusion that it is always wrong to make or take an oath. They see the command of Christ to be clear and unequivocal: 'Do not swear at all.' The difficulty with such a view lies in the way that Jesus himself accepted without objection the fact that he himself was put on oath. Indeed, it was only then that he opened his mouth to answer the high priest (Matthew 26:63–64). There is also the fact that on a number of occasions Paul seems to affirm a point by an oath, or a virtual oath in God's name: 'I call God as my witness' (2 Corinthians 1:23; cf. Romans 9:1; Galatians 1:20; 2 Corinthians 11:31). In another instance he actually put his readers on oath: 'I charge (*henorkizō*) you before the Lord to have this letter read to all the brothers' (1 Thessalonians 5:27). These passages would suggest that our Lord did not intend to countermand the provisions of Old Testament law and that Paul did not understand him to have done so. Rather he must have proscribed oaths of the kind which tried to evade the implications of swearing by the divine name and which were, of course, practised by the Pharisees.

It may well be that what our Lord was attacking was not solemn oaths needed to establish the integrity or guilt of an accused person, but more trivial swearing indulged in to impress hearers and convince them that the speaker was being honest. For our Lord such swearing is quite unnecessary. His followers should be men of their word, whose 'Yes,' means 'Yes', and whose 'No,' means 'No', without the addition of an oath. To have to strengthen a promise with an oath is, as the Living Bible suggests, an indication that something is wrong.

We must constantly watch our words and make sure that we conform to the standard set for us here by Jesus. Our 'Yes,' must mean 'Yes', and not something else. Our 'No,' must mean 'No', and not be spoken tongue-in-cheek with intent to deceive. If, as sometimes happens, we are in situations where we are called upon to speak on oath, we should not feel obliged to refuse, as by law in Britain and other countries we would be entitled to do on grounds of conscience, but we should then ponder well every word we say and see to it that we do not perjure ourselves by swearing falsely. If the oath involves the name of the Lord or some synonym by which divine power in witness or retribution is invoked, then perjury would be a misuse of God's name.

Magic

Magicians and magical practices are mentioned on a number of occasions in the New Testament. In general, there is clear and definite rejection of the whole business, even if there is genuine compassion for the personal well-being of those concerned.

The party of men who came to welcome the infant Jesus are introduced as 'Magi (or "wise men") from the east' (Matthew 2:1). The Greek word *magos* (plural *magoi,* Latin *magi*) was originally used of priests in Media but later came to mean a magician, a wizard, a sorcerer, one who practises *magia* or magic. There are several views of the identity of the wise men, but the most commonly accepted one is that they came from Mesopotamia, where they specialized in observing the stars and where their astrology marked them out as diviners or *magoi.* They might well have been Babylonian Jews who had imbibed astrological arts and who linked the Messianic hope with a reading of the stars. There is no suggestion, however, that they actually practised magic of the type we have seen to be prohibited by the third commandment, but neither is there ground for denying that they had done so.

In the Acts we find the apostles meeting two men of whom the same word, *magos,* is used. The first is Simon, often called Simon Magus, who had so long and so effectively practised sorcery (*magia*) that the people of Samaria acclaimed him as 'the divine power known as the Great Power' (Acts 8:10). This Simon was converted under the ministry of Philip but did not at once leave behind all his magical ideas. When, therefore, he saw that the Holy Spirit was received through the prayer and the laying-on of hands of the apostles, he wanted to get this power for himself. He was, we can be sure, honestly seeking to go forward in the Christian way, but he was as yet unable to discern between spiritual and magical power, and thought that he could purchase the spiritual kind of power in the same way as in the past he had purchased magical know-how. Peter dealt with him firmly and the genuineness of his conversion is shown by the humble and the penitent way in which he accepted rebuke. He had to learn, and it seems did learn, that magic could have no place in the Christian life.

The second case is that of Elymas or Bar-Jesus who is described both as a sorcerer (a *magos*) and as a Jewish false prophet (Acts 13:4—12). No details of his magical activities are given but it is probable that in opposing the apostles, he had cast a spell or used a curse of some kind. It would seem that he was in the employ of Sergius Paulus, the Roman proconsul in Cyprus, or in a position of influence with him, so that he feared dismissal or loss of position if Sergius heeded Paul's preaching. Paul's response was to address him as a child of the devil and an enemy of everything that was right, implying that, whatever his activities, he was doing Satan's work on earth. The apostle went on to accuse him of perverting the right ways of the Lord (v. 10), which might well mean that by the use of magic he was intruding into realms forbidden to men and trying to manipulate divine power for his own ends. As a Jew he would probably have invoked the divine name, YHWH, and would in that event have been guilty of misusing that name. The way in which Paul pronounced his punishment by temporary blindness convinced Sergius that divine power was on the side of the apostle: 'When the proconsul saw what had happened, he believed.'

A further incident involving magic is recorded in Acts 19:11—20. A Jewish family who engaged in exorcisms saw certain miracles associated with Paul's ministry in Ephesus and began to use the name of Jesus to invoke divine power apparently in a magical fashion. A spirit they sought to exorcise responded by rejecting their authority: 'Jesus I know and Paul I know about, but who are you?' Then the man turned on them and overpowered them. Here indeed was misuse of the name of Jesus, and no miracle was accomplished by those who thought they could use it as a success formula for magic-style incantation. However, the outcome was a victory for the Lord in that his *name* was held in high honour as great fear fell on Jews and Greeks, and as a considerable number of believers confessed sins, which included the practice of sorcery presumably like that of the sons of Sceva. The relevant literature, worth fifty thousand pieces of silver, was publicly burned and the Word of God progressed with new liberty. Again magic was shown to be worthless and totally unworthy of those who profess the name of Christ. Its paraphernalia, however costly, is fit for but one fate, the fire, and where any relic of it is found in the life of a Christian, public confession and repudiation like that at Ephesus is essential to complete deliverance and to a proper and full honouring of the name of Jesus.

The New Testament has five other references to witch-craft or those who practise magic, and in each case the Greek words belong to a group from which we derive words like pharmacy or pharmaceutical, and which could mean not just medicines or drugs, but spells and potions used in magic for charming or poisoning. It is generally believed that in the New Testament their main reference is to magicians and their arts. In the Galatian Epistle 'witchcraft' (*pharmakeia*) is one of the works of the flesh and a mark of those who shall not inherit the kingdom of heaven (Galatians 5:20). Incidentally, it is mentioned immediately after idolatry, a juxtaposition which might suggest that Paul was thinking of breaches of the second and third commandments — idols being images and sorcery being a wrong use of God's name. Similar ideas obtain in Revelation, where those who practise magic are listed with those who will have no part in eternal bliss (Revelation 9:21; 18:23; 21:8; 22:15).

The incidents in Acts and the references to magic arts in Galatians and Revelation unite to demonstrate the total incompatibility of magic with Christianity. It involves a turning to some power other than God or the use of his name in an attempt to manipulate his power. As such it either makes fellowship with him impossible because of reliance on another god, or it misuses his name and incurs guilt before him.

In an age when there is an alarming resurgence of occult practices including magic, Christians need to be alert to its dangers and to avoid it like they would avoid the plague. Sometimes it is presented as if it were Christian, the spell-binders calling on God or even using the name of Jesus in their incantations and charms. But clearly it is totally in opposition to true Christianity, a dangerous practice which, when using the divine name or any appellation relating to the persons of the Trinity, must involve a breach of the third commandment, a misuse of God's name.

Most Christians will pride themselves on being free from many of the sins we have been discussing. They try to live

for God and would be offended to be told that their profession of the Lord's name is hollow. They would never
dream of perjuring themselves or of loosely using the name
of God or of Christ in oaths or cursings. As for magic, they
have no part in it and mercifully do not even know what it
is. In their book they do not misuse God's name.

But let us make sure we really do keep the third commandment in its spirit as well as to the letter, that our profession
of the name of Christ is real and not empty, that we do not
fall into habits which, even without the direct use of his
name, actually profane it. Let us see to it that our behaviour
patterns, our life-styles, our words and our deeds are totally
consistent with the name we are privileged to bear and to
use. Let us see to it that we give to the name of God, and
to the three Persons of the Trinity to whom it applies, all
the honour and reverence that is due.

The fact is that this command makes ultimate demands on
each of us. It admits of no compromise and demands that
our all be on the altar for God. 'Through Jesus, . . . let us
continually offer to God a sacrifice of praise — the fruit
of lips that confess his *name*.' The best, the only, way to
avoid misusing his name is to acknowledge his name and to
do so with constant reverence and self-giving.

'You shall not misuse the name of the Lord your God . . .'

6. The sabbath
The Fourth Commandment

'Remember the Sabbath day, by keeping it holy. Six days you shall labour and do all your work, but the seventh day is a Sabbath to the Lord your God. On it you shall not do any work, neither you, nor your son or daughter, nor your manservant or maidservant, nor your animals, nor the alien within your gates. For in six days the Lord made the heavens and the earth, the sea, and all that is in them, but he rested on the seventh day. Therefore the Lord blessed the Sabbath day and made it holy.'

The fourth commandment prescribes the observance of one day in seven as a day of rest from work. It has three imperatives, two of which are cast in a positive form. The third, 'On it you shall not do any work,' is negative and directly comparable with the prohibitions of the other commandments. It is a fairly long commandment, incorporating a series of extensions to ensure that the privilege of rest is enjoyed throughout the whole family and community. The record preserved in Deuteronomy shows a number of variations from that in Exodus and these have to be taken into account as we seek to grasp the significance of the command.

The Deuteronomic version reads as follows, the words in italics being either additions to, or alterations of, that found in Exodus: '*Observe* the Sabbath day by keeping it holy, *as the Lord your God has commanded you.* Six days you shall labour and do all your work, but the seventh day is a Sabbath to the Lord your God. On it you shall not do

81

any work, neither you, nor your son or daughter, nor your manservant or maidservant, nor your *ox, your donkey* or any of your animals, nor the alien within your gates, *so that your manservant and maidservant may rest, as you do. Remember that you were slaves in Egypt and that the Lord your God brought you out of there with a mighty hand and an outstretched arm. Therefore the Lord your God has commanded you to observe the Sabbath day'* (Deuteronomy 5:12—15).

This commandment, alone of the ten, clearly spells out obligations that are both God-ward and manward. Sabbath was to be kept 'to the Lord', but it was also to be kept for the good of one's fellows and, indeed, for the good of those animals which were used to work for man's benefit. There is thus something of a transition here between the vertical or God-ward dimension of the first three commands and the horizontal or manward dimension of the later ones.

The meaning of sabbath

The Hebrew word *shabbath*, which English versions render as 'sabbath', is usually understood to mean a day or a period of rest. The associated verb *shabath*, however, means 'to desist', 'to cease' or 'to make an end'. The emphasis seems to be on breaking a routine and so making a division in time or bringing a series of activities or a cycle of time to an end.

In Israel the word was mainly used of the seventh day, on which this fourth commandment prohibited work. There was a cessation of the routine of the other six days and therefore what we know as 'rest'. But there were other days which were also to be 'sabbaths', even though they did not fall on the last or seventh day of a seven-day week. In the great festival of Passover, for example, the fourteenth and twenty-first days of the first month were to be days marked by rest and holy convocations. They were sabbaths and would fall on different days of the week (Exodus 12:14—20; Leviticus 23:4—8). The same applied to the fifteenth day at harvest time — the day after the sabbath, and so in fact the first day of a new week (Leviticus 23:15—21). Similarly the first, tenth, fifteenth and twenty-second days of the seventh

month were days of religious observance at sacred assemblies
and marked by rest from regular work (Leviticus 23:23—44).
These dates were important dividing points in the calendar —
the beginning of a new half-year, the Day of Atonement
and the first and final days of the Feast of Booths or Tabernacles. Occasionally, one or even two of them might fall on
a regular sabbath day, but more often than not they would
be on other days. They were thus additional sabbaths, 'in
addition to the Lord's sabbaths' (Leviticus 23:38).

These additional sabbaths would suggest that the word is
not restricted to the one day of rest following six days of
work. It must be somewhat broader and embrace any day
which broke an established routine and divided between one
cycle of time and another.

There can be little doubt that the idea of a break in labour
was common in the ancient world. The Babylonians had their
shabbatu or *shappatu* which some have tried to identify with
the Israelite sabbath. The routine and the significance were
different but the idea of a break in the time cycle is probably
common. Abraham may well have brought some such ideas
with him from Mesopotamia to Palestine, but we have no
record of him or of any of the patriarchs observing a seventh-
day sabbath to the Lord.

We can say with certainty that sabbath as a seventh day of
the week routine was established as a covenant obligation
after the deliverance from Egypt. As the Deuteronomic
version of the commandment concludes, 'Therefore', that is,
because of the divine deliverance of Israel from Egypt, 'the
Lord your God has commanded you to observe the Sabbath
day' (Deuteronomy 5:15). Centuries later Ezra confirmed
that the sabbath was instituted at Sinai when he prayed, 'You
came down on Mount Sinai . . . You gave them regulations
and laws that are just and right, and decrees and commands
that are good. You made known to them your holy Sabbath
and gave them commands, decrees and laws through your
servant Moses' (Nehemiah 9:13—14).

Whatever Israelites or others may have known of sabbath
before Moses' time, the sabbath as one day in seven, holy to
the Lord, was introduced by him, and the world owes its
seven-day week, independent of its annual and monthly
calendars, to him. It is thus difficult to accept the contention

that sabbath was known and obligatory from the creation
onwards. That the creation narrative (Genesis 2:1–3) tells
of God resting on the seventh day is not in itself proof that
the earliest men knew that fact or that they knew themselves to have a duty to follow suit.

The sabbath prescriptions

A day holy to the Lord
'*Remember (observe) the Sabbath day by keeping it holy.*'
In Exodus the verb is '*zakar*', the standard Hebrew word
for calling to mind or having something actively in one's
consciousness. In Deuteronomy it is '*shamar*' meaning
'to take heed', and so to observe or keep a rule or a law.
Either way the implication is that the people of God were
not to neglect the sabbath. They were to give it a proper
place in their thinking and so make sure that they observed
what God had commanded.

The content of the command at this point is simply that
the sabbath be kept holy, that it be distinguished from, or
set apart from other days as a day of cessation and rest, a
day peculiarly for the Lord: 'It is a Sabbath to the Lord
your God.' By setting it apart for the Lord, Israel would
properly remember and properly observe the sabbath.

By laying claim to one day in seven, the Lord was asserting that man's days were all his gift and belonged to him.
The sabbath kept holy to him was a token that every day and
every hour were meant to be used for his glory. It was somewhat parallel to the tithe, in which by the giving to him of
one tenth of the produce of the land and of herds and
flocks, he was honoured as the source of these benefits. In
sabbath one seventh of a man's time is specially consecrated
to him as the Source and Sovereign of man's life. It was in a
way a 'tithe on time'.

In Leviticus 23 we have a calendar which links the weekly
sabbath with the great annual festivals at which, by appropriate ceremonies, Israel was to express and maintain its
covenant relationship with God. The sabbath is put first as
an indication perhaps of the fact that its observance is
required in the ten commandments. It was to be marked by

a sacred assembly as well as by an absence of work. This suggests that at this point the sabbath was taken over into *the ceremonial law* and that some sort of religious gathering, an assembly similar to that required on the great festival occasions, was expected. Sabbath, thus envisaged, was not a day of complete inactivity, but one in which together, in assembly, the people of God rested and honoured him by appropriate acts of worship.

The Old Testament gives very little indication about the occurrence of such sabbath assemblies or of what they involved. It would seem that it was an accepted custom in Elisha's day to visit his house at new moon and sabbath (2 Kings 4:23) and it might be that this was for instruction or acts of worship. Isaiah pours scorn — divine scorn — on the same festivals, new moon and sabbath, and the assemblies called on them, because those assemblies were marked by acts of religious devotion, offerings, incense and prayers which were meaningless, because made insincerely and inconsistently by people involved in iniquity, injustice and oppression (Isaiah 1:12–17). Whatever the aberrations, the message was that these improper assemblies or convocations be replaced by gatherings of people whose hearts and hands were cleansed and who could sincerely worship God and humbly bring their petitions to him. Worship and prayer of a corporate nature but, of course, following the ceremonial patterns of the Levitical system, would seem, then, to have been prominent parts of sabbath observance.

That the sabbath day became incorporated in the ceremonial calendar points to an important distinction which we must make between the principle of our commandment — that a day be kept holy to the Lord — and the ceremonial expression of that requirement in Israelite observances. For the Israelite the two things were often so interlocked as to be inseparable, but for us separation is essential if we are to avoid imposing on ourselves, and requiring of others, ceremonials which God intended only for the period between Moses and Christ.

Six days of work
'Six days you shall labour and do all your work.' This second imperative is an integral part of the commandment.

Indeed, a day of cessation from labour would be meaningless
apart from a regular daily routine of work. Here, then, is a
firm declaration of the duty of man to work, a reiteration
indeed of the ordinance given at creation when God put
Adam in the Garden of Eden specifically 'to work it and
take care of it' and when man as the cultivator of the ground
was authorized to maintain himself by eating of its fruit
(Genesis 2:15–16). The Fall introduced an element of
unpleasantness and drudgery into man's work: 'Through
painful toil you will eat of it . . . By the sweat of your
brow you will eat your food' (Genesis 3:17–19), but it
in no way cancelled the creation ordinance. Man, in short,
was made for work.

At Sinai there might well have been a temptation for
those who had suffered so much at the hands of Egyptian
slave-drivers to relax, to make every day a rest day, but this
was not to be. God's requirement was clearly stated: 'Six
days you shall labour.' In addition, work that might have
arisen on the seventh day was to be performed during the
six days leading up to it: 'Six days you shall labour and *do
all your work*.' As manna for the sabbath had to be collected
on the sixth day, so labour in general was to be completed,
so that the sabbath could be free, not only from work but
from the anxiety caused by tasks left undone.

This emphasis on work is never lost sight of in the Old or
New Testaments. Nowhere is it more underlined than in
the book of Proverbs. One paragraph will be sufficient:

> 'Go to the ant, you sluggard;
> consider its ways and be wise!
> It has no commander,
> no overseer or ruler,
> Yet it stores its provisions in summer
> and gathers its food at harvest.
> How long will you lie there, you sluggard?
> When will you get up from your sleep?
> A little sleep, a little slumber,
> a little folding of the hands to rest –
> and poverty will come on you like a bandit
> and scarcity like an armed man.'
> (Proverbs 6:6–11; cf. 24:30–34 etc.).

Clearly then, if one day was to be set apart and kept specially for the Lord, the other six days were also subject to divine claim. They were to be used profitably in honourable work and only by so using them could God's people keep the essential spirit of this commandment. Thus an Israelite had to realize that he was responsible to God for the use he made of all his time, the six days as well as the one. Whatever else the fourth commandment had to say, it certainly taught men that they had time as a stewardship for which they were accountable to God.

One day's abstention from work

The third imperative of the commandment reads,
'On it [the seventh day] you shall not do any work.'

This is the one negative element in this commandment. It shows that a vital aspect of keeping sabbath as a day holy to the Lord was a cessation of labour: 'On it you shall not do any work.'

From the pages of the Old Testament we gain the impression that proper sabbath observance required a fairly strict interpretation of the prohibition on work. Manna was neither to be collected nor cooked (Exodus 16:5, 22–30) and there is the case of a man found gathering sticks on the sabbath during the wilderness wanderings and subsequently condemned to death by stoning (Numbers 15:32–36). Some think that this man could not have been condemned simply for the gathering of sticks, but for an underlying high-handed act of reviling the Lord, such as is dealt with in the preceding verses (Numbers 15:27–31). There may well have been such rebellion in the man's heart, but it is the breach of the commandment which is given as the ground of his being put to death. The application of the death penalty was in harmony with the solemn pronouncement of Exodus 35:2 that whoever did work on the sabbath day was to be put to death.

The references to the death penalty point to the incorporation of sabbath observance into *the civil law* of Israel, under which death was inflicted on one adjudged to have committed a criminal offence. The commandment itself does not carry any stipulated or mandatory penalty because it was given to show an appropriate spiritual response by a redeemed people. The civil law, which related to Israel's national life, and which no longer applies in the Christian dispensation, made sabbath-breaking a criminal offence as well as a spiritual and, as we have seen, a ceremonial one.

Subsequent references to sabbath-breaking in some cases name specific offences and so show something of the kind of work which was forbidden. Jeremiah towards the end of the seventh, or in the beginning of the sixth century before Christ, points to the transporting of goods, presumably for commercial purposes. He says, 'Be careful not to carry a load on the Sabbath day or bring it through the gates of Jerusalem. Do not bring a load out of your houses or do any work on the Sabbath, but keep the Sabbath day holy . . .' (Jeremiah 17:21–22). The covenant made in the days of Ezra involved an undertaking not to buy wares or grain from people who might bring such things on a sabbath day (Nehemiah 10:31). The sins rebuked by Nehemiah included the treading of winepresses, the transporting of grain and other loads and the selling of food (Nehemiah 13:15–18). These were, of course, matters of ordinary everyday living, in no way wrong in themselves, but they were not activities permitted to the covenant people on the sabbath. To stop them Nehemiah as governor closed the gates of Jerusalem from sunset to sunset and threatened with arrest any traders who hung around hoping he would relent (Nehemiah 13:19–21).

Several references in the prophets point to the fact that sabbath was often treated as the occasion for self-indulgence and mirth rather than for solemn remembrance of God's grace in redemption. The letter of the law may have been kept and the civil penalty for doing work avoided, but the spirit of the commandment and of a day kept holy to the Lord was conspicuous by its absence. One of the earlier prophets, Hosea, proclaimed God's intention to put an end to the mirth of Israel's feasts and sabbaths (Hosea 2:11). Later on Isaiah called for a change in the way sabbath was observed:

> 'If you keep your feet from breaking the Sabbath
>   and from doing as you please on my holy day,
> if you call the Sabbath a delight
>   and the Lord's holy day honourable;

and if you honour it by not going your own way
  and not doing as you please or speaking idle words,
then you will find your joy in the Lord . . .'

(Isaiah 58:13—14).

The point seems to be that God's day was being given over to self-seeking, to pleasure and to idle chatter, activities that in no way met the demand of the commandment that sabbath be 'holy to the Lord'. It was in fact as needful to cease from these things as from what would more naturally be called work.

There is difficulty in the fact that the commandment itself does not spell out precisely what is meant by work and does not indicate what activities were to be regarded as legitimate on the sabbath. Some scholars are of the opinion that domestic chores essential to feeding a family were excluded from the prohibition and would cite in support of this view the fact that the words extending the command to a man's household do not mention his wife. Whatever the truth in the suggestion, the ban on lighting fires (Exodus 35:3), which was to apply in every Israelite habitation, would surely affect wives and would limit severely the kind of cooking that they could do on the sabbath.

The measures taken by Nehemiah against those profaning the sabbath were clearly aimed at profit-making or commercial activities. The same was probably the case in the regulations governing the special sabbaths which arose in connection with the great festivals when 'regular work' was forbidden (Leviticus 23:7, 8, 21, 25, 35, 36; Numbers 28: 18, 25; 29:1, 12, 35). The word translated 'regular' (AV 'servile') is *'abodah'* meaning 'service' and suggesting occupational or bread-earning activities rather than those essential to personal survival. This word is not used in Leviticus 23:3 which deals with the regular sabbath and which seems to prohibit all work on that day. It may be, however, that the instructions given to Moses for the first and seventh days of unleavened bread, which were in effect sabbaths, set a pattern which is assumed in the later sabbath laws: 'Do no work at all on these days, except to prepare food for everyone to eat — that is all you may do' (Exodus 12:16).

We can see, then, the possibility that 'works of necessity'

in relation to the preparation of food may well have been permitted, but because this is nowhere spelled out there must remain some degree of uncertainty.

Rest as a right

The command is expanded to provide rest for the entire working community but it does not, as mentioned already, specifically refer to wives. '. . . On it you shall not do any work, neither you, nor your son or daughter, nor your manservant or maidservant, nor your animals nor the alien within your gates.' In the Deuteronomic version the words 'or your animals' are further expanded to read, 'nor your ox, your donkey, or any of your animals'. Some scholars regard these phrases as later insertions, but for our purpose the point is that the essential prohibition on work is extended to embrace the entire household. Male and female, children and servants, together with working animals, were to be given a rest day. As Exodus 23:12 puts it, 'On the seventh day do not work, so that your ox and your donkey may rest and the slave born in your household, and the alien as well, may be refreshed.' The command could not be circumvented by getting someone else, whether an Israelite or a non-Israelite, to work on one's behalf. An Israelite was obligated to regard a rest day, one in seven, as a duty for himself and as a right due to other people and, indeed, to that section of the animal world which he made to work for him.

There is thus enshrined in this commandment a fundamental human right, the right to rest from labour on one day in seven. This right was to be respected even in times of great pressure when the temptation would be strong to keep on working: 'Even during the ploughing season and harvest you must rest' (Exodus 34:21b).

The giving of such a right to rest was clearly an act of God's grace and can be seen as providing a measure of relief from the effects of the Fall. It will be remembered that a curse was then pronounced: 'Cursed is the ground because of you; through painful *toil* you will eat of it . . . By the *sweat* of your brow you shall eat your food' (Genesis 3:17–19). As a result man's work became a burden, a toil, a labour, but now on one day in seven there was to be a mitigation of the burdensome drudgery of unbroken toil. Seen this way, the sabbath was a blessing accruing from redemption, an institution designed to make life more pleasant for the redeemed people of God.

At any event sabbath was a provision for the good of God's people. 'The Sabbath,' as Jesus said, 'was made for man.' It was for man's benefit and, indeed, for the benefit of working animals and even of the land. As such it was an institution to be enjoyed and not an imposition to be endured.

The theological basis

Three distinct statements ground sabbath observance respectively in creation, covenant and redemption.

The pattern of creation
The version of the commandment found in Exodus grounds sabbath observance in the pattern of the seven days of creation: 'For in six days the Lord made the heavens and the earth, the sea, and all that is in them, but he rested on the seventh day. Therefore the Lord blessed the Sabbath day and made it holy' (Exodus 20:11). This links up very closely with Genesis 2:1–3, 'God blessed the seventh day and made it holy, because on it he rested from all the work of creating that he had done.' The point surely is that as God himself had acted — six days of creative work followed by one in which he did not engage in such work — so men should work for six days and follow this by one free from the responsibilities and toil of the preceding six. The parallel between the seventh day of God's creative work and the weekly sabbath cannot, of course, be complete: that was a once-for-all event; sabbath is a recurring one. However, the fourth commandment makes the underlying principle permanent. The sabbath break in labour is presented as part of the divine purpose in creation. The Lord has blessed the sabbath day and hallowed it.

A sign of the covenant relationship
Sabbath was also a sign of Israel's covenant relationship with

the Lord. It marked the nation off as his own people. He
said, 'It will be a sign between me and the Israelites for
ever . . .' (Exodus 31:17). This became especially important
when the Jews went into exile in Babylon in the sixth century before Christ. Their temple had been destroyed and,
being far from Jerusalem, they were unable to observe their
pilgrimage festivals or to offer the Levitical sacrifices. In
that situation sabbath observance became one of the things
which marked the Jews off from other races. Ezekiel, who
prophesied in Babylon to the exiles, reminded them of the
fact that God had given the sabbath as a sign of his covenant
with them: 'I gave them my Sabbaths as a sign between us,
so that they would know that I the Lord made them holy'
(Ezekiel 20:12). It was thus a reminder to the Jews that
they were set apart for God, that they belonged to him, that
they were his covenant people.

A reminder of redemption
When Moses repeated the decalogue to Israel just before his
death, he made the remembrance of God's redemptive act,
rather than an acknowledgement of his creative purpose, the
basis for the observance of the sabbath. It reads thus:
'Remember that you were slaves in Egypt and that the Lord
your God brought you out of there with a mighty hand and
an outstretched arm. Therefore the Lord your God has commanded you to observe the Sabbath day.'

The Israelites had been redeemed by a marvellous demon-
stration of God's power, but they could easily forget God's
goodness. Too often, indeed, during the wilderness wanderings, they had failed to act with the gratitude that becomes
the recipients of God's grace. Now before they settled in the
promised land the sabbath was given a new dimension: it was
to be a regular occasion when redemption from the bondage
of Egypt was remembered. In other words, it was to be
observed with the positive spiritual purpose of celebrating
with thankfulness God's redemptive act and the resultant
privileged status of his people.

Sabbatical years

The principle of cessation and rest was extended in

subsequent legislation to provide a fallow year, one in seven, for the land, and a jubilee of very special significance every fiftieth year. The jubilee was to involve a further year of rest for the land and meant two such years following consecutively every half-century. The main passages providing for the sabbatical year are Exodus 23:10−11, and Leviticus 25:1−7, 20−22. (Those concerned with the jubilee are Leviticus 25:8−17, 22−55; 27:16−25.)

There seem to have been a number of reasons for the years of sabbath. One, we can be reasonably sure, was the well-being of the land itself, 'The land is to have a year of rest' (Leviticus 25:5). Another was to give an opportunity for the needy to benefit from the spontaneous growth of the countryside, 'the poor among your people may get food from it' (Exodus 23:11). A third and probably more important purpose is suggested by the regulations for the year of jubilee, which was itself an additional sabbatical year and which was observed to ensure that Israel recognized divine ownership of the land. Every letting or mortgaging of land had to be priced according to the number of years remaining until the jubilee. Indeed, it was not the land, but the right to cultivate and take a crop from it, which was subject to contract (Leviticus 25:8−17). While the ordinary sabbatical year did not involve the liberation of land that had been hired or sold it would, like the special sabbath of the fiftieth year (that is, the jubilee) remind the people that they were tenants and not owners of the land. They would farm it and eat of its fruits as a provision of God's grace and the fallow year would be a recognition that they could only touch it and use it in accordance with his pleasure. Failure to observe the sabbath year would be an act not just of ingratitude but of usurpation. It would be tantamount to claiming as one's own what belonged to God. It would in fact be a way of robbing God.

It is also possible that the septennial reading of the law prescribed in Deuteronomy 31:10−13 and accompanied by the ceremony of 'release' at the Feast of Tabernacles took place at the end of this year. In that event the sabbath year may have been intended as giving rest from agricultural work with a view to enabling full participation in covenant renewal ceremonies.

The provision that Israelite slaves be released after six
years of service (Exodus 21:1–6) is sometimes thought to
have been related to the sabbatical year. This is rather doubtful since six years of service could end in different years,
but the principle of cessation, of making an end, of granting
release, and so of giving rest after six years, comes through
and would seem to be an extension or application of the
sabbath idea.

It is generally agreed that the Israelites did not keep the
sabbath year in any meaningful way, at least up to the time
of the exile. There is no record anywhere in the Old Testament of it or of the year of jubilee actually being observed.
The chronicler did however describe the seventy years of
Jewish exile in Babylon as giving the land seventy years of
rest which had previously been denied to it (2 Chronicles
36:21). The Levitical laws did in fact assert that if Israel
did not walk with God she would be scattered among the
nations and her land left to enjoy sabbaths denied to it
while the people were in occupation (Leviticus 26:34,
35, 43).

Nehemiah, a century or so after the end of the exile, led
the Jews in a solemn covenant which included an undertaking to 'forego working the land' every seventh year
(Nehemiah 10:31). It seems that thereafter there was greater
loyalty to the sabbatical year and after the Roman conquest
Julius Caesar is reported by Josephus as having excused the
Jews from taxes for one year bcause of it. We do not, however, find any reference to it in the New Testament.

New Testament presentation

Jesus and the sabbath
Anyone who has even a cursory knowledge of the Gospels
knows that our Lord frequently and seriously clashed with
the Pharisees over the observance of the sabbath. Much of
his teaching on the subject actually arose on occasions when
he refused to conform to the petty and pettifogging rules
which the rabbis had devised to safeguard the institution
and which were given an authority equal to, or indeed
superior to divine law. In this situation things tended to be

turned upside down and man became the slave of the sabbath institution rather than the enjoyer of its privileges. It appeared that man had been made for the sabbath, rather than the sabbath for man.

His religious habits

We can be quite certain that Jesus was brought up in a godly home where religious duties were performed with meticulous care. He was circumcised on the eighth day, the normal purification rituals then took place and year by year his parents attended the Passover Feast at Jerusalem. He formed the habit of attending the synagogue in Nazareth and when he returned from the wilderness where he had been tempted he went *as was his custom* to that synagogue on the sabbath day (Luke 4:16).

Clearly he did not by any means agree with the teaching of the scribes and Pharisees who controlled the synagogues, but nevertheless he joined in sabbath worship with the communities in which he moved. As opportunity arose, he read the Old Testament Scriptures and taught in the synagogues, first at Nazareth (Luke 4:16–30; cf. Mark 6:2) and then in Capernaum (Mark 1:21–29; Luke 4:31–38). Leaving the latter on one occasion, he healed Simon's mother-in-law who was suffering from a high fever. This was an acute illness and his healing act seems therefore to have been acceptable to the Jews, as were those of a more general nature which followed at sundown, when officially the day after sabbath began (Mark 1:29–34 etc.). Later he toured Galilee and seems to have made a point of preaching in the synagogues as he went (Matthew 4:23; Mark 1:39). Clearly he was often found in the synagogues and there can be no doubt that he was regularly there on the sabbath and involved in whatever elements of true worship took place in them.

When he was in Jerusalem he participated in the worship of the temple and used it also as a public forum in which to preach and teach. His attendance at the great feast would have involved sabbaths and some participation in the acts of worship then performed. At his trial he referred to having been 'day after day' in the temple teaching, again implying his presence on some sabbaths (Matthew 26:55; Mark 14:49; Luke 19:47; cf. John 18:20).

When our Lord requested baptism John was at first reluctant but agreed when Jesus said, 'Let it be so now; it is proper for us to do this to fulfil all righteousness' (Matthew 3:15). He seems to have been saying that he wished to submit to every requirement for righteousness expected of those around him, a principle on which he would also feel obliged to keep sabbath as a day specially holy to the Lord and marked by the appropriate acts of corporate worship.

His teaching
There is no record of our Lord actually mentioning the fourth commandment but this does not mean that it did not have his endorsement. In fact his general endorsements of the law of God must include this commandment, for had that not been his intention he would have had to qualify what he said so as specifically to exclude it. The sermon on the mount has an important passage: 'Do not think that I have come to abolish the Law or the Prophets; I have not come to abolish them but to fulfil them. I tell you the truth, until heaven and earth disappear, not the smallest letter, not the least stroke of a pen, will by any means disappear from the Law until everything is accomplished. Anyone who breaks one of the least of these commandments and teaches others to do the same will be called least in the kingdom of heaven, but whoever practises and teaches these commands will be called great in the kingdom of heaven' (Matthew 5:17–19).

When a scribe asked him to say which commandment was first of all the commandments he replied, 'The most important one is this: "Hear, O Israel, the Lord our God, the Lord is one. Love the Lord your God with all your heart and with all your soul and with all your mind and with all your strength" ' (Mark 12:29–30; Matthew 22:37). He was, of course, citing Deuteronomy 6:4–5, words which summarize the God-ward elements of the decalogue and which required, among other things, a proper keeping of the sabbath day as holy to the Lord. By so stating the first and greatest commandment, he was endorsing the fourth as a vital spiritual duty for all who would live for God.

Jesus' first clash with the Pharisees on the sabbath arose when he was going through fields of grain with his disciples who began to pluck and eat ears of grain (Matthew 12:1–8; Mark 2:23–28; Luke 6:1–5). The civil laws of Israel had permitted travellers to do what the disciples did, presumably as a means of satisfying their immediate hunger, but to put in a sickle and take a quantity of grain was an offence (Deuteronomy 23:25). The Pharisees, however, listed grain plucking among 'works' not permitted on the sabbath and told our Lord that his disciples were doing what was not permitted to be done on the sabbath (Matthew 12:2). This 'extra' traditional law clearly displeased our Lord, who answered by reminding those concerned of how hunger had justified one of their heroes, David, in breaking a ceremonial law governing the consecrated bread. Their laws on sabbath were also ceremonial and they should have known that such laws must always take second place to the spiritual and moral laws, which can never be waived. 'If you had known' said our Lord, 'what these words mean, "I desire mercy [loving concern for a neighbour], not sacrifice [ceremonial]", you would not have condemned the innocent' (Matthew 12:7).

To reinforce this teaching our Lord made two firm pronouncements. In the first he declared that the sabbath was made for man, that is, for man's benefit, an expression of redemptive grace, mitigating for one day in seven the curse which made work unpleasant and giving man a day to be enjoyed in fellowship with God. Man was not made to serve the sabbath as an irksome tyrant, robbing him of all freedom and burdening his conscience with guilt for the infringement of impossibly detailed rules. The second pronouncement was to the effect that he, the Son of man, was Lord even of the sabbath. He claimed sovereignty over it and therefore the right to demonstrate to and through his disciples the essential principles of its observance and, as necessary, to amend or suspend its ceremonials, whether found in the traditions of the elders or in the Old Testament itself.

Each of the three synoptic Gospels follows this with another sabbath-day incident in which Jesus healed a man suffering from a withered hand (Matthew 12:9–14; Mark 3:1–6; Luke 6:6–11). This man had a chronic disability rather than an acute disease, and according to the traditional laws of the scribes and Pharisees only the acutely ill could receive medical or other assistance on the sabbath. Jesus asked if it was lawful to do good to a man on the sabbath, but got no answer! He then asserted that it was far more important to do good than to lift a sheep out of a pit, which in Jewish eyes was an acute or crisis situation legitimately tackled on a sabbath day. Mark tells us that in response to their silent refusal to commend the good work of healing the man, 'He looked round at them in anger. . . deeply distressed at their stubborn hearts' (Mark 3:5). The thing which grieved him was their hard legalistic insistence on the ceremonial avoidance of work on the sabbath and their total lack of compassion for a man in need. The lesson was clear that ministering to human need, whether of an acute or of a chronic nature, takes and must take precedence over any requirement to rest on the sabbath.

Similar principles emerge in virtually every other instance where it is recorded that our Lord performed a miracle of healing on the sabbath day. The Jews sought to kill him (John 5:16) because he had healed the man who had suffered an infirmity for thirty-eight years and had told him to take up and carry his bed on the sabbath day. For the Pharisees this involved work. His rather enigmatic response, 'My Father is always at his work to this very day, and I, too, am working' (v. 17), was probably a claim to sovereignty over the sabbath similar to the pronouncement: 'The Son of Man is Lord of the Sabbath.' The same incident is possibly the background to the occasion on which our Lord pointed out that his hearers allowed a child to be circumcised on the sabbath day, if that happened to be the eighth day of his life, but inconsistently marvelled angrily over his one work of making a man whole on the sabbath (John 7:19–24). They were in fact making a judgement that was based purely on outward appearances, on ceremonial criteria, rather than an inward and real righteousness.

The man born blind and given sight by Jesus (John 9: 1–41) was another case of chronic illness, as was that of the woman who for eighteen years had been bent in two and was unable to straighten herself (Luke 13:10–17). In the latter case the ruler of the synagogue accused him of *working* on the sabbath and he retorted by calling the ruler a hypocrite because he and his friends actually engaged in

work on the same sabbath day when they led their animals
to places of watering. Not long after this, he was having a
meal in the home of a Pharisee where there was a man
suffering from dropsy (Luke 14:1–6). He was being carefully
watched and before the man appealed for help, or the Pharisees tried to prevent his giving it, he took the initiative and
asked them to state the law on the matter: 'Is it lawful to
heal on the Sabbath or not?' (v. 3.) They kept quiet and he
healed the man and then asked them another and very perti-
nent question: 'If one of you has a son or an ox that falls
into a well, on the Sabbath day will you not immediately
pull him out?' (v. 5.) His point was that if emergency action
to save life, even if it were animal, was legitimate on the
sabbath, the thing he had done in making a suffering man
well must surely be equally legitimate.

Our Lord thus took a stand against the hard legalism of
the Pharisees. For him the needs of men took precedence
over every ceremonial law. His example of humanitarian
action showed that God never intended the sabbath to be a
day of idleness or of cold indifference to the needs, chronic
or acute, of fellow men. Rather it was to be a day of rest
from the routine occupations of making a living, a day when,
in addition to acts of corporate worship, loving one's neighbour as oneself would be given practical expression in deeds
of kindness and compassionate care.

The apostles and the sabbath

Initial observance
In the early days of their ministry, the apostles retained
their Jewish identity. Despite the fact that they held a view
of Jesus unacceptable to other Jews, they continued to
attend the temple daily and to participate in the special
prayer times held there (Acts 2:46; 3:1). Without a doubt
some sabbath observances would have been included.

When persecution arose after the death of Stephen things
became more difficult, but neither then nor later is there
any suggestion that Jewishness was given up. To the end the
apostle Paul remained a Jew and engaged in some Jewish
religious practices. Wherever he travelled in Asia Minor or
Europe, he found the local synagogue and as a matter of

custom joined in its sabbath services of worship. His out-
spoken witness to Christ sometimes led to his expulsion
from these synagogues, but when he went to another town
he simply repeated the process and went to worship and to
speak as opportunity was afforded in the synagogue. This
happened at Antioch in Pisidia (Acts 13:14—42, 44) and
again at Thessalonica and Corinth (Acts 17:2; 18:4). At
Philippi there may have been no synagogue, so on their first
sabbath there he and his companions sought out a place
where a group of women, presumably Jewish, gathered for
prayer (Acts 16:13). In each case we see Paul giving due
respect, due Jewish respect, to the sabbath. It was a day in
his calendar to be different from other days, a day for meeting with others to worship God and to declare his truth.

Break-away from Jewish observances
The advent of Gentile converts changed the picture considerably and forced to the forefront the question of whether or
not such converts should be required to become proselytes
to Judaism. There were Jewish believers who taught that
faith in Christ was not enough and that no one could be
saved without circumcision and the acceptance of the whole
body of Jewish law. This provoked the discussions of the
Jerusalem Council when Paul and Barnabas, representing the
Antioch church, were assured that the burdens of circumcision and Jewish law need not be imposed on Gentile
believers.

Paul further develops this theme in the Epistle to the
Galatians, in which he reproaches readers there who had
fallen under the spell of Judaizers who wanted to impose
circumcision and scribal law on them. Christians who became
circumcised took the yoke of this law upon themselves and
in so doing espoused a principle of salvation through law-
keeping rather than through faith. Paul chides such in no
uncertain terms: 'How', he asked, 'is it that you are turning
back to those weak and miserable principles? Do you wish
to be enslaved by them all over again? You are observing
special days and months and seasons and years! I fear for
you, that somehow I have wasted my efforts on you'
(Galatians 4:9—11). The behaviour of those who had turned
to Jewish law-keeping made Paul feel his evangelistic efforts

among them had been in vain. They were more Jewish than Christian and he was in serious doubt about the reality of their conversion.

Writing to the Colossians, Paul put the matter somewhat differently: 'Do not let anyone judge you by what you eat or drink, with regard to a religious festival, a new moon celebration or a Sabbath day. These are a shadow of the things that were to come; the reality, however, is found in Christ' (Colossians 2:16—17). The questions on which he feared his readers might be criticized certainly included Jewish ceremonials, some connected with the sabbath. Paul insisted that the Old Testament ceremonial law provided only a shadow, an illustration, and that the reality projecting the shadow is Christ. Those who now have Christ have the substance, the fulfilment, and no longer need the shadows. Believers are not, then, required to observe the ceremonial shadows of pre-Christian times and are not to allow others to judge them by the canons of Jewish belief or practice. Similar principles emerge in Romans 14:1—12 but without specifically mentioning the sabbath. No doubt, however, the days observed or not observed in honour of the Lord in verses 5 and 6 were days of festival, new moon or sabbath, exactly as in Colossians 2:16—17, and it is in relation to these days that Paul gives his readers the freedom to make up their own minds. Indeed, he imposes on them a duty to do so responsibly, as those who will one day give account to God.

This teaching clearly gave the Christian considerable, or even complete liberty to observe or not to observe the Jewish sabbath. In Christ he had the substance, the rest, of which sabbath was but a shadow.

Throughout the apostolic era Jewish antagonism to Christ and those following him frequently flared up, as when persecution arose after the death of Stephen, or when Paul and his friends were expelled from synagogues in Asia Minor and Europe. More and more it was becoming impossible for followers of Christ to live within the confines of Judaism. Indeed, they were being pushed out and some disenchantment with Jewish institutions was almost inevitable. While there is no strong anti-sabbatarianism in the apostolic writings we get the impression that Christians were being encouraged to choose whether or not they would observe sabbath.

In due course there were more Gentile than Jewish believers, and as time went on the Judaistic religion, in which Christianity had been cradled, fell into the background. Christianity became a distinct new religion standing on its own feet and completely independent of Judaism. The new wine of the gospel needed and got a new wineskin because the old skin bottle of Judaism could not contain the powerful pressures generated by the new faith.

The first day as the Lord's day

Among Christians there soon developed a new emphasis on the first day of the week which took on a new importance because on it our Lord rose from the dead (Matthew 28:1; Mark 16:2, 9; Luke 24:1; John 20:1). He had even appeared to the disciples in the upper room on the evening of that day and again eight days later on the first day of the next week (John 20:19–25, 26–29). The Day of Pentecost, fifty days after the Passover sabbath, was also on the first day of the week. This day, then, spelt atonement and life in the Spirit, redemption and regeneration, and became as time went on the one day in seven which believers sought to keep as 'holy to the Lord'.

It was on the first day of the week that Paul and his friends gathered to break bread during a seven-day stay at Troas (Acts 20:7) and it was on the first day of each week that he wished his Corinthian readers to set aside some money in store for the collection he hoped to take back to Jerusalem (1 Corinthians 16:2). These references do not prove that the first day had ousted and succeeded the seven-day sabbath, but they do seem to indicate that it was becoming the really meaningful day for believers.

Further evidence is usually found in the fact that John introduces his great apocalyptic visions by saying that he was in the Spirit *on the Lord's day* (Revelation 1:10). The phrase *'en tē kuriakē hemera* occurs nowhere else in the New Testament but it is closely parallel to the phrase 'The Lord's supper' (*kuriakon deipnon*) in 1 Corinthians 11:20. In both cases Christ seems to be clearly designated 'Lord' and the day and the supper are specifically and specially *his*. It is even possible that the practice of observing the supper on the first day of the week (Acts 20:7) led to that day being called 'the Lord's day'.

John does not, of course, mention any act of worship taking place on what he calls 'the Lord's day', but the very fact of his receiving a revelatory vision on it would not be out of harmony with its recognition as the Christian successor to the sabbath. In any event, it seems clear that Christians, like the Jews, recognized a seven-day week with one of those days marked out as specially dedicated to the Lord. How far they were able to rest from daily toil is not clear and probably varied from place to place. It may be that their celebration of the supper took place, or at least usually took place, on the evening of the first day at a time when the work of the day had been completed. Even if we do not know how far abstention from work was possible for believers in apostolic times, the celebration of Christ and his redemption one day in seven, and particularly through the supper, would seem right in line with the spirit of the fourth commandment.

The Lord's day thus provided a continuation of the theological emphases of the fourth commandment and as a celebration of redemption has a close parallel with the sabbath. But the two days are different and should not be regarded as of identical significance. Indeed, the apostolic church, in contrast to that of later times, refused to identify them. The Lord's day was a new institution enshrining the essential sabbath principle, but with new ones of its own and without the sabbatarian rules imposed by both Old Testament and Judaistic ceremonial law.

Jesus insisted that in God's eyes it was right and necessary to do good, to be kind and helpful on the day set apart for rest and worship. The Pharisees gave priority to ceremonial rectitude and added a near infinite number of ceremonial requirements of their own to those of the Old Testament. Jesus, by contrast, put ceremonial law, even divinely ordained ceremonial law, in a subordinate place to spiritual and moral law, which required that man give God first place in his affections and duly love his neighbour as himself.

The apostles, as we have seen, moved on to teach that Christians are free to observe or not to observe sabbath and to put alongside it and ultimately in its place 'the Lord's day' celebrated on the first day of each week. There is, however, no injunction of any kind to the effect that abstention from work, as required on sabbath, was an essential part of the Lord's day. Indeed, as already indicated, it would seem unlikely that many early Christians had the privilege of being free from work on that or any other day. It was not in fact until the fourth century, when Constantine made Christianity the religion of the Roman Empire, that provision was made for a shut-down of work on Sundays.

There is no biblical support for the view that Sunday succeeds the Jewish sabbath and attaches to itself the requirement of a cessation from work. What is clear, however, is that man needs at least one day in seven off work. He needs this for health reasons and to maintain efficiency at his daily work. He needs it for social reasons to maintain in a relaxed atmosphere a meaningful form of family life. He needs it for spiritual reasons to receive instruction in the things of God and to contribute to the worship of God's people. By keeping Sunday as the Lord's day Christians can meet these needs in combination with a positive acknowledgement of the great truth of the day — that Christ has risen. That gatherings to do these things are vital to spiritual life is affirmed by the exhortation not to neglect to meet together, as was the habit of some, but rather to meet and encourage one another (Hebrews 10:25). Where by necessity work schedules frequently clash with such gatherings, or where a Christian becomes careless about them, some measure of spiritual loss is inevitable, both in individual experience and in the corporate life of the church from which he or she is absent.

The New Testament thus leaves the way in which the individual Christian spends Sunday very much an open question. The only pattern which emerges is in terms of gathering together for fellowship, observance of the supper, the sharing of material possessions and, no doubt, other acts of worship. No instructions are given for the rest of the day and if we or any other Christians decide to make such instructions we are simply dropping back from New Testament Christianity to Pharisaic Judaism.

Some evangelical Christians will feel that such a position

involves a risk that they, or others, might become careless and desecrate the day! They are correct, of course, for there is indeed risk in the New Testament stance, but that is how God has ordered things for this gospel era. He expects his children to use the minds he has given them and the spiritual insights he gives them to work out for themselves how they can best glorify him on this and every other day. It is not our place to question this revelation or to try to improve it by devising sabbatarian-type rules for the Lord's day.

How the principle is worked out will vary from individual to individual and from community to community, for each of us sees things through the personality and the temperament he possesses and also in the context of the norms of his family and community. God does not want his children to be a collection of identical sausages churned out of a machine, but individual persons of infinite variety, each dedicated to love him with the whole heart, each deciding intelligently and spiritually how best to use the Lord's day. Some who normally engage in heavy manual work may need extra time in bed or relaxing without muscular activity. Those who have sedentary occupations may need to spend part of the day in fairly energetic forms of relaxation which will keep body and heart muscles in tone. The advent of a five-day working week has, of course, made provision for these needs to be met on another day.

No laws can be laid down as binding on all believers simply because God has not seen fit to give even one. No criticism can be made of believers who, while loving the Lord as we do (or more dearly than we do), yet behave differently on the Lord's day.

One of the most neglected passages of Scripture is Romans 14 which has as its background the criticism of Christians who did not conform to Jewish ceremonial observances. The principles it enunciates are equally valid in relation to Christian traditions, which have often hardened into expected norms of behaviour for the Lord's day or for other occasions. A series of quotations will give the main impact of Paul's teaching.

'Accept him whose faith is weak, without passing judgement on disputable matters.'

'Who are you to judge someone else's servant? To his

own master he stands or falls. And he will stand, for the Lord is able to make him stand.'

'One man considers one day more sacred than another; another man considers every day alike. Each one should be fully convinced in his own mind. He who regards one day as special, does so to the Lord. He who eats meat, eats to the Lord, for he gives thanks to God; and he who abstains, does so to the Lord and gives thanks to God. For none of us lives to himself.'

'Why do you judge your brother? Or why do you look down on your brother? For we will all stand before God's judgment seat.'

'So then, each of us will give an account of himself to God.'

'Therefore let us stop passing judgement on one another. Instead, make up your mind not to put any stumbling-block or obstacle in your brother's way.'

'For the kingdom of God is not a matter of eating and drinking, but of righteousness, peace and joy in the Holy Spirit, because anyone who serves Christ in this way is pleasing to God and approved by men.'

'So whatever you believe about these things keep between yourself and God. Blessed is the man who does not condemn himself by what he approves. But the man who has doubts is condemned if he eats, because his eating is not from faith; and everything that does not come from faith is sin.'

The Lord's day and civil law
In ancient Israel the sabbath became part of the nation's civil law and its breach was to be punished most severely (Exodus 31:12–17). In the teaching of our Lord and of his apostles civil law does not come into the picture at all. The kingdom of God has become a purely spiritual entity and the duties falling on believers are presented in spiritual and moral terms.

There is therefore no suggestion that the Roman authorities should adopt a first day of the week holiday to facilitate Christians. Rather the believer had to live out his Christian faith and keep the Lord's day in a world that was often hostile. He had no grounds for thinking that that world owed him anything, much less a workless day each week!

Constantine made Christianity the official religion of the

empire and Christendom proceeded to think in terms of influencing and controlling state law. Since then church interference in the civil realm has been frequent and there are still those who have a Constantinian view of the church and who expect the state to have laws forcing Old Testament and Judaistic regulations about sabbath on the entire population. Recent times have seen this view wane and more and more Christians take the more biblical one that church and state are separate realms, the Christian taking his place in the state as an ordinary citizen and no more.

At the same time Christians must be interested in the well-being of one another and of their fellow men. They can and should ask that the state organize its life so as to give proper freedoms to its citizens and in particular to allow believers and others to have one day in seven, where possible on Sunday, for rest and worship. This is not the same as forcing sabbatarian laws on unwilling fellow countrymen. The onus is on the individual to use the Lord's day aright, rather than on the state to legislate for such use.

'Remember the Sabbath day by keeping it holy . . .'

7. The sanctity of the family
The Fifth Commandment

'Honour your father and your mother, so that you may live long in the land the Lord your God is giving you.'

The fifth commandment, like the fourth, imposes both God-ward and manward obligations. Whereas, however, in the fourth, sabbath observance is primarily a responsibility man owes to God, in the fifth the duty imposed is primarily in the realm of a human relationship, namely the giving of due honour to one's parents. Thus we have a further stage in the transition from the exclusively God-ward reference of the first three commandments to the predominantly interpersonal reference of the last five.

Honour for parents enjoined

The fifth commandment, again like the fourth, is positive in form: 'Honour your father and your mother.' It strongly affirms the sanctity of the family as the basic social unit of human life and as that on which the stability of society itself depends. It is also couched in terms that are quite general. It does not ask small children or adolescents to honour their adult parents. It does not ask adult men and women to honour their ageing parents. It is addressed to all and sundry and to all without exception. No human being can evade it.

The honour required

The Hebrew verb translated 'honour' in our commandment is *kabed*. It and related nouns and verbs occur fairly frequently in the Old Testament and always emphasize that the one honoured is accorded considerable personal dignity and given the appropriate measure of respect. It is used of man-to-man relationships, where one party is in a position of seniority or authority. Thus Saul wanted Samuel to *honour* him before the elders of Israel (1 Samuel 15:30). Thus indeed it was laid down that the Israelite rise in the presence of the aged and show respect for the elderly (Leviticus 19:32).

The 'honour' commanded to be given to parents, and indeed to senior citizens in a more general way, undoubtedly involved submission to the authority of the person concerned. In ancient Israel the father was the head of the house and had full authority within that household. Anyone who did not submit to that authority was in revolt and was doing the opposite of giving honour. The provision in the laws of Deuteronomy for a mother and father to bring such a son before the elders for judgement and condemnation to death (Deuteronomy 21:18) shows how seriously such rebellion was viewed and demonstrates in the process the underlying importance of submission.

The same verb, *kabed*, is also used for the response due from man to God. 'Those who honour me', said the Lord, 'I will honour' (1 Samuel 2:30). The last book of the Old Testament links honour for fathers and masters with the honour required by God. 'A son honours his father and a servant his master. If I am a father, where is the honour due to me? If I am a master, where is the respect due to me?' (Malachi 1:6). Similarly, the Lord invites men to call on him for deliverance and declares that they will then *honour* him (*kabed*, Psalm 50:15). This psalm concludes with the declaration: 'He who sacrifices thank-offerings *honours* me' (v. 23). Sometimes, when the reference is to God the word is translated into English as 'glorify', or 'bring glory to'. To glorify the Lord is to respect and honour him by giving him willing submission of the heart. Thus it is affirmed that all nations will bring glory to his name (Psalm 86:9) and that the psalmist himself will glorify God's name for ever (Psalm 86:12).

It would seem, then, that the honour to be given to parents is of a similar kind to that due to God, so similar indeed that the same Hebrew word can be used for both. This is confirmed by the use made of another Hebrew verb,

yare, meaning 'to fear' or 'to revere'. This is, in fact, synonymous with *kabed* and is substituted for it when the fifth
commandment is repeated in Leviticus 19:3: 'Each of you
must respect (AV 'fear') his mother and father.' Later in
the same chapter it is used of fearing God: '. . . Revere your
God. I am the Lord' (v. 32b). Similarly, in Psalm 111:9 we
have the words: 'Holy and awesome (literally, to be feared,
yare, AV 'reverend') is his name.'

In the light of these facts it seems reasonable to conclude
that the obligation imposed by the fifth commandment is
not simply manward in direction. As those through whom
life is received and norms of belief and practice are provided,
parents are in some sense mediators between the individual
and his Maker. Honour given to parents is not simply a
matter of loving one's neighbour, but also to some degree a
matter of loving God. This is why some scholars prefer to
join the fifth with the first four commandments as express-
ing a God-ward obligation. However, like the fourth, it does
seem to have both God-ward and manward dimensions and
it is perhaps wise to think of both of them as providing a
transition from the purely God-ward direction of the first
three to the primarily manward direction of the last five.

The respect required for parents had the sanction of Israelite criminal law. The ill-treatment of parents was punishable
by death. 'Anyone who attacks his father or his mother must
be put to death . . . Anyone who curses his father or mother
must be put to death' (Exodus 21:15, 17). In the package of
laws given at Sinai to supplement the decalogue, the same
offences committed against other persons carried no death
penalty unless the victim died as a result of his injuries
(Exodus 21:18—25). This shows that ill-treatment of a
parent was regarded as a very much more serious offence.
Such behaviour was always regarded as utterly reprehensible:
'He who robs his father and drives out his mother is a son
who brings shame and disgrace' (Proverbs 19:26).

Another aspect of honour for parents is the imprecation
of woe on anyone who questioned their reproductive role:
'Woe to him who says to his father, "What have you
begotten?" or to his mother, "What have you brought to
birth?"' (Isaiah 45:10). There is a sanctity attaching to
parenthood which precludes intrusion by others. Children

who honour their parents as required by the commandment will grant those parents complete freedom from enquiry or criticism in relation to this aspect of life. Indeed their respect for their parents will parallel their respect for God — the thing made will not ask the potter what he is doing!

A number of passages in Proverbs focus on the honour due to parents and are worthy of careful consideration. By way of example we quote one passage only:

> 'Listen to your father, who gave you life,
>> and do not despise your mother when she is old.
> Buy the truth and do not sell it;
>> get wisdom, discipline and understanding.
> The father of a righteous man has great joy;
>> he who has a wise son delights in him.
> May your father and mother be glad;
>> may she who gave you birth rejoice!'
> (Proverbs 23:22—25; cf. 10:1; 15:5; 17:25; 19:13; 30:17).

In most cases these proverbs link father and mother together and insist that both are honoured in the way required by our commandment: 'Honour your father and your mother.'

Authority in the Israelite family

In ancient Israel the family was the basic element in social structure. In earlier times the concept seems to have involved a fairly large group of people stemming from some common ancestor, an extended family. In later times, when there appears to have been an increased emphasis on the individual, the family was rather closer to what we know today as the nuclear family, a smallish unit made up of a man, his wife and their children.

The husband or father was the person of supreme importance in the family. He was often called *'ba'al'* meaning 'master' or 'possessor' and was literally the heart of family life. His was the ruling will; his was the authority that kept the family functioning in an orderly manner and that gave coherence to its life.

Wives came firmly under the authority of their husbands. While tender relationships could develop between husbands and wives, a woman had to recognize that she was his possession and he her master. She, too, called him *'ba'al'*. Thus she was in a position of subordination and could not inherit his property. Any vow she might make was only valid if it had his tacit agreement.

Yet a wife was different from a chattel or a slave. She could not be sold even if she was a captive taken from a foreign nation (Deuteronomy 21:14). She could not be driven away by an irate husband, as was the case among most races in ancient times, and she could only be divorced by a proper legal procedure which gave her written proof of her freedom to remarry (Deuteronomy 24:1–4). By her work in the home and on the farm and particularly by the bearing and rearing of children she gained respect in the family. Her position was safeguarded by laws which prohibited offences against her by her children on exactly the same terms as similar offences against fathers: 'Anyone who attacks his father or his mother must be put to death . . . Anyone who curses his father or mother must be put to death' (Exodus 21:15, 17; cf. Leviticus 20:9; Deuteronomy 21:18–21; 27:16). In the fifth commandment equal honour is commanded for both father and mother: 'Honour your father and your mother.' In the Israelite family, then, the wife or mother seems to some degree to have had an equality of status with the husband or father.

It seems that in the time of the patriarchs a father had more or less absolute authority over his family. Indeed, even the wives and children of his grown-up sons who lived with him on the family land were subject to this authority. Thus Judah was able to condemn to death Tamar, his daughter-in-law, the penalty only being avoided when she cleverly exposed his own involvement in her sin (Genesis 38:24). Later on, however, the Deuteronomic laws reserved the right to pronounce and execute the death penalty to elders acting as civil magistrates. The father and mother of a transgressing son could and, indeed, should chastise him, but the right to take his life was no longer theirs (Deuteronomy 21:18–21).

The family and covenant life

An Israelite child was born into a family which itself was part of the community in covenant with God. The family was the sphere in which it was nurtured in the essential facts of covenant life and parents had a solemn duty to teach those facts of faith and religion to their offspring. Some scholars think that such instruction is one of the main purposes for the fifth commandment because in the long run it is those who truly honoured their parents who would share and preserve the faith of those parents and observe the obligations of the covenant. Any repudiation of parents would in effect have led on to a repudiation of the Lord and would have done damage to the covenant relationship.

Both father and mother seem to have shared in the instruction of children, though it is generally believed that when boys became more mature the father was specifically responsible to pass on religious truth. The verses normally quoted to support this view (Exodus 10:2; 12:26; 13:8; Deuteronomy 4:9; 6:7; 32:7 etc.) do not, however, specify fathers as distinct from mothers except possibly in one case, in the song of Moses where we read,

> 'Remember the days of old;
>> consider the generations long past.
> Ask your *father* and he will tell you;
>> your elders, and they will explain to you'
>>> (Deuteronomy 32:7).

It is, however, very doubtful if this reference is to be interpreted in terms of fathers instructing their sons. In the previous verse it is God himself who is Father to Israel and this could also be the case here. Instruction about the past history of the nation would be obtainable from the Lord possibly through the elders who kept and preserved the records of those events. Alternatively the father in question might be a wise sage whose role in life was to teach God's people, rather than a biological father. Even if the father as family head was to be the main transmitter of truth about God's leading of his people, there is no exclusion of mothers from that role. It would indeed be quite natural for fathers to instruct their adolescent sons in matters normally regarded

as male responsibilities and likewise for mothers to instruct
their daughters, but this is not to say that fathers alone were
able to teach religious truth to their sons. The writer of
Proverbs makes it clear that a man is to hold firmly to the
teachings he receives from both parents:

'Listen, my son, to your father's instruction,
and do not forsake your mother's teaching.
They will be a garland to grace your head
and a chain to adorn your neck'
(Proverbs 1:8–9; cf. 6:20–22; 23:22, 25 etc.).

In the light of the general teaching in the Old Testament
on the instruction of children in the virtues of covenant
life, it would seem reasonable to think of the fifth commandment, with its emphasis on honour for parents, as safeguarding not only family life but the transmission of
covenant faith. Certainly closely-knit families do pass on and
retain beliefs and practices unacceptable to the wider world,
and modern Jewry is itself an evidence of this. So, too, are
groups like the Amish and the Hutterites in America. Such
preservation and transmission of religious values seems to
need the kind of family structure which gives authority
and respect in a proper biblical sense to parents.

Many today would, of course, see such structures as
reactionary hindrances to change and would try to undermine the family institution so as to eliminate from society
the values which are preserved in it. Their efforts in a very
real way highlight the value of family life and should alert
all who are anxious to live by God's pattern to all-out efforts
to exemplify and preserve that pattern.

While strong family life, structured so as to give submissive
respect to parents, is undoubtedly the best way to keep
cherished values alive, it is by no means always successful.
Many a good family has its 'black sheep', one or more way-
ward sons or daughters who neglect or discard the beliefs
and practices of their parents and espouse ideas and ways
diametrically opposed to those in which they were brought
up. Equally, weak or bad families have members who have
conversion experiences and adopt better ways than those of
their parents.

Because life is such a complex affair it is difficult, if not impossible, to assess all the factors involved in the life history of an individual. Family is a very strong one but there are influences from outside the family and from within the personality which also affect what each person is and which may precipitate either rebellion against family norms or increased conformity to them. When we try to analyse the factors which contributed to successful or unsuccessful transmission of Israel's covenant faith, we discover that in most cases we have inadequate information to enable us even to begin to assess whether parental authority was exercised or filial respect paid. Nevertheless, the overall picture is that instruction within the family was the main way in which covenant life and covenant ways were preserved.

The commandment in Israelite history

While family life was clearly of supreme importance in Israel, there is a singular lack of evidence as to how this commandment was observed in the Old Testament era. It may be that respect for parents was so normal that it was taken for granted and received little mention. Malachi's words, 'A son honours his father,' were probably so true to life that they provided a ready basis for God's complaint that he himself was not being properly honoured.

Two positive cases of honour for parents or parents-in-law can be mentioned. Jotham, youngest son of Gideon or Jerubaal, displayed great courage and great respect for his father when he took to task those who had made his half-brother Abimelech king and had killed seventy other sons of Gideon in order to do so (Judges 9:16–21). Ruth showed great respect and indeed great love for her mother-in-law Naomi, to whom she seems to have been thoroughly devoted. 'Don't urge me to leave you or to turn back from you. Where you go I will go, and where you stay I will stay. Your people will be my people and your God my God . . . May the Lord deal with me, be it ever so severely, if anything but death separates you and me' (Ruth 1:16–17). Clearly Ruth was fulfilling the spirit of the commandment and doing so for one who, while not her own natural parent, was in fact mother to her in a legal sense.

On the negative side of the picture, there are several

instances of sons whose behaviour towards their parents was thoroughly dishonourable. One was Abimelech, son of Gideon by a concubine from Shechem, who persuaded his mother's family to give him money to have seventy other sons of Gideon killed so that he himself might be declared king, an office his father had refused to accept because the Lord and the Lord alone was King in Israel. Abimelech showed complete disregard for his father, not just by the way he treated his father's sons, but by his repudiation of his father's view of theocracy.

Absalom, the son of David, was another rebellious son who dishonoured his father. David seems to have been rather lenient with him and this lack of parental authority may have contributed to the disastrous feud which dragged on for a considerable time and ended with the death of Absalom (2 Samuel 13–18). The sons of Eli have gone down in history as worthless men who had no regard for the Lord (1 Samuel 2:12) and who would not listen to the voice of their father (1 Samuel 2:25). Samuel had two sons who took over some of his responsibilities when he became old but who did not walk in his ways. They turned aside after dishonest gain, accepted bribes and made a mockery of justice (1 Samuel 8:1–3). They were not carrying on their father's principles of self-effacing service and so were not honouring him as they ought to have done.

Clearly then, Israelite history is tinged with instances of failure in family life. This, as ever in human life, is the product of man's fallen nature, but nevertheless the commandment sets the standard and was the ideal at which Israelites were to aim, and indeed to which many must have conformed with considerable success.

Reinforcement of promise

The full commandment reads, 'Honour your father and your mother, so that you may live long in the land the Lord your God is giving you.' The subordinate clause, 'so that you may live long in the land . . .' may be read as indicating the reason why parents are to be honoured, that is, as giving a motivating purpose to such honour: 'If you want to live long on the land the proper honouring of parents is the way.' It may also be read as indicating by way of a promise the result that will accrue if due honour is given to parents: 'Honour your parents and you will live long in the land.' No doubt both purpose and promise are in view, but Paul seems clearly to have understood the emphasis to be on promise. He said emphatically that the fifth is 'the first commandment with a promise' (Ephesians 6:2). What he meant by 'first' is somewhat obscure, since no other commandment in the ten has such a qualification, but it may be that he was thinking of the whole body of Mosaic legislation containing many subsidiary commands and that he is saying that, of all the laws which have or imply a promise, this one, being in the decalogue, has priority; it is first, primary, chief.

The promise is even more explicit in the form in which the command is recorded in Deuteronomy: 'Honour your father and your mother, as the Lord your God has commanded you; that you may live long, and that it may go well with you in the land the Lord your God is giving you' (Deuteronomy 5:16). Here it is not just longevity, but prosperity, which is promised and both of those elements are mentioned when Paul cites the command in his letter to the Ephesians: 'Honour your father and mother . . . that it may go well with you and that you may live long on the earth' (Ephesians 6:2–3).

The original sense of the promise seems to have been that Israel's tenure of Palestine and her prosperity there depended heavily on a proper observance of this commandment. Within the nation the land was to be portioned out among the various families and the enjoyment of their inheritance depended in great measure on the stability of family life. In effect God was saying that if family life should decay, if respect for parents should disappear, society itself would disintegrate and other people would soon claim and occupy Israel's inheritance.

In ancient Israel personal longevity or length of days was, of course, regarded as a mark of God's favour. Indeed God told Solomon that if he walked in God's ways God would lengthen his days (1 Kings 3:14). Wherever long life was enjoyed it could only be attributed to the gracious purpose and providence of God. But this did not mean that all who had God's blessing lived to a ripe age. Neither could it be asserted that those whose lives ended earlier had not been the objects of his favour or that they had not duly honoured their parents.

Extension to teachers and rulers
In Old Testament times the respect due to, and the authority vested in parents extended beyond the nuclear family unit. This is expressed in general terms in an injunction already cited: 'Rise in the presence of the aged, show respect for the elderly . . . ' (Leviticus 19:32). It emerged in much more specific terms in relation to two groups in Israelite life — the sage-teachers and the rulers.

There were always wise teachers or sages in Israel, men dedicated to the distillation, preservation and communication of common-sense laws for living. They were known as 'the wise' and very often also functioned in other roles as prophets, priests or kings. The wise were renowned as counsellors and were looked up to, respected and honoured as fathers. Thus Joseph in Egypt became a father to Pharaoh, not in any biological sense, but as the source of wise counsel which Pharaoh followed. So Elisha, as he watched his tutor Elijah go up to heaven in a whirlwind, exclaimed, 'My father! My father!' (2 Kings 2:12.) Later, when Elisha himself lay dying, King Joash visited him and 'wept over him. "My father! My father!" he cried' (2 Kings 13:14). The simple fact was that anyone whose ideas were followed by another was 'father' in an educational sense, in a spiritual and moral sense, to the one in whom these ideas were reproduced. Equally the pupil who followed those ideas was a child, a son, of the teacher.

As an example of a ruler cast in the role of father to those he ruled, we have the rather enigmatic prophecy of Isaiah that Eliakim, son of Hilkiah would replace the renegade Shebna as the king's steward: 'He will be a father to those who live in Jerusalem and to the house of Judah' (Isaiah 22:21). Eliakim was to rule with great authority, as a peg driven in a firm place, and was to be honoured as a father. Earlier David had shown great respect, respect indeed of the kind due to a father, to King Saul whom he knew to be rejected by God. At every point David behaved in a way that displayed honour to Saul. In the end, when Saul had been killed, he called on the daughters of Israel to weep over him (2 Samuel 1:24).

Thus teachers and rulers were joined with old people in general and parents in particular as those to whom honour was to be given. The underlying implication is that there was a pattern of authority and of respect for those holding it, beginning with the family and extending in widening circles to the nation, the house or family of Israel. Each individual was expected to take his or her place within these circles and to submit respectfully to those who exercised authority over him or her. Thus there was a structure which provided for orderly living rather than disordered chaos. Wisdom was passed on and restraints were imposed, and those responsible to exercise these roles, whether immediate parents, wise teachers, elders, princes or kings, were to be duly respected and honoured. The fifth commandment was thus a prescription not just for stable family life but also, with these extensions, for stable national life.

New Testament endorsement

The fifth commandment, like the others, was included in our Lord's overall endorsements of the decalogue. It also received specific mention in his teaching and thorough exemplification in his relationships with Joseph and Mary.

Jesus' teaching
Answering a ruler who wanted to know what he needed to do to inherit eternal life, our Lord pointed to six commandments, the sixth to the tenth and the fifth (Mark 10:19; cf. Matthew 19:18–19; Luke 18:20). It is not at all clear why he put the fifth at the end of the list, but for our purpose the important thing is that he quoted it and did so in a way which firmly endorsed it.

He was equally emphatic on an occasion when he responded to a group of Pharisees, who criticized the fact that his disciples ate food without first ceremonially purifying their hands. He told them that in this they were holding not to God's commandment, but to the tradition of men, and went on to show that they were guilty of the same error in following a tradition which effectively watered down their responsibilities under the fifth commandment:

'And why do you break the command of God for the sake
of your tradition? For God said, "Honour your father and
mother," and, "Anyone who curses his father or mother
must be put to death." But you say that if a man says to his
father or mother, "Whatever help you might otherwise have
received from me' (literally — whatever you might be owed
by me — that is, in terms of obligation under the commandment) 'is a gift devoted to God" (Mark — is *Corban*) he is
not to "honour his father" with it. Thus you nullify the
word of God for the sake of your tradition' (Matthew 15:
3–6; cf. Mark 7:9–13).

Under the traditional laws of the Pharisees a portion of
money could be promised to God by a vow of *Corban*. The
money did not need to be paid over immediately to the
treasurer of the temple but could be held in the possession
of the person making the vow. However, because it was
subject to solemn vow the vower was excused from giving
financial support to his parents. The rationalization was
that giving to God, or rather the intention to give to God,
was a sacred act more important than supporting aged
parents. In our Lord's eyes this device involved blatant
deceit and was a shirking of responsibilities given by God
in the law of Moses. By saying that the Pharisees by their
tradition were nullifying the law of God, our Lord was
himself endorsing that law. He was asserting that the fifth
commandment could not be circumvented on the pretence
of a religious demand on one's resources.

The way in which our Lord dealt with the *Corban* issue
brings into focus the fact that the honour due to parents
involves financial or material support in old age. This does
not emerge so positively in the Old Testament, but it is a
fair assumption that in a society which gave such a prominent position to family life, ageing and aged parents were
properly cared for and supported. The response of one man
called to serve the Lord Jesus illustrates the kind of concern
and loyalty that must have obtained: 'Lord,' he said, 'first
let me go and bury my father' (Luke 9:59). The man was
probably quite sincere in this and felt such a loyalty to his
father that to leave him in the eventide of life was unthinkable.

In societies where family life is strong and where the wider unit — the extended family — lives in close proximity, the care and support of the elderly is no great problem. The old folk simply fit into the total family and find companionship and a way of using their remaining energies. There is no need for old people's homes! In the Western world of the late twentieth century, with its emphasis on the nuclear family and with its great mobility, things are more difficult. Relatives live far apart and with more and more people surviving to advanced years the problem of care is acute. But the obligations imposed by our commandment cannot be shirked. Offspring must ensure that in old age their parents have adequate material resources, that they have companionship and such specialist help as they may need, and that, as far as possible, they be assured that their affairs will be looked after properly and fairly when they die.

On a number of occasions our Lord made pronouncements which showed that while he fully endorsed the fifth commandment and objected to any weakening of its force, he would not allow its obligations to take precedence over man's true responsibility to God. 'Anyone who loves his father or mother *more than* me is not worthy of me; anyone who loves his son or daughter *more than* me is not worthy of me; and anyone who does not take his cross and follow me is not worthy of me' (Matthew 10:37; cf. Luke 14:26). At first sight this might seem to be in direct contradiction of what he had said to the Pharisees about *Corban,* but in fact the two strands in his teaching complement each other and his emphasis on giving priority to God-ward responsibilities puts honour due to parents in its proper place as an expression of love to God. By demanding first place in the lives of his followers he was saying that their *priority* must be to love God and to do his will and to be primarily under his influence, rather than to be fettered to the whims and influences of parents. He did not in any way abrogate the fifth commandment, but rather corrected an abuse which was just a pretext for incomplete commitment to God and to himself.

The behaviour of Jonathan towards his father Saul illustrates the balance to be maintained. Jonathan respected and honoured and died with his father, but he knew God's will for David and put loyalty to the outworking of God's

cause above allegiance to his father. He helped David while
remaining a faithful son. The calling of James and John to
discipleship also illustrates the proper balance of priorities.
They were mending fishing nets with Zebedee their father
and honouring him by contributing their work to the family
income, but the call of God took precedence. We read,
'Immediately they left the boat and their father and followed
him' (Matthew 4:22).

By contrast, there is the man mentioned above who
responded by saying, 'Lord, first let me go and bury my
father.' If, as seems probable, this was a genuine statement
of his feelings, he had his priorities wrong and was putting
his father before God. The good had become the enemy of
the best. Our Lord's reply called forth that best: 'Let the
dead bury their own dead' (Luke 9:60). Another man's case
was similar. He actually wanted to follow the Lord but would
first say farewell to his family. Again our Lord's challenge
was that he put the call of God first: 'No one who puts his
hand to the plough and looks back is fit for service in the
kingdom of God' (Luke 9:61—62).

Thus our Lord publicly and emphatically endorsed our
commandment and opposed beliefs and practices which
nullified it or which gave it more importance than it was
due.

Jesus' example
The Lord Jesus kept this commandment himself. Despite
the uniqueness of his person, he seems to have played his full
part in the life of the home of Joseph and Mary in which he
spent his childhood and youth. We read that during his
youth, that is between the ages of twelve and thirty, he was
obedient to his parents (Luke 2:51). Even after the 'inaugura-
tion' of his public ministry, when he was, of course, pursuing
an independent path, there was frequent contact with his
family and particularly with his mother, Mary, who may by
then have been widowed. On the cross just before his decease
he made provision for her to be cared for in future days. We
read, 'When Jesus saw his mother there, and the disciple
whom he loved [probably John] standing near by, he said
to his mother, "Dear woman, here is your son," and to the
disciple, "Here is your mother." From that time on, this
disciple took her into his home' (John 19:26—27).

Thus his example, like his teaching, endorsed the commandment and highlighted its application. He was in no way perfunctory in the honour he gave to his parents. It was submissive and it was marked by loving concern and the positive provision of care. He was indeed fulfilling righteousness by keeping the fifth commandment.

Apostolic teaching
Paul's letters to Ephesus and Colossae both have passages giving instructions about family relationships, including that of children to their parents. In Ephesians the word is 'Children, obey your parents in the Lord, for this is right' (Ephesians 6:1). The fifth commandment is then quoted with the comment that it is the first commandment with a promise. The promise is given in a form close to that of the version in Deuteronomy: 'That it may go well with you and that you may enjoy long life on the earth' (Ephesians 6:3).

It is difficult to be sure whether or not Paul is putting a new meaning on the promise, but this seems likely because long life in the land of Palestine would be a meaningless expectation for the believers in Asia Minor to whom he wrote. The Septuagint, a translation of the Old Testament into Greek, used the word *gēs* for 'land' and Paul also uses it. This word can mean the solid earth, as distinct from the heavens or the sea, and it can also mean a particular area like the land of Palestine. That Paul drops the qualifying phrase, 'the Lord your God is giving you,' would seem to indicate that he uses it with a new and wider meaning of 'earth' or 'world'.

In Colossians there is no quotation of the commandment but the teaching is virtually the same as that of Ephesians: 'Children, obey your parents in everything, for this pleases the Lord' (Colossians 3:20). In both Epistles the word 'children' (Greek, *tekna*) could be used either of physical offspring or of pupils or disciples. The context of family matters shows that it is actual offspring who are in Paul's mind and who are exhorted to obey their parents. His requirement of obedience makes submission to parents a Christian duty: *'This pleases the Lord.'*

It is probable that in these passages Paul was thinking only of junior members of a household still living at home with their parents. He recognized, as did the people of God in Old Testament times, that through marriage a man set up a new household in which he was head and over which his father had no direct or overriding authority. Some verses earlier, in a discussion of marriage, Paul had quoted Genesis 2:24 which required a man to leave his father and mother and cleave to his wife. There had to be a break in the authority structure to allow the setting up of a new home, and in a world where the girl would be taken from her parents to live with and under the authority of a husband it was most significant that Scripture required a formal 'leaving home' on the part of the bridegroom. This reduced the father's authority over him and lessened proportionately his obligation to obey his father. It did not, however, relieve him of the responsibility to honour his parents by giving them love, respect and such help as they might need.

In a society such as ours, in which some people, male and female, never marry at all or remain unmarried until relatively late in life, it is surely reasonable to conclude that the same kind of independence is God's will for the unmarried adult. Paul can hardly mean that such are to be submissively under the authority of their parents until those parents die. The permission he gives widows to remarry in the Lord would suggest that one group of adult singles was to be regarded as having such freedom.

The apostles follow the Old Testament in presenting an extended concept of fatherhood and of the honour due to parents. Thus Timothy was told not to rebuke an older man but to exhort him as he would a father. Similarly, he was to treat 'older women as mothers' (1 Timothy 5:1–2).

Those who point souls to Christ and who instruct the people of God are spiritual fathers and spiritual mothers and are to be duly honoured as such. Thus Paul could tell the believers at Corinth who had been converted through his ministry that he had become their *father* in Christ Jesus through the gospel (1 Corinthians 4:15). He similarly thought of Timothy as his 'true son in the faith' (1 Timothy 1:2).

There is thus a real parent-child relationship in spiritual things and in this, as in the family, the child has a duty to honour those who are his parents. Said Paul, 'The elders who direct the affairs of the church well are worthy of double *honour,* especially those whose work is preaching and teaching' (1 Timothy 5:17). The honour in question involved the same elements as are needed in family life — a recognition of personal dignity, a submission to the authority of the one honoured and adequate material support: 'The worker deserves his wages.' This being so, it is not without significance that candidates for office as elders or bishops and as deacons were to be men who had demonstrated an ability to rule their own households well. Those who did not pass that test could hardly in the wider circle of church life earn the respect, the honour, that properly belongs to such officers.

In the Old Testament civil authorities operated within what was ideally God's kingdom. In the apostolic era civil government rested in the hands of the Roman overlord but respect for those in positions of authority in that government was still affirmed. Peter says, 'Submit yourselves for the Lord's sake to every authority instituted among men: whether to the king, as the supreme authority, or to governors, who are sent by him . . . For it is God's will that by doing good [i.e., in submitting to these authorities] you should silence the ignorant talk of foolish men' (1 Peter 2:13—15). Paul has a similar emphasis in Romans 13:1—7: 'Everyone must submit himself' (and so give honour) 'to the governing authorities, for there is no authority except that which God has established. The authorities that exist have been established by God . . . Give everyone what you owe him. If you owe taxes, pay taxes; if revenue, then revenue, if respect, then respect; if honour, then honour.'

The picture which emerges from apostolic teaching is thus very similar to that of the Old Testament. Parents are to be honoured by the citizens of the kingdom of God and this obligation is extended to spiritual teachers and leaders and to civil governors. Across the board in relation to family, church and state, the principle of respect for those in positions of authority is affirmed. Without such respect society would disintegrate.

The Christian has an obligation to work for stability in social institutions. Indeed, he is to pray for people in positions of authority so that he and his fellow believers might be able to 'live peaceful and quiet lives in all godliness and holiness' (1 Timothy 2:3). 'This' (the praying, the stable social order and the godly living) Paul continued, 'is good, and pleases God our Saviour.'

These extensions do not mean, however, that the Christian is committed to the *status quo* and therefore to opposing all change in the family or in wider aspects of social life. He is not required to approve or bolster up corrupt or weak systems, but to support principles of good order within which orderly change is possible without destruction of the framework of a stable authority structure. The submissive obedience of the Christian to those in authority over him in family, church or state will exemplify to the world the honour required by the fifth commandment for parents and responsible leaders.

Concomitant parental duty

Though not specifically stated in the commandment itself, there is a second side to a healthy child-parent relationship, namely the attitude and behaviour of the parents to the children. In the home there is an interaction of personal wills and a reaction of one will to another. The honour which is required of children can only be given if conditions are conducive to respect and obedience.

The apostle Paul goes straight from the duties of children to the duties of parents towards those children. We read, 'Fathers, do not exasperate your children; instead, bring them up in the training and instruction of the Lord' (Ephesians 6:4), and again, 'Fathers do not embitter your children, or they will become discouraged' (Colossians 3:21). The simple fact is that parents must by a benign exercise of authority create the atmosphere in which children can give them the honour required by our commandment. The biblical pattern of authority is maintained. Discipline is not shirked: 'Bring them up in the training [or discipline] and instruction of the Lord,' but discipline will be applied fairly and without provocation and in the context of proper instruction in the things of the Lord. It is, indeed, only as young people grow up with a sense of accountability to God that they can properly see the need for moral restraint and for obedience to God's laws.

Parents who are themselves God-fearing will treat their children honourably, giving a growing respect to their developing personalities. They will avoid on the one hand the follies of over-indulgence or of leaving them too much to their own devices (as, alas, some missionary parents may have done when leaving their children for years in the care of strangers). They will avoid on the other hand a possessiveness which demands the constant presence or attention of a child and that gives a young person no freedom to make choices for himself or for herself, and is, in fact, a subtly selfish form of repression.

A properly ordered home life, which involves a due observance of this commandment, provides a large measure of security for children. If they are to honour parents, those parents must, by their careful adherence to and transmission of the ways of God, prove themselves worthy of honour. There is a mutuality of responsibility.

Paul's insistence on the nurture of children in the things of God carries forward the emphases of the Old Testament on the preservation and transmission of the verities and values of the faith through the family. This raises important questions in a modern world where the education of children is so much in the hands of professional educators, who are only rarely committed Christians, and who in many cases directly or indirectly undermine teaching given in the home. Indeed, modern educators dedicated to training the pupil to think for himself often speak as though values handed down in a family or in some wider community are the cause of all our ills. They undoubtedly cause children to question and in some, perhaps many cases to reject the faith and the moral norms of their parents. In some cases they influence pupils towards materialistic or anarchical philosophies and in others leave them with such a welter of alternatives that they do not know what to believe and end up believing nothing and with few, if any, ethical norms.

These dangers need to be faced positively by all Christian parents. The anti-God forces which abound today are now directing their guns against the institution of the family and against its age-long role of transmitting beliefs and values. If that is a biblical role, as undoubtedly it is, Christian parents must exemplify it by teaching Christian truth to, and by living out Christian ethics before their children. It is a tough assignment and steadily, it would seem, becoming tougher.

The God-ward priority
Where parents are not what they ought to be, when they
oppose the Christian, or other convictions of their offspring, when by their actions they forfeit all reasonable
right to a child's respect and honour, when to give such a
parent support might be to become party to his evil deeds,
what does a son or a daughter do? Similarly, when ecclesi-
astical authorities become apostate or when civil authorities
are incompetent or engage in activities that are morally
evil, what does the God-fearing Christian do? How can
honour be given in such circumstances?

Submission to parents and to duly appointed leaders is
important but not as important as submission to God in
Christ. Where a clash arises between loyalty to God and
loyalty to parents, to church leaders, or to the state, the
higher law of total commitment, of loving God with the
whole being and doing so by following Christ, takes precedence over the law that demands special honour for parents
and for others in authority over us.

When a conflict of loyalty does arise, God must ever be
given first place. Our Lord said, 'Love the Lord your God
with all your heart and with all your soul and with all your
mind. This is the great and first commandment' (Matthew
22:37–38). The fifth commandment, 'Honour your father
and your mother,' is subsidiary to it. Ideally there should
never be conflict since love for God includes a proper respect
for parents. Where in a non-ideal world conflict does arise,
parents can and must be given respect and due honour, and
other authorities, religious or civil, can and must be treated
similarly. The priority is love for God, and everything else,
including obedience to the fifth commandment, must be
kept in proper balance with it.

'Honour your father and your mother . . .'

8. The sanctity of life
The Sixth Commandment

'You shall not murder.'

At first sight this seems to be one of the simplest and most straightforward of all the commandments. Closer study shows, however, that it has far-reaching implications which are not always immediately obvious and which can give rise to problems of great magnitude.

The Old Testament understanding

The vocabulary
The main Hebrew word in the command is a form of the verb *ratsach* meaning 'to kill'. Occurring rather infrequently in the Old Testament, it was used only of the taking of human life and invariably of killings in which the victims were fellow Israelites. It was probably, therefore, one of those words which were reserved for Israel's covenant life as the chosen people of God.

In some instances deliberate murder is in view as, for example, in Elijah's rebuke of Ahab over his dealings with Naboth: 'Have you not murdered (*ratsach*) a man and seized his property?' (1 Kings 21:19.) In others the killing was unintentional, as in the regulations providing for cities of refuge to which 'anyone who had killed a person could flee and find refuge if he had unintentionally killed (*ratsach*) his neighbour without malice aforethought' (Deuteronomy 4:42).

The killings for which this verb was used seem almost always to have been personally rather than communally

initiated. At no point in the Old Testament is capital punishment or the slaughter of enemies in war referred to by this
word, which was presumably inappropriate for these com-
munal actions. The one possible, but by no means certain,
exception to this is the provision for a figure known as the
avenger of blood (*go'el hadam*) to kill (*ratsach*) an accused
person found outside the confines of a city of refuge. If, as
has traditionally been believed, the avenger was a relative,
he presumably had a family obligation and may not have had
to act purely on his own initiative or responsibility. If he was,
as some scholars think, a public official, he would act on the
authority of the community and in that event his deed would
seem to come even closer to judicial execution.

It is somewhat difficult to provide an exact English equivalent to *ratsach* in the commandment. If it is translated 'You
shall not kill', the commandment is made to appear broader
than the verb would allow because capital punishment, war
killing and the slaughter of animals would be included. If,
however, the verb is translated 'You shall not commit
murder,' (as in the New International Version), the commandment is narrowed and the accidental or unintentional killings
included in the range of meaning of the verb are excluded.
Something like 'You shall not on your own initiative kill a
human being,' or 'You shall not commit homicide,' might
provide a suitable alternative. On the whole, it is probably
best to use the traditional 'You shall not kill' (RSV – cf.
'Thou shalt not kill' in AV) and this will be done on a
number of occasions in the pages that follow.

The prohibition of homicide
There can be no doubt that the sixth commandment put an
absolute prohibition on the privately initiated killing of a
fellow Israelite. If, as seems possible, the avenger of blood
was a public official, a kind of guardian executioner, the
pentateuchal laws have to be seen as outlawing the blood
feud from Israel and thus as depriving even the relative of
the right to take the life of his brother's killer. Only the
properly constituted civil courts could pronounce the death
penalty and no private citizen, however just his cause, could
on his own initiative effect it.

In any event deliberate acts of murder were forbidden. The

ordinances which follow the commandments confirm this by prescribing a mandatory death penalty for the murderer: 'Anyone who strikes a man and kills him shall surely be put to death . . . If a man schemes and kills another man deliberately, take him away from my altar and put him to death' (Exodus 21:12—14). Even if the murderer sought refuge by clinging to God's altar, he could not evade the penalty due for his crime. When a man killed his own slave and in essence damaged his own possession he was to be punished, and should a pregnant woman suffer fatal injury at the hand of a quarrelling male, life was to be given for life, his life in effect for hers (Exodus 21:22—25). These early regulations show respect for human life and a total antagonism to any act calculated to bring it to a premature end. Murder was clearly understood to be worthy of the ultimate penalty. Thus Joab, military commander of great daring in David's time, was put to death by Solomon for the murder of Abner, the son of Ner, and Amasa, the son of Jether (1 Kings 2: 28—35).

The prohibition of the commandment was not understood simply in terms of premeditated murder, but as relating to every act, positive or negative, intentional or unintentional, that could cause death. It was a general prohibition on homicide. Thus the Old Testament placed an obligation on everyone to make sure that none of his fellows was incidentally, accidentally or unnecessarily deprived of life. It demanded, for example, that a man building a house put a parapet round the roof lest someone fall off and bring guilt of bloodshed on the builder and his house (Deuteronomy 22:8). Similarly, the owner of an ox which killed a man was held responsible for the death if he knew that the animal was dangerous and had failed to keep it under control (Exodus 21:28—29). So, too, anyone who struck and killed a thief some time after his crime was held guilty of murder (Exodus 22:2—3). This suggests that those who apprehended offenders or suspected offenders had to respect life and so plan their operations as to avoid the coincidental death of any of those concerned.

It is important to realize that both the murderer and the person who killed unintentionally were guilty of homicide, but that a different degree of guilt attached to each. Anyone

found guilty of premeditated murder, evidenced by ante-
cedent hatred, had to pay the price by forfeiting his own life
(Numbers 35:16–21 etc.). Someone whose act was found to
be without premeditated malice, an accidental or even an
impulsive killing, was given asylum in the city of refuge to
which he had fled (Numbers 35:22–28). In a sense this
became a form of imprisonment because such a man could
not leave that city without serious risk of losing his life at
the hand of the avenger of blood. He was thus spared from
death but at the same time punished by incarceration in a
city of refuge for as long as the high priest should live. Manslaughter, even if accidental, was thus a crime carrying a
definite penalty of imprisonment, or at least of restricted
movement, but its guilt was not as great as that attaching
to deliberate murder.

The sacredness of human life

We noticed earlier that the verb *ratsach*, which gives this
commandment its meaning, seems to have been restricted
to the killing of fellow members of the covenant between
Israel and God. This must not be taken, however, as meaning
that Israelites were free to kill willy-nilly people of other
races or that the commandment does not have a universal
validity. The fact of the matter is that this commandment
simply reiterated laws of human life known from the earliest
times. Cain learned that in taking the life of Abel he had
violated something absolutely sacrosanct in God's sight:
'Your brother's blood cries out to me from the ground. Now
you are under a curse and driven from the ground, which
opened its mouth to receive your brother's blood from
your hand. When you work the ground, it will no longer
yield its crops for you. You will be a restless wanderer on
the earth' (Genesis 4:10–12). More striking, perhaps, is the
solemn divine vow of protection on Cain himself. The fact
that he had murdered his brother did not confer on anyone
else the right to kill him by way of reprisal. 'If anyone kills
Cain,' said the Lord, 'he will suffer vengeance seven times
over' (Genesis 4:15). In addition God put a mark on him,
'so that no one who found him would kill him'. This would
seem to suggest that from the very beginning God had set
his face against tit-for-tat killings, against the blood feud and
the avenging of a brother's death.

Later on, but still before the covenant with Abraham was inaugurated, God told Noah that he would require an accounting (NEB. 'a satisfaction') for the shedding of human blood and said that the penalty for such an offence was to be the shedding of the offender's own blood: 'Whoever sheds the blood of man, by man shall his blood be shed' (Genesis 9:6). This would seem to have been an authorization for the community acting through its rulers and judges to impose the death penalty on those guilty of culpable homicide. It was grounded on the fact that man had been made in God's image and as such had a sacred duty to preserve and propagate life and at all costs to avoid taking it. 'As for you, be fruitful and increase in number; multiply on the earth and increase upon it' (Genesis 9:7). The provision of the death penalty for murder was clearly to show the great worth of a human life and to declare every such life sacrosanct. Anyone who dared tamper with another's life interfered with something uniquely created in God's image, something uniquely representing and revealing God on earth, and so must pay the supreme penalty. This was another way of saying what the sixth commandment later said: 'You shall not kill.'

What God had seen fit to reveal to the whole human race through Noah was essential also for those chosen to be in a special covenant relationship with himself. If the Israelites would live aright before him, if they would behave as a redeemed people, they must respect human life and see to it that no one was denied his natural life-span. In effect this commandment made each man his brother's keeper and conferred on every human being the right to live. It declared life sacred.

In harmony with this are the many laws enjoining kindness to strangers. Some of these refer to resident aliens and not just to itinerant Israelites. The stranger was neither to be wronged nor oppressed (Exodus 22:21; 23:9). Gleanings were to be left for him (Leviticus 23:22; Deuteronomy 24:19). The stranger was to be loved and provided for because God had loved and provided for Israel when she was a stranger in Egypt (Deuteronomy 10:18—19). There was to be one law for the stranger and for the native (Leviticus 24:22) showing not only that courtesy and kindness were to be extended to him, but that his life was to be respected. He, as much as an Israelite, was not to be killed. His life, too, was sacrosanct.

The sanctity which attached to life is shown by the many condemnations in the pages of the Old Testament relating to acts of murder and to those who perpetrated them. The sixth commandment was clearly in mind when Hosea wrote of priests who were banded together to murder (*ratsach*) on the way to Shechem (Hosea 6:9), or Isaiah of the city once marked by righteousness but now full of murderers (Isaiah 1:21). Especially strong are the words of Jeremiah spoken on the steps of the temple in Jerusalem at a time of great spiritual and moral declension when God's patience with Judah was coming near to breaking point: 'This is what the Lord Almighty, the God of Israel, says, ". . . Will you steal and murder (*ratsach*), commit adultery and perjury, burn incense to Baal and follow other gods you have not known, and then come and stand before me in this house . . . to do all these detestable things?"' (Jeremiah 7:9—10.) The same revulsion comes out against wicked men who slew the widow and the alien and murdered the fatherless, and who boasted that God did not notice their deeds (Psalm 94:6—7). Such had to learn that God did indeed see what they were doing and would not forsake his people. He would bring back on the wicked their iniquity and wipe them out for their wickedness (vv. 8—11, 23).

For the entire Old Testament life was sacred and murder was the ultimate crime. That it became common was an indication of departure from devotion to the Lord. His command was not being obeyed because he himself was not being feared. But those who knew their God and who sought to teach his Word have left abundant evidence of their acceptance of, and loyalty to this commandment. They knew that human life was sacred.

While the sixth commandment forbids homicide, the pages of the Old Testament abound in records of judicial and war killings which do not seem to have been regarded as violating it. To some this seems to indicate inconsistency, but, as we have already noticed, the verb *ratsach* used in the commandment is never applied to such killings. This suggests that they were not regarded as coming within the scope of either the verb or the commandment.

There was, in fact, a whole series of offences for which Israelite civil law prescribed death by stoning. These included enticement to serve other gods (Deuteronomy 13:10), cursing God (Leviticus 24:13–15), sabbath breaking (Numbers 15:35), murder (Exodus 21:12) and adultery (Leviticus 20:10; Deuteronomy 22:23–24). In each case the offender had to be given a proper trial and had to be condemned on principles of evidence designed to ensure justice. In the case of murderers the punishment by death simply carried on the principle enunciated in Noah's time: 'Whoever sheds the blood of man, by man shall his blood be shed.' The stoning was a community rather than a private act and in the laws of the Israelite state carried divine authorization and was not at any point seen to be in conflict with our commandment. It did not come within the definition of homicide and so was excluded from the application of the commandment.

The killings inflicted on Israel's enemies in war were very considerable and more than once included large numbers of women and children. Sometimes, indeed, those killings are presented as being in obedience to God's command (Joshua 6:21; 1 Samuel 15:1–3). To modern minds they seem out of harmony with the concept of a God of love and they do, undoubtedly, create one of the great moral problems of the Old Testament. To say, as many do, that God picked up his people in the cultural setting of their times and worked with them in that culture, progressively showing them a higher way of life, does not solve the problem, though for some it does mitigate it somewhat. That the Old Testament records these acts of war alongside denunciations of murder, which obviously affirm the sixth commandment, and does so without any indication of the one being inconsistent with the other, would suggest that the commandment was not understood as forbidding them. They too, then, appear to have been regarded as outside the application of the sixth commandment.

New Testament endorsement

Murder and manslaughter
When we move into the New Testament we find several

quotations of this commandment. Our Lord endorsed it in
the sermon on the mount by his general affirmation that not
the smallest letter, not the least stroke of a pen, would pass
from the law, and by specific mention: 'You have heard that
it was said to the people long ago, "Do not murder, and anyone who murders will be subject to judgement"' (Matthew
5:21). Though as we shall see, he immediately developed the
inward implications of this, he did not for one moment
weaken it or set it aside. It was not a temporary civil or
ceremonial enactment or a Pharisaic addition to the law,
which he found himself obliged to set aside or reverse, but
a divine command, a moral absolute, that none could break
with impunity.

To a young man who asked what he should do to gain
eternal life our Lord said, 'Obey the commandments,' and
when asked which commandments, he gave the man a list,
putting this one first: 'Do not murder' (Matthew 19:18;
Mark 10:19). In Luke 18:20 murder is in second place but
the implication of the record is the same as in the other
two Gospels.

The apostles similarly cited the commandment leaving
no doubt about its abiding validity in the new Christian era.
Says Paul, 'He who loves his fellow man has fulfilled the
law. The commandments, "Do not commit adultery," "Do
not murder," . . . are summed up in this one rule: "Love
your neighbour as yourself"' (Romans 13:8–9). Says James,
'Whoever keeps the whole law and yet stumbles at just one
point is guilty of breaking all of it. For he who said, "Do not
commit adultery," also said, "Do not murder"' (James 2:
10–11). The point is that love for one's neighbour involves
keeping all the commandments which relate to human
relationships and 'You shall not murder' is one of them.

In the New Testament murder is viewed with the same
disgust and condemned with the same firmness as in the
Old. It is the fruit of an evil heart (Matthew 15:19; Mark
7:21). It is a mark of those who have rejected God and
whom he has given up to a depraved mind and to improper
conduct (Romans 1:28–29). It is a work of the flesh, the
perpetrators of which have no inheritance in the kingdom of
God (Galatians 5:21; 1 John 3:15; Revelation 21:8; 22:15).
It is a most heinous sin which Christians must avoid at all

costs. 'If you suffer, it should not be as a murderer . . .'
wrote the apostle Peter to believers who at the time were
suffering, or in imminent danger of suffering persecution
(1 Peter 4:15). For such to have committed murder would
have been to betray Christ by giving the world around justification for its antagonism and persecution.

The New Testament seems to have very little to say about
accidental or unintentional killings, the manslaughter of Old
Testament and of much modern civil law. The lack may,
however, be more apparent than real, because in citing and
endorsing the sixth commandment our Lord and the apostles
were in fact affirming its Old Testament implications and
therefore prohibiting for the Christian all privately initiated
killing. A follower of Christ was no more at liberty to be
careless about life than to take it deliberately. His duty was
to respect, to preserve, to enrich the life of his neighbour –
in short, to love that neighbour as himself. The Christian,
like the Israelite of old, is to be his brother's keeper.

In the teaching of the New Testament, as of the Old, there
are a host of positive injunctions requiring followers of Christ
to work for the well-being of fellow Christians and of all mankind. There is to be brotherly love and hospitality to
strangers (Hebrews 13:1–2); there is to be no partiality,
favouring the rich and influential as against the poor and
insignificant (James 2:1–7); there is to be prayer for all
(1 Timothy 2:1–2) and there is to be good conduct among
unbelievers so that they will be brought to give due glory to
God (1 Peter 2:12). Such requirements call for an attitude of
caring concern and active love for other men which is the
direct antithesis of hatred and of killing and which would
make homicide unthinkable.

A very special instance of malicious killing is that of our
Lord. There was, of course, a trial, or a series of trials, and
therefore a community responsibility for his death. But
those who clamoured for and persuaded the Romans to
effect that death bore some personal responsibility for it.
Their crime may not have been murder in the full sense, but
their intention was the same, and Peter did not hesitate to
tell them so on the Day of Pentecost and on subsequent
occasions: 'You, with the help of wicked men, put him to
death by nailing him to the cross' (Acts 2:23; cf. 2:36; 3:14,

15; 4:10). Even though Peter knew that our Lord had died by the will of God, and even though he understood that spiritual ignorance was a mitigating factor, he had no doubt that those responsible were guilty of intentional homicide and that their only hope before God lay in genuine repentance: 'Repent, then,' he said, 'and turn to God, so that your sins may be wiped out . . .' (Acts 3:19).

Serious as is the New Testament view of murder, there is a clear hope of forgiveness for the penitent murderer. Peter offered this to those who had instigated the crucifixion of our Lord, and in Revelation 9:21 the same possibility seems to be implied when men who escape a series of plagues are presented as yet unrepentant of sins which include murder. The implication seems to be that such could have, and indeed ought to have repented, and that without doing so they, like those not surviving the plagues, would miss the forgiveness and the salvation they could have enjoyed.

Without a doubt then, the New Testament emphatically endorses the sixth commandment. As with other truths firmly held by the Jews, it does not argue the case but simply accepts and reaffirms it. 'You shall not kill' is a law of the kingdom.

The deeper application to hatred
In the sermon on the mount our Lord showed that this commandment is concerned with something deeper than actual acts which cause or could cause the death of other persons. It requires also that Christians banish from their inmost beings the thoughts and attitudes that lead to murder. He said, 'You have heard that it was said to the people long ago, "Do not murder, and anyone who murders will be subject to judgement." But I tell you that anyone who is angry with his brother [without cause] will be subject to judgement . . .' (Matthew 5:21–22). The words 'without cause', it should be noted, are absent from some early manuscripts and so are not clearly attested as being actual words of Jesus. In that event the force of the passage is strengthened and we have an affirmation that every expression of anger by which, no doubt, is meant malicious or hateful anger, will be brought to the bar of divine judgement and be treated as on a par with actual acts of murder. This linking

of anger with murder stresses the inward nature of Christian morality and tells the Christian that it is not enough to be innocent of physical acts of homicide. What is rather needed is a tamed temper and the veritable excision of anger and hatred and every similar vice, a heart so transformed that it could never be party, not just to murder, but to the vicious thoughts which give it birth.

The New Testament constantly teaches that hatred is totally out of keeping with the Christian life. This is shown by direct condemnation and by the emphasis on its opposite, love. Paul tells how he and Titus had once lived spending their days 'in malice and envy, being hated and hating one another' (Titus 3:3). In the goodness of God they had been saved from that way of life. Writing to the Galatians the same apostle lists hatred, discord, jealousy and fits of rage among the works of the flesh and puts them in stark contrast to the fruit of the Spirit which is to characterize the Christian. An injunction to the Ephesians makes the same contrast: 'Get rid of all bitterness, rage and anger, brawling and slander, along with every form of malice. Be kind and compassionate to one another, forgiving one another, just as in Christ God forgave you' (Ephesians 4:31—32).

In 1 Corinthians 13 Paul has a paragraph which sets down the characteristics of love. Some of these are directly opposite to the inner hatred of which we are thinking. 'Love', he says, 'does not envy . . . is not self-seeking, it is not easily angered, it keeps no record of wrongs . . . It always protects . . . always perseveres' (vv. 4—7). Men who have these qualities will certainly not allow their hearts to harbour hatred.

The evil of hatred is seen in sharpest focus in the First Epistle of John. The writer is blunt in the extreme and leaves us in no doubt that hatred is completely incompatible with Christianity. In fact, he says that anyone who hates his brother (not specifically a sibling or a fellow believer) is still in spiritual darkness (2:9, 11). If such a person makes a profession of loving God his profession is quite simply invalid; he is a hypocrite! 'If anyone says, "I love God," yet hates his brother, he is a liar. For anyone who does not love his brother, whom he has seen, cannot love God, whom he has not seen' (1 John 4:20).

These are strong words and there are still more to come: 'Anyone who hates his brother is a murderer, and you know that no murderer has eternal life in him' (1 John 3:15).

Neglect of the inward application of this commandment, and indeed of the whole biblical ethic, was the great error of the Pharisees, and Christians frequently display the same characteristic. They measure spirituality in terms of the worldly pleasures and vices from which they abstain, in terms of external cleanliness rather than a wholesome, God-glorifying spirit of love. So often, alas, those who boast of separation from the world harbour harsh and hateful thoughts about others which are the very antithesis of Christianity.

The sixth commandment demands that the follower of Christ say a resounding 'No' to every thought involving hatred. He must not kill in a physical sense and he must not have thoughts that involve hatred. The words of the Lord Jesus are clear: 'I tell you that anyone who is angry with his brother will be subject to judgement.' This is the inward, the deeper, the more ultimate meaning and application of the command, 'You shall not murder'.

No homicide today

The sixth commandment, with its establishment of a right to life, has incredibly far-reaching implications on which volumes upon volumes have been written. For our present purpose we can only examine briefly some of the issues which arise for the Christian who seeks to keep this commandment in a modern environment.

Before we attempt to do so, it will be well to recall that the New Testament does not lay down canons of civil law. While the Christian is entitled to stand for and to urge that the laws of his particular community be based on principles of righteousness, and ultimately on divinely revealed absolutes, his primary concern must be with his own behaviour. His duty is to behave aright in all his relationships with his fellows and to accord to them every right and every benefit he would wish for himself. As our Lord put it, 'In everything, do to others what you would have them do to you, for this sums up the Law and the Prophets' (Matthew 7:12).

Intentional killings

It is abundantly clear that this commandment prohibits the individual Christian from killing another person, whoever he be and whatever might be the motive. Revenge or retaliation arising as a result of an offence committed by someone else never justifies the killing of that person by the one who has been offended. In this we have the incomparable example of the Lord Jesus, the Lord of glory, who when reviled, 'did not retaliate', who when suffering, 'made no threats. Instead, he entrusted himself to him who judges justly' (1 Peter 2:23).

The imposition of the death penalty as a matter of civil law and the infliction of fatal injuries in war are community rather than personal matters and need very careful and very detailed consideration which is just not possible here. Issues which do, however, call for some attention are suicide, euthanasia and abortion.

Suicide

Suicide, the taking of one's own life, is not discussed at all in the Bible, though one or two instances of it — some of them quite heroic — are recorded. There was Samson who by bringing down a Philistine palace killed not only himself but a great number of Philistines (Judges 16:28—30). There was Saul (1 Samuel 31:2—5) who to avoid ignominy at the hands of the Philistines took his own life. Ahithophel, adviser to Absalom, hanged himself when his counsel was frustrated and Zimri, king of Israel for seven days, ended his life by burning the king's house over him with fire (1 Kings 16:18). The only case in the New Testament is that of Judas who hanged himself after betraying our Lord, but the record (Matthew 27:5), like those in the Old Testament, gives no teaching on the moral issue involved.

Suicide seems to be a taking into one's own hands of something which by right belongs to God. Man is God's creature; conception and birth are his gifts; breath and all the essentials of life are his provisions: 'In [the Lord's] hand is the life of every creature and the breath of all mankind' (Job 12:10). If so, it is surely God's place, his prerogative,

to call men and women from this life to the next. It is when
he takes breath away that death occurs (Psalm 104:29).
Since man is prohibited by the commandment from personally initiating homicide, and since at no point is his own life
excluded from the prohibition, it seems reasonable to conclude that he has no right to determine the time or the
circumstances of his own departure. To do so either by self-
inflicted suicide or by the assisted form we know as
euthanasia would seem to be a clear violation of the biblical
absolute for personal morality: 'You shall not kill.'

A less deliberate form of suicide must also be noticed. It
results from indulgence in pleasures which prove destructive
ultimately of all that is good and of life itself. Drugs, from
tobacco and alcohol to heroin, have this effect. So, too, does
gluttony. In each case compulsive addiction can arise and
the victim finds himself in a prison of his own making and
committing suicide on an instalment plan. Many argue that
men must be free to indulge in these pleasures even if they
prove self-destructive, but for the Christian this argument
cannot be applied to his own life which is only his on trust
from God. It is to be lived not for pleasure but for God's
glory and this means that every part of his being must always
be at its optimum usefulness for the Lord. God is to be
glorified in the body of the believer (1 Corinthians 6:19–20)
which is to be a temple worthy of the Spirit of God. It is
very difficult to see how God is glorified when there is an
indulgence which damages the person, weakening and ultimately destroying his body.

Euthanasia
The word 'euthanasia' simply means 'dying well' and in
modern parlance refers to measures aimed at expediting the
demise of a person deemed beyond recovery and for whom
continued life would involve great, and perhaps intolerable
burdens of suffering. For this reason it is sometimes called
'mercy-killing'.

The arguments for euthanasia assume either that the
individual has the right to decide when or in what circumstances his life should end, or that society or some group of
experts within it has such a right. We are told that if a person
freely expresses a wish to be put to sleep at a point where he

becomes incurably ill, the incurability being confirmed by a panel of competent medical authorities, the wish should be granted. On this basis euthanasia is a kind of assisted suicide. We are also told by more radical advocates that even where no such wish has been expressed the incurably ill could be and should be disposed of without fuss or delay. Some have gone further and argued for the elimination of the senile, the insane, the badly deformed and the criminal in the interests of a purer and a more efficient society.

Such views are open to very strong objections on medical, social and legal grounds. From the theological point of view they are totally unacceptable because the kind of killing they envisage is quite simply a direct violation of the commandment: 'You shall not kill'.

This is not to say, however, that it is right for medical skill to be used in such a way as to extend life abnormally, or, as could more accurately be said, to extend unnaturally the process of dying. It would seem, indeed, as unchristian to keep people alive, medicinally or mechanically, when every possibility of meaningful living has gone, as to take life from them prematurely. It is to say that, however compassionate euthanasia is made to appear, it involves an intrusion into a realm which belongs ultimately and alone to God. Man does not have the right to take his own life or the life of anyone else. His duty is to make life as meaningful and pleasant as is possible for as long as God is pleased to give it to him and to his fellows.

Abortion

This is sometimes seen as a method of population control, sometimes as a way of ending an unwanted pregnancy within marriage and more frequently as a way of dealing with an illegitimate one. On occasions it is advised on medical grounds if the pregnancy endangers the mother's health or if there are strong indications that it will produce a severely defective child.

Artificially induced abortion was totally alien to the cultures of the ancient Near East but it did have considerable place in classical Greece and in Rome. It is not specifically mentioned in either the Old or the New Testament, but one passage in the Old does have some bearing on it. This is

among the ordinances which follow and apply the decalogue
and relates to a woman who aborts or miscarries following
injury: 'If men who are fighting hit a pregnant woman and
she gives birth prematurely' (or 'she has a miscarriage') but
there is no serious injury, the offender must be fined whatever the woman's husband demands and the court allows. But
if there is serious injury, you are to take life for life, eye for
eye, tooth for tooth, hand for hand, foot for foot, burn for
burn, wound for wound, bruise for bruise' (Exodus 21:
22—25). The implications of this seem to be that the loss of
the unborn child was to be regarded as a relatively small
matter, which could be settled by a legally agreed or imposed
fine, but injury to the mother was to be treated much more
seriously. In that case 'serious injury' had followed the
affray, and there was to be an equal retribution. If the
woman died, her assailant's life was to be taken; if she lost
an eye, he must lose an eye. These words surely imply that
death of the mother was regarded as murder and that death
of the foetus was not so regarded. Indeed, it would seem that
the death of the foetus when resulting from the violence of a
brawl was not even regarded as a case of unintentional manslaughter.

What this passage seems to do is to make the life of the
mother more important, more valuable than the life of an
unborn child. It does *not* make any pronouncement at all
on the kind of deliberately induced abortion which is so
common in many countries today. If, in fact, it indicates
that the life and well-being of the mother has priority over
that of the foetus, it might provide scriptural endorsement
for therapeutic abortion effected for the good of the mother.
The argument might, indeed, be extended to cover preg-
nancies resulting from rape, where the psychological health
of the mother, both in the immediate and in the long-term
future, is a most important matter, whatever her physical
condition at the time a decision has to be made.

Such endorsement seems less clear where the health of the
mother is not at stake but there are indications that the
child will be malformed. It can be argued that the care
needed by such children is often in the long-term damaging
for the mother and that for her sake the pregnancy may be
terminated. It can also be argued that in the long term such

termination is the most compassionate thing for the child, but the Christian has to ask if in any sense the abortion of such a foetus could be a violation of the command, 'You shall not kill.'

A question which has to be faced concerns the point at which life actually begins. Is it at conception or at birth or at some intermediate point like quickening? Scripture does not answer this question but if it could be shown that personal life begins not at conception but later on early abortion would not need to be regarded as the taking of a human life. Exodus 21:22—25, which certainly implies that a foetus is less significant than an actual human life, would tend to confirm this. In that event Scripture may be understood as leaving somewhat open the issue of whether or not the abortion of a foetus involves the killing of a human being.

At the same time it has to be recognized that abortion involves the termination of a life process and therefore the killing of a potential, if not of an actual human being. In some sense human life is taken and this a Christian with a biblically-orientated conscience could not easily contemplate. It would seem to be absolutely unacceptable as a method of birth control. In cases where the health of the mother is at stake or where the prognosis for the child is one of severe incapacity and suffering Christian people can be faced with awesome dilemmas and need great sympathy and loving support. Those who disagree with their decisions must respect their consciences, recognizing that to some degree Scripture leaves the issue open.

Incidental and accidental killing

We have seen that the Old Testament interpreted the commandment as requiring men to act in such a way that incidental or accidental killings did not follow their actions. The regulations concerned teach us that across the board, in personal, commercial, judicial, social and medical activities, the sanctity of life must be an overriding consideration. Life can never be treated as expendable. No end, however good, can ever justify a means which does not give due respect to the sacredness, the inviolability, of existing lives. 'You shall not kill.'

The Christian, who lives under the laws of God's kingdom,

like the Israelite of old, is obligated to avoid any and every
action that could cause or contribute to death for himself or
for someone else. To a high degree he must be orientated
towards safety because of his responsibility to love his
neighbour as himself. In practical terms four areas of life are
of great importance.

The home
Accidents in the home claim many lives each year. Elderly
people and young children are the most vulnerable, but
others are by no means free of risk.

In the home, then, we must take maximum safety pre-
cautions. The proper control of fires and of naked lights,
the avoidance (particularly with children) of inflammable
garments, the correct installation and use of electric and gas
appliances and the proper care of medicines and other
dangerous items are all part of our obedience to the sixth
commandment.

The roads
The toll of death and injury through road accidents is fan-
tastic but somehow we seem to have become inured to its
enormity. Daily we hear of a carnage which could be avoided,
or at least greatly reduced, if drivers and pedestrians were
less thoughtless and showed more concern for the safety of
themselves and others. Too many people take risks, driving
recklessly, or using cars or cycles that are mechanically
defective and that should have been repaired or serviced.
Often folk drive when their competence is impaired by failing
capacities, by fatigue, by drink or by drugs — any one of
which often dulls a man's ability to recognize his impaired
competence. Surely it is right for Christians to give a lead to
the whole community by exercising the utmost care and by
encouraging everybody to work more responsibly for the
safety of all who use our roads. I am my brother's keeper.

Industry
In the world of commerce and industry the Christian must
again exhibit the maximum concern for safety. It is easy for
employers and workers to cut corners in order to save
time, money or effort. Where love of gain or love of ease

are more important than the lives of men and women, the sixth commandment is broken or in danger of being broken.

Employers who fail to provide protection for their workers are like the builder who put up a house without a parapet, and who was held responsible for the death of anyone who subsequently fell off the roof. The workers who fail to use protective equipment or who fail to follow safety regulations are likewise guilty of culpable neglect. From the drawing-boards where factories and workshops are planned, to the operation of band-saws or cement mixers, from the boardrooms to the shop-floor, the safety of human life is the moral priority. Each man is his own and his brother's keeper. He must not kill by oversight or neglect, any more than by a deliberate act of murder.

Medicine
Neglect or indifference to the worth of a human life can have disastrous results in medicine. The fact that a patient's life is often literally in the doctor's hands heightens the latter's responsibility to ensure that no action, or lack of action on his part contributes to premature or untimely death.

While there is no doubt whatever about the deep devotion of the vast majority of medical workers to the care of their patients, there have been and inevitably always will be exceptions. Sometimes, for example, the pressures of research, the desire to break through some barrier to knowledge can cause men to take risks which they justify in terms of the ultimate good of others. Occasionally the burden of caring for long-term patients or the pressures of understaffing have led to a measure of neglect. We can understand how such things happen, but this is not to excuse them. The men and the women who take on themselves the role of medical care must remember that the first command in the moral law is 'You shall not kill.' Administrators in charge of medical services and their political bosses must see to it that staffing is at such a level that neglect of patients does not occur. The Christian, in whatever area he is involved, must set an example in patient care, treating each individual as a person whose life is inviolate.

. . . But forgiveness

Incidental and accidental killings are by nature unintentional. They are not cases of murder and must not be regarded as such. Often people who in some indirect way have contributed to a death of this kind develop an undue feeling of guilt. It is good, of course, that they have sensitive consciences, but for the Christian there is a way of forgiveness and of being at peace with God and with himself. This involves a frank acknowledgement of his own failure, whether of neglect or of misguided activity, and an acceptance of God's gift of forgiveness. 'If we confess our sins, he is faithful and just and will forgive us our sins and purify us from all unrighteousness' (1 John 1:9).

While we must heed the warnings implicit in the sixth commandment and so order our lives that we allow no avoidable neglect that could cause a fatality, let us never become burdened or depressed by a sense of guilt over past failures. Rather let us by faith claim and enjoy God's forgiveness and go forward with peace in our hearts. If justification by faith means anything it means that 'we have peace with God through our Lord Jesus Christ' (Romans 5:1).

Hatred also proscribed

The New Testament outlawing of hatred stands as absolutely in the late twentieth century as it did in the days of our Lord and his apostles. The Christian just must not give it a place in his thinking. Yet today, as in every generation, it constantly raises its ugly head and in several areas of life is particularly catastrophic.

Race relations

Race relations have become a factor of immense importance in the modern world. This is especially the case where the white and negro races confront each other, but there are often equally acute problems elsewhere.

Whatever we may think about racial integration or apartheid, the Bible makes it absolutely clear that we have to give proper respect to those whose race is different from our own. In the Old Testament law the Israelites were required to make provision for strangers who came temporarily or permanently to their land. They were prohibited from exploiting the stranger on the ground that they themselves had been strangers in Egypt. In the New Testament the gospel reaches out across racial barriers, bringing together both Jew and Gentile and producing a new people of God whose unity in Christ transcends the division of race. Says Paul, 'There is neither Jew nor Greek, slave nor free, male nor female, for you are all one in Christ Jesus' (Galatians 3:28).

The Christian will not imagine that racial identity has ceased to exist any more than he will think that on becoming a Christian a man ceases to be a man or a woman is no longer a woman. But he will see that these distinctions are secondary and will seek to show true Christian love to others, whatever their race, whatever their colour, whatever their social status.

At no point is hatred more apparent or more violent than where racial, political and religious factors coalesce. Northern Ireland is an example and as a result has been marked by suspicion, fear and antagonism between two communities. In many hearts there is real hatred. But Northern Ireland has no monopoly of these things. In our Lord's day Jews and Samaritans detested each other, and human history is filled with similar stories. Cyprus provides a relatively recent parallel.

Such a situation requires that hearts be changed and that hatred be replaced by love. The only way to create a bridge between rival groups is through loving concern. This has to begin at the level of the individual but it must extend to community action. Each side has to become interested and has to work for the well-being of the other. Each has to give up selfish aspirations in order to accommodate to the other. Often in history peace has only come when one party literally devoured the other or when extensive intermarriage effectively produced a new hybrid group. But surely it is possible for alien communities to accommodate to and live alongside each other in mutual respect and without one dominating the other. Within a given society the Christian, with his ethic of love, has a vital role to play. He should set the tone and become what in God's purpose he is meant to be — the salt of the earth and the light of the world.

Church life
Church life is often plagued by the squabbling of believers.
It is indeed strange that evangelicals, who claim to enjoy
experimentally the blessings of God's love, find it so hard to
love one another! Perhaps we have allowed ourselves to slide
into an excessive individualism which tends to make every
man think he is his own master and that he need not consider anyone but himself. Perhaps we attract people of an
aggressive temperament, people who feel strongly over
their beliefs and who are prepared to stand up and fight for
them. Whatever the explanation, such squabbling and such
hatred are not honouring to God and must be eliminated
from all our hearts.

The church is a sphere in which there are differences of
gift and differences of function, just as in the human body
there are many different organs, each with its own role. Each
Christian must therefore recognize the worth of his fellow
believers and, in things where God has not clearly spoken,
respect their views where different from his own. Love and
not hatred must be the guiding principle. As the apostle
John writes, 'He has given us this command: Whoever loves
God must also love his brother' (1 John 4:21).

New Testament application of the sixth commandment to
our inner attitudes absolutely precludes us from hating one
another. Most Christians accept this teaching but often, in
fact, they fail to see that the absence from their hearts of
love for those whom they dislike and with whom they
disagree is really an evidence of destructive emotions. They
hate rather than love and in so doing, whether they know it
or not, they break the sixth commandment.

'You shall not kill.'

9 The sanctity of marriage
The Seventh Commandment

'You shall not commit adultery.'

'Adultery' is the name we give to a sexual relationship established by a married person with someone other than his or her legal spouse. The context is the violation of a marriage. Whether the offence is casual or established on a more permanent basis, the adulterer is unfaithful to a partner to whom he or she is bound by personal troth and by legal provision.

Creation ordinance of marriage affirmed

The word 'adultery' is not mentioned at all in the records of antediluvian or patriarchal times. Nevertheless in the book of Genesis there is impressive testimony to the fact that it was God's intention that husband and wife live together in a permanent relationship and without the superimposing of adulterous ones. In the story of creation (Genesis 2:18−24) we learn how God brought to the first man, Adam, the first woman, Eve, as bone of his bones and flesh of his flesh. Because they both, the man and the woman, shared a common human flesh, they could be united in a lasting and exclusive relationship of marriage which set a pattern for all time: 'For this reason,' that is, because of the way they had been created, 'a man will leave his father and mother and be united to his wife, and they will become one flesh' (Genesis 2:24).

Subsequent history shows that men in general did in fact respect the institution of marriage. Cain, Seth, Enoch and the others were family men and Noah had a wife, as did each of his three sons. When Terah and Abraham left Mesopotamia,

Sarah, Abraham's wife, went with them and was Abraham's constant companion till she died. Respect for marriage was also demonstrated when Abraham made Sarah identify herself in Egypt as his sister (Genesis 12:10—19). She was taken into Pharaoh's harem but as soon as the truth became clear Pharaoh told Abraham to take his wife and be gone. He did not want the ire of Abraham's God as punishment for violating another man's marriage! Even more impressive was the response of Joseph to the machinations of Potiphar's wife (Genesis 39:6b—18). Because she was his master's wife he would not on any account be inveigled into a sexual relationship. Even if the word is not used, the fact is that he would not commit adultery.

The seventh commandment is a direct prohibition of adultery. 'You shall not commit adultery.' It is in fact the earliest use of the Hebrew word, *na'aph*. Throughout the Old Testament this word and its various derivatives refer either to a sexual relationship which violated a marriage covenant, or to a spiritual apostasy which broke Israel's covenant with the Lord. The commandment, like the sixth and those which follow, is concerned with interpersonal human relationships and relates specifically to the sexual dimension. It prohibited the formation of a sexual union which transgressed the exclusive commitment of one party to a marriage.

There is general agreement that the command primarily prohibited a man from having sexual relations with a woman who belonged by marriage or betrothal to another Israelite. Where the woman had been a willing or even a non-resisting partner, she too was regarded as guilty of adultery and under Israelite civil law both were liable to the death penalty. 'If a man commits adultery with another man's wife — with the wife of his neighbour — both the adulterer and the adulteress shall be put to death' (Leviticus 20:10). The same death penalty was to apply where the girl was a betrothed virgin. The man was then regarded as violating his neighbour's wife and the girl was held guilty if she did not cry for help (Deuteronomy 22:23—24).

It would thus appear that adultery only arose where the woman was married or betrothed. If she was unmarried and unbetrothed and forced by an aggressive man, a different definition applied and the man was simply required to pay to the girl's father the normal marriage present or bride price and to take her as his wife. If her father refused to give her to him he was to pay the father an equivalent sum as a fine (Exodus 22:16–17). In the later Deuteronomic laws the emphasis was on paying the fine and on a measure of further deterrence effected by the fact that the man concerned was denied the privilege of divorcing that wife in the way that in normal circumstances other men could do. He would have to live with her, whether he liked it or not, for the rest of his, or her life. Nevertheless because the girl involved had no marital commitment the man's offence was not regarded as adultery.

This picture will, no doubt, seem to fall short of the Christian standard of morality, but it must be remembered that in Moses' time and in later Old Testament times every woman had to be the ward of a man, normally her father or her husband. To have an illicit relationship was therefore an offence against her father or her husband. At the same time polygamy, the marriage of a man to more than one woman, while not encouraged, was tolerated, with the result that there was nothing criminal in a man forming a relationship with more than one woman, so long as the women concerned were themselves free from a marriage covenant.

What the commandment did was to make Israelite marriage sacrosanct by prohibiting adventurous men from violating the marriage bonds of women and the rights of husbands in relation to their wives. In doing this the commandment provided a basis for stable home life. It was a defence against the intrusion of a second man into the home and a preventative of divided loyalty among the mothers of Israel. It gave to every man the right to be assured that his wife was his and his alone and gave to the wife the confidence that she was the possession of one man and not the plaything of many. At the same time it sought to give rising generations of Israelites the security of a home not disrupted by disloyalty or maternal neglect.

The sin of David
The sin of David with Bathsheba is probably better known than any other case of adultery in the Bible. It was a terrible blot on the life of a man of God. The record (2 Samuel

11:2—12:25) is remarkable for its honest portrayal of how
David was tempted and of how he schemed to extricate himself once his sin had begun to catch up with him.

David saw a beautiful woman bathing and deep in his soul
sexual desires were aroused. He enquired who the woman
was and then, using the weight of regal authority, sent for
her and an adulterous union took place. Bathsheba soon
informed David that as a result of her visit to him she had
become pregnant and this started off his attempts to effect
a cover-up. He arranged to get her husband leave of absence
from the army so that he would appear to be the father of
the child. When Uriah refused to play ball David gave
instructions that he be put in the front line where he was
likely to be killed by enemy action. This ploy worked and
David added the crime of murder to that of adultery. Then
he took Bathsheba into his own house as an additional wife
and in due course a son was born.

The thing of special interest to us is the way in which the
divine disapproval of David's actions endorsed both the sixth
and the seventh commandments. We read, 'The thing David
had done displeased the Lord' (2 Samuel 11:27b) and learn
how Nathan was sent with a parable which aroused David's
anger and brought him to see his guilt. The Lord said through
Nathan, 'You despised me and took the wife of Uriah the
Hittite to be your own' (2 Samuel 12:10b). David said,
'I have sinned against the Lord.' Thus the adultery and the
murder to which it led were recognized for what they were,
sins against the Lord.

The denunciations of the prophets

Hosea knew the bitterness of having an unfaithful wife and
was equipped by that experience to understand God's grief
over his spiritually adulterous people. Indeed, he linked
spiritual adultery with the physical and taught that the
defection of the nation from the Lord was the root cause
of all the nation's troubles, not least the one from which he
was suffering, namely, the infidelity of a wife who had
become a virtual whore. Thus we read, 'A spirit of prostitution leads them astray; they are unfaithful to their God.
They sacrifice on the mountaintops and burn offerings on
the hills [that is, sacrifices to the Baals] . . . Therefore

your daughters turn to prostitution and your daughters-in-law to adultery' (Hosea 4:12—13). The point was that backsliding from the Lord led inevitably to the abandonment of the Lord's standards of morality. Once Baalistic religion was adopted, the fear of God waned in men's hearts and the marriage bond lost the sanctity given to it by God at creation and through the seventh commandment. The women of Israel became adulteresses and many other evils flourished. Hosea's appeal that the people return to the Lord, confessing and forsaking their sins (Hosea 14:1—2), shows that these evils were serious offences against God, which could not be glossed over and which he could only forgive if there was genuine repentance.

Jeremiah is another prophet in whose oracles apostasy is often spoken of as 'adultery' but the physical variety was obviously all too common at his time, about 620—580 B.C., or 140—160 years after Hosea's prophecies. In one passage we read, 'They have done outrageous things in Israel; they have committed adultery with their neighbours' wives' (Jeremiah 29:23). In another he asserts that they were stealing, murdering, committing adultery, etc., and yet daring to stand before the Lord in his house (Jeremiah 7:9). Again it is clear that adultery was viewed as a despicable sin and a clear violation of the law of God.

The warnings of the wise

The wisdom of the Old Testament is all too often neglected by Christians. It is mainly concentrated in three or four books — Proverbs, Job, Ecclesiastes and Song of Songs — and has a great deal to say about the relationship of man to woman in marriage and against the violation of that relationship through adultery.

In Proverbs we have down-to-earth maxims which were easy to remember and which the wise men of old were inspired to record for the learning of future generations. Many of these warn against the machinations of a loose, an adulterous woman. Chapter 5 is a good example, giving almost all of its twenty-three verses to this theme and stressing in the process the positive worth of a stable marriage.

'. . . May you rejoice in the wife of your youth.
A loving doe, a graceful deer —
May her breasts satisfy you always,
    may you ever be captivated by her love.
Why be captivated, my son, by an adulteress?
    Why embrace the bosom of another man's wife?
For a man's ways are in full view of the Lord,
    and he examines all his paths.
The evil deeds of a wicked man ensnare him;
    the cords of his sin hold him fast.
He will die for lack of discipline,
    led astray by his own great folly'
                                    (Proverbs 5:18—23).

In the very vivid language of chapter 7 the writer describes how a loose woman entices a young man with seductive speech to an orgy of lovemaking that proves a snare and costs him his life. Thus the whole weight of poetic wisdom is used to warn men against the sin of adultery. The advice of the sage puts the issue very clearly:

Now then, my sons, listen to me;
    pay attention to what I say.
Do not let your heart turn to her ways,
    or stray into her paths.
Many are the victims she has brought down;
    her slain are a mighty throng.
Her house is a highway to the grave,
    leading down to the chambers of death'
                                    (Proverbs 7:24—27).

New Testament endorsement

In New Testament times the dominant power was Rome. Judea was mostly under direct Roman rule, while Galilee and Peraea were continuously under a client king who ruled by favour of his Roman overlord.

Millions of Jews lived outside Palestine in settlements all over the Roman Empire and to the east in Babylon and Persia. Among these scattered Jewish communities known as the 'Dispersion' or 'Diaspora' much of the witness of the apostles and their associates took place. The early churches to which the New Testament Epistles were addressed were made up of dispersion Jews and of Gentiles who had come from various backgrounds to faith in Christ.

In the light of these facts it has to be recognized that in the New Testament there is no single cultural unit such as obtained in ancient Israel. Accordingly terms like marriage, adultery and sexual immorality may have had somewhat different connotations according to the context in which they were spoken or written, or in which they were heard or read.

Our Lord's ministry took place in Palestine among Jewish people who were divided into a number of religious sects, each of which involved a considerable measure of deviation from the religion of the Old Testament. One extremist group among those known as the Essenes even practised celibacy. The dominant influence, however, came from the Pharisees, for whom celibacy was sinful disobedience to God's command: 'Be fruitful and increase in number' (Genesis 1:28). The ordinary people (known as the *'am haaretz'* or 'people of the land') greatly admired the Pharisees but were not prepared to join them because of their insistence on the observance of finicky traditions which were extra to the various laws of the Old Testament.

We have some evidence of Pharisaic traditions as these are mentioned in the Gospels, but the main source of our information is the Mishnah, which was produced around 200 A.D. This committed to writing teaching which was previously transmitted by oral methods and some of which went back to our Lord's time. The Mishnah shows that in the main 'adultery' was still regarded as the sin of a man with a married woman and as an offence against the woman's husband. Its regulations were designed to give redress to the husband and provided that a guilty wife be put away (Sotah 1:5). Thus divorce seems to have taken the place of the death penalty prescribed by the Old Testament, a change precipitated, or at least encouraged, we may surmise, by the fact that under Roman rule the Jews were no longer free to impose capital punishment. There were different views about the grounds on which a man could divorce his wife but all the rabbis were agreed that adultery was a valid ground for it.

The teaching of our Lord

This is mainly found in two passages, Matthew 5:27–32 and
Matthew 19:3–12 (with parallels in Mark 10:2–12; Luke
16:18). At the same time there is considerable additional
evidence that our Lord fully accepted and fully endorsed
the seventh commandment. This appears, for example, in
the sermon on the mount in his remarks about the Mosaic
law, 'Do not think that I have come to abolish the Law or the
Prophets; I have not come to abolish them but to fulfil them'
(Matthew 5:17). It appears also in his response to the rich
young ruler: 'You know the commandments: "Do not
murder, do not commit adultery . . ."' (Mark 10:19;
Matthew 19:18; Luke 18:20). For him the Old Testament
law was the eternal law of God, and any teacher who sought
to relax its application prejudiced his own position in the
kingdom of heaven (Matthew 5:19).

Inward application

In the sermon on the mount our Lord brought out the full
meaning of the commandments and in this case did so with
devastating effect. He began, 'You have heard that it was
said, "Do not commit adultery"' (Matthew 5:27). To this
his hearers would all give assent. They knew the law. Then
came the new teaching: 'But I tell you that anyone who
looks at a woman lustfully has already committed adultery
with her in his heart.' Our Lord thus struck at the very root
of adulterous behaviour, at the lustful looks with which it
begins. There could be a moral offence even where no act
of adultery had taken place! The look that springs from lust
or that is accompanied by lust is sinful.

What is not clear is whether or not our Lord at this point
was also widening the scope of the commandment. The word
recorded here is *gunē*, which can mean an adult female,
whether single or married, but which in fact often means a
wife. Indeed, when he used it again four verses on, it must
have meant 'wife' because a man could not divorce a woman
who was not recognized as his wife! It is probable then that
the 'look of lust' in verse 27 is a look directed not at an
unmarried woman, but at the wife of another man. At any
event the inward application of the command is brought
to the fore.

Our Lord then took up another Old Testament provision, that which enabled a man to divorce his wife (Matthew 5:31). He was again establishing common ground with his hearers. Then he added his own extension of the law: 'But I tell you that anyone who divorces his wife, except for marital unfaithfulness[1], causes her to commit adultery, and anyone who marries a woman so divorced commits adultery' (Matthew 5:32).

The point which emerges so clearly here is that if a man divorced his wife for the wrong reason (that is, for some other reason than her having committed adultery with another man) he was making that wife available to be married to someone else when in fact she should properly still have been his own wife. In so doing he forced the woman into an adulterous relationship with the other man. Our Lord thus extended the meaning of adultery to include a relationship which in the practice of the Old Testament and of the rabbis was regarded as a valid marriage.

The basis of this extension becomes clearer when we examine Matthew 19:3−12 and Mark 10:2−12. The Pharisees had come to our Lord with one of their 'trick' questions: 'Is it lawful for a man to divorce his wife for any and every reason?' More accurately translated they said, 'Is it lawful to divorce one's wife for *every* cause?' The question reflects a dispute between rabbinic schools, one of which allowed divorce only to a man whose wife was unchaste, while others allowed it on much more trivial grounds. The Pharisees wanted our Lord to take sides and on this occasion he did just that, coming down in favour of the more rigid school. In doing so, he explained the divine will starting with creation. God made man male and female with a view to a permanent union between the two. A man is to be joined to his wife and the two are to be one. In God's purpose this is what happens in marriage; the two become one and are not to be separated: 'Therefore what God has joined [or yoked] together, let man not separate.' It is thus the sanctity of each marriage within the wider divine institution which is the basis of our Lord's teaching and of his extension of the scope of our commandment.

This led to a further question from the Pharisees: 'Why then did Moses command that a man give his wife a

certificate of divorce and send her away?' Our Lord's answer
was that Moses had allowed divorce as a concession to the
sinful hardness of men's hearts. This, our Lord affirmed, was
not the position from the beginning. Divorce is no part of
God's ideal; it is a concession to men and the fact that it has
been permitted must in no way be taken as encouraging it.
Indeed, our Lord went out of his way to discourage it and
at this point further extended the application of our commandment. 'I tell you that anyone who divorces his wife,
except for marital unfaithfulness, and marries another
woman commits adultery' (v. 9). It is not just that the man
who divorces his wife for the wrong reason forces her and
another man into an adulterous relationship. When he himself marries another woman he also commits adultery; he
also sins.

This was clearly something new and even the disciples
found it hard to swallow. They said, 'If this is the situation
between a husband and wife, it is better not to marry.' They
saw for the first time that God did not regard marriage as an
experiment from which a man could extricate himself by
issuing a certificate of divorce. It involved commitment, lifelong commitment, to a woman. There was to be no release
unless she should commit an offence against the marriage by
sexual union with another man.

At this point our Lord surely rejected polygamy, that is,
the marriage of a man to two or more wives at the same time.
By defining marriage in terms of the union of one man with
one woman till one or other dies or destroys the marriage
by sin, he made it an exclusive relationship that can allow
no intrusion by a third party. If it is adultery for a man to
marry a second wife after wrongly divorcing a former one, it
must also be adultery if he marries a second wife while still
married to the first one. Among the Jews in the first century
polygamy was allowed (Herod had some eight wives at one
stage!) but it was not common among the ordinary people.
Our Lord's teaching here seems to rule it out completely.

Mark's account of this incident has a sentence which adds
another emphasis. It acknowledges that a woman could
initiate divorce and in the event of her then marrying another
man places on her shoulders the precise guilt which is
imputed in the previous verse to a man who does the same

thing. This introduces into these matters an element of equality between men and women which was not at all evident in the Old Testament.

The fact that neither Mark nor Luke (Mark 10:11; Luke 16:18) mention the clause, 'except for marital unfaithfulness' (Matthew 5:32, 19:9 — AV 'except it be for fornication'), has occasioned much discussion. Some scholars have argued that this was never spoken by our Lord but was inserted into the text of Matthew by someone who wanted to have in Scripture a saying of our Lord that would justify divorce in the case of a sexual offence against a marriage. If this were true, then our Lord would in fact have cancelled the Mosaic permission of divorce. However, in the absence of textual evidence which would put the authenticity of the exceptive clause in doubt, we must accept it as genuinely spoken by our Lord and thus as giving the stamp of his approval to the continuance of divorce as a way of relief for a husband, and indeed for a wife, whose marriage has been violated by the adultery of a spouse.

The woman taken in adultery

This incident is recorded in John 8:1–11, a passage which, as most modern versions indicate, is absent from the most important of the ancient Greek manuscripts, though several have it at the end of John's Gospel and others after Luke 21:38. We cannot discuss textual problems here and can only say that there is a possibility that when manuscripts were being copied it somehow became misplaced. For our present purpose we can assume that it is a genuine part of Scripture even if we are not sure where it should be placed.

Again the scribes and the Pharisees seem to have been setting a trap for Jesus. They dragged before him a woman who had been caught in the very act of adultery and, citing the requirement of the Mosaic law that such be stoned, they asked, 'Now what do you say?' If he had said, 'Stone her,' they would have charged him with sedition before the Roman authorities, and if he had denied the validity of the Mosaic punishment they would have condemned him as a false teacher.

Our Lord proved more than a match for them. He bent down, perhaps to avoid even looking at the pious humbugs before him and, writing on the ground, said, 'If any one of you is without sin, let him be the first to throw a stone at her.' He continued writing on the ground and by the time he looked up the woman's accusers had gone. None had the moral right to cast a stone; none would have dared to do so, for that would have been to incur the ire of Rome they had hoped might come to our Lord.

The accusers gone, Jesus addressed the woman. 'Woman, where are they? Has no one condemned you?' She answered, 'No one sir.' To this he replied, 'Then neither do I condemn you. Go now and leave your life of sin.'

Some have taken this as indicating that our Lord did not regard adultery as a serious sin. Such a view is quite unjustified. What Jesus declined to do was to act as civil judge. He would not usurp the power of the courts. Thus in saying to the woman, 'Neither do I condemn you,' he was not for one moment saying that she had no guilt before God or before her husband. She was undoubtedly an adulteress and our Lord recognized the fact when he told her, 'Go now and leave your life of sin.' There was no harshness in the way he handled the woman, but there was a firm rejection of what she had done. It was sin and, as such, something to be abandoned: 'Go and leave your life of sin.'

We see our Lord then as endorsing, deepening and extending the significance of our commandment. He warns us, as he warned his original hearers, of the heinousness of adultery and of the lustful look which gives birth to it. To those who have fallen he would say, as to the woman accused by the scribes and Pharisees, 'Go now and leave your life of sin.'

Apostolic teaching
Christian churches were quickly formed in Syria, Asia Minor and Europe. They drew into their membership both Jews and Gentiles, with many of the latter coming from a very profligate and permissive background. Rome itself was famous for its wife-swapping and its high incidence of divorce. In Corinth and other places licentious cult prostitution was rampant.

The instructions given by the apostles to the churches inevitably dealt with marriage and its implications. The marital infidelity and the sexual licence of the contemporary scene were strongly disapproved of and the Christian view of a lifelong and exclusive commitment of husband to wife and wife to husband was clearly presented.

General opprobrium for sexual sin

Without exception, apostolic references to adultery endorse the seventh commandment and call on Christian people to observe the purity of sexual relationships which it demands. James, whose first readers were undoubtedly of Jewish origin, affirms that adultery is a transgression of God's law (James 2:11). The writer to the Hebrews, also writing to converted Jews, warns that God would judge those who polluted the institution of marriage.

'God will judge the adulterer and all the sexually immoral' (fornicators) (Hebrews 13:4b). This is why Paul, in urging his readers at Rome to conduct themselves becomingly, says, 'not in sexual immorality and debauchery' (Romans 13:13 — AV, 'chambering and wantonness', literally, 'in beds', i.e., in illegitimate sexual intercourse and unrestrained indulgences). Paul also asserts that observance of the seventh commandment, together with the other laws of morality, is an expression of love for one's neighbour (Romans 13: 9—10). Love will do no wrong to a neighbour and, therefore, rules out adultery. Writing to Corinth, he includes the sexually immoral and adulterers in a list of those who will be excluded from God's kingdom (1 Corinthians 6:9). The list of what he calls 'the acts of the sinful nature' (Galatians 5:19) also includes sexual immorality. Paul adds firmly that those who so behave will not inherit the kingdom of God. Some less important manuscripts, followed by the Authorized Version, also include adultery in the list but more recent versions, like the RSV and NIV omit it as not being part of Paul's original text.

The inclusion of fornicators (Greek *pornoi*, NIV 'the sexually immoral') in Paul's lists probably refers to a form of immorality that was all too common in Corinth and in Asia Minor. The Greek word refers primarily to men who frequented brothels and whose sin was with harlots. This reflects the fact that oriental fertility cults had become established at temples which were, in part, religious brothels with a permanent establishment of cult prostitutes. Men

who were involved in these cults presented sacrifices to the
deities concerned and indulged in ritual prostitution. Paul's
attitude to such practices was absolutely uncompromising:
'Flee from sexual immorality' (1 Corinthians 6:18; cf. 1
Corinthians 10:8; Ephesians 5:3; Colossians 3:5; 1 Thessalonians 4:3). In the light of our Lord's extended application
of the commandment we can take such cult prostitution as
offending against an existing marriage and thus as a form of
adultery.

The messages of the risen Christ to the churches in Pergamum and in Thyatira give us further evidence of these things.
The Pergamum church had within it some who held 'the
teaching of Balaam' which had caused Israel to combine
idolatrous sacrifices with cult prostitution (Revelation 2:14;
cf. Numbers 25:1–5; 31:16). At Thyatira there was a woman
called Jezebel who claimed to be a prophetess and who was
similarly beguiling the Lord's servants to practise immorality
and to eat food sacrificed to idols (Revelation 2:20).

The close association of immorality with idolatry at pagan
temples accounts for the way in which sexual immorality was
included in the list of four forbidden things circulated from
the council of elders and apostles which met Paul and
Barnabas to discuss the position of Gentile believers in
relation to Jewish ceremonial and traditional law. The
council knew only too well that many of the Gentiles had a
background of idolatry and of cult prostitution and they
made absolutely sure that it was conveyed to them that
these things were totally out of keeping with Christian
discipleship. So the message went out clearly: 'Abstain
from food sacrificed to idols, from blood, and from the
meat of strangled animals and from sexual immorality'
(*porneias,* fornications) (Acts 15:29).

The writer to the Hebrews surely gathers up in one short
sentence the opprobrium of the apostolic writers against
these sins when he says, 'God will judge the adulterer and
all the sexually immoral' (the *pornous,* the fornicators)
(Hebrews 13:4b).

The specific exclusion of licentious living
In Paul's first letter to the Corinthian Christians, principles
are laid down which totally exclude sexual licentiousness

from the life-style of the Christian. These are in chapter 6
verses 12–20 and follow almost immediately after the list
of vices which can and do exclude men from God's kingdom — vices from which, indeed, the readers had been
delivered (1 Corinthians 6:11).

It seems likely that some in Corinth were justifying licentious behaviour on the grounds of Christian liberty — 'Everything is permissible for me' was apparently their slogan. Paul
might even have used this slogan to counter the idea that
salvation was a matter of law observance, but here he quali-
fies it in two ways. First he says that while all things are
permissible for him all things are not necessarily helpful.
Indeed some things not forbidden by law and therefore
lawful in themselves are to be avoided because they do not
befit the Christian life. Secondly, he says that while all
things were permissible for him he would not be mastered by
any. He saw a danger that in the exercise of liberty he or any
Christian could come under the authority of some enslaving
habit and so lose the very liberty he claimed to have.

Paul further argues that Christians' bodies (*somā*, probably
meaning 'their whole personalities') are not meant for
immorality but belong to the Lord and are members of
Christ. He asserts that it is absolutely preposterous to take
the members of Christ and to unite them with a prostitute.
Whatever else he had in mind, he was certainly thinking of
the cult prostitution of Corinth which was so closely related
to the worship of idols. For a believer to become involved in
those practices would be not merely a matter of physical
adultery but of spiritual treachery. 'Shall I then take', he
asks, 'the members of Christ and unite them with a prostitute?' 'Never!' (*mē genoito*, 'let it not be so') is his emphatic
reply.

In verses 16–20 he develops his argument in more general
terms and shows all fornication and adultery, all sexual
immorality, to be totally inexpedient for a Christian. First of
all, he asks if his readers are not aware that a man who joins
himself to a prostitute becomes one body with her. Even a
single act of sexual intercourse creates a union, and to back
up this assertion he quotes Genesis 2:24, 'The two will
become one flesh.' Such a union is in stark contrast and
total opposition to the spiritual union between a believer

and his Lord and is to be avoided at all costs. 'Flee from
sexual immorality', says the apostle (v. 18a) or, more literally, 'Flee (and keep on fleeing) from fornication.' A man
must not trifle or temporize with sexual temptation.

The fact that Paul regards a man's association with a
prostitute as effecting a 'oneness of flesh', to which the
words of Genesis 2:24 can be applied, creates a problem. It
seems as if he is saying that every casual sexual relationship
creates a union of the same kind as that which occurs in
marriage. But clearly those who indulge in prostitution do
not become emotionally united. Their passing physical union
involves no oneness of spirit and no acceptance of family
responsibilities. Some have tried to get over the difficulty
by arguing that the unity of man and woman first mentioned
in Genesis 2:24 is to be understood not in terms of a
permanent relationship but simply of the immediate experience enjoyed in sexual embrace. This would undermine, however, the whole biblical view of marriage, making it a matter
merely of mating and not of loving. It seems therefore that
we must regard the relationship between a man and a prostitute as somehow the same type as the union arising in
marriage, but yet as different from full marital union because
it does not have the ingredients of exclusive love and permanent fidelity which are of the very essence of marriage.

Paul has another reason for excluding extra-marital sex
from the Christian life. It is that sexual sin is different from
all other sins. He says, 'All other sins a man commits are
outside his body; but he who sins sexually sins against his
own body' (v. 18b). The meaning seems to be that sexual
sin does damage to the personality (*sōma*, 'body', but again
probably meaning 'personality'). God's purpose is that man
and woman come together in marriage and find personal
completion and fulfilment each in the other. Sexual sin
deviates from that purpose and frustrates its fulfilment
and in so doing damages the personality which can never be
the same again.

Paul reminds his readers that their bodies, their persons,
are the dwelling-place of God's Holy Spirit and belong not to
themselves, but to God. Their prime responsibility then is to
live to God's glory, something with which sexual sins like
fornication and adultery are wholly inconsistent. It is

impossible to break the seventh commandment and at the same time glorify God in one's body.

The Christian options

Chapter 7 of the same Epistle (First Corinthians) sets out to answer questions which Paul had received from his readers. Some of these concerned the advisability or otherwise of marriage in the situation of stress or impending stress then obtaining.

For our present purpose the main point of interest is that the options open to Paul's readers completely exclude fornication and adultery. Those who possess an appropriate gift from God are entitled, if they so wish, to remain unmarried: 'It is good [acceptable] for a man not to marry' (v. 1), 'Are you unmarried? Do not look for a wife' (v. 27b, cf. vv. 7–8, 32–35). Paul would like his unmarried readers to remain single as he is, but while he says this for the benefit of the readers, he does not wish to place any restraint on them that would make those who wish to be married feel guilty about doing so. Quite simply he was saying that the unmarried state for those who have the gift of continence and can live singly without being consumed by burning passions is an acceptable and, in the circumstances of the time, a desirable option.

The second option is marriage and Paul acknowledges that this is the normal thing and that it is indeed necessary as a bulwark against immorality: 'Since there is so much immorality, each man should have his own wife, and each woman her own husband' (v. 2). The married are not permitted to separate or to deprive their partners of conjugal relations except for short mutually agreed periods. The husband has control over his wife and the wife over her husband and there is certainly no room for a third party. When a Christian wife voluntarily separates from her husband she must either remain single or be reconciled to him. A new relationship with a second man, that is, an adulterous liaison, or an adulterous marriage, is an option that is not open to her.

The sanctity of marriage is thus clearly affirmed and any extra-marital sexual relationship is rejected as inappropriate and sinful. The prohibition on the dismissal of an unbelieving partner by a believing husband or wife (vv. 12–16) again stresses the importance of maintaining a stable marriage and, indeed, the danger of causing a wrongfully dismissed partner to contract an adulterous relationship later on.

Clearly the writings of the apostles exclude adultery and all other forms of sexual immorality and leave the Christian with but two possible states in which to live – marriage and celibacy. The seventh commandment and the teachings of our Lord are fully upheld. No sexual union outside marriage is allowed: 'You shall not commit adultery.'

The antidote to adultery

In our consideration of the sixth commandment we saw that the prohibition of murder was a negative formulation of man's most fundamental right, the right to life. Similarly, the commandment, 'You shall not commit adultery,' has a strong affirmative aspect. It, too, confers a right, or rather a group of rights, giving a man the right to the sole possession of his wife and (as extended by our Lord) giving a woman the right to the exclusive possession of her husband. At the same time it safeguards home and family life by giving children a right to the continuing security which is properly provided when father and mother live together in mutual trust and loyalty, and together take full responsibility for their care.

What we are saying is that the seventh commandment safeguards stable marriages and in so doing safeguards family life. It is essential, therefore, that we give some thought to the biblical picture of marriage as that which is the normal antidote to adultery.

A biblical form of marriage
The biblical picture of marriage is, of course, that of an ideal, from which men in Bible times all too often departed, and which men today all too often fail to realize. Since we are fallen creatures our best endeavours are tainted by sin. We transgress God's laws and we fall short of his standard. But the ideal is the standard and we must work, and work hard, to attain it. We owe it to ourselves, to our wives or husbands, to our children, to society and above all to the Lord, to make

our marriages the happy, holy and blessed relationships God intends them to be. Our duty is to see that his purposes for our marriages are fulfilled.

Fulfilling God's purposes
In the creation narratives we learn that man was made male and female, in the image of God and that God's first command was 'Be fruitful and increase in number; fill the earth and subdue it. Rule over . . . every living creature that moves on the ground' (Genesis 1:28). While the main thrust of this relates to man's headship over every other living creature, fulfilment implies the union of men and women in marriage to produce the necessary increase in the human population. We can thus affirm that *procreation* was an essential element in the divine purpose for the human race.

The second chapter of Genesis gives us a more detailed account of man's creation and includes the story of God taking a rib from Adam's body to make Eve (Genesis 2: 18–24). In these verses the emphasis is on *companionship* but the idea of procreation is clearly still present. The record tells us that God saw the man he had made as needing a suitable companion: 'The Lord God said, "It is not good for the man to be alone. I will make a helper suitable for him." ' No other creature was fit and so God took one of the man's ribs and from it made a woman. Adam at once recognized that Eve met his need for companionship, that with her he would no more be alone. 'This,' he said, 'is now bone of my bones and flesh of my flesh; she shall be called "woman", for she was taken out of man' (v. 23).

Marriage rests on the fact that by himself man, the male, was incomplete. He needed, and God gave him, man, the female, or woman as a complement. Eve was created from Adam, bone of his bones, flesh of his flesh, and thus shared with him all the essentials of human nature. She was an integral part of man and in no way inferior to him, as were the animals, none of which was found to be a helper fit for the man. Man is thus to be thought of as a whole, consisting of two parts, one male and one female and each indispensable to the other. In togetherness and companionship husband and wife can be what God intended they should be.

Another element in the creative purpose of God is that

marriage is meant to be a permanent union. A man is required to leave his father and mother, or, to put it another way, to leave the parental home, and to be so joined to a wife that he becomes one with her. The words of Genesis 2:24 suggest a strong and a lasting bond — he is to 'be united' or 'cleave' to his wife. The two are to be inseparable because, in fact, they become and are 'one' in a unity which involves the entire personalities of both.

The union of husband and wife in marriage is more than the physical conjoining of a man and a woman. It involves personal fulfilment with each finding his or her deepest needs met in the other as they together become 'one whole human being'. This personal fulfilment is expressed at every level of life — physical, psychological, spiritual. It is seen in a oneness of purpose and will, in a sharing together in the making of a home and the rearing of a family and in common faith and united worship.

It would seem reasonable to infer that Adam and Eve had such a permanent union and indeed that this was true of many of the great men of Scripture. Clearly, too, the first marriage was to be the pattern for all time and for the whole race. 'For this reason' (that is, because of how God made Eve and brought her to Adam and of Adam's reception of her as his wife — companion), 'a man will leave his father and mother and be united to his wife, and they will become one flesh' (Genesis 2:24).

What a man does, then, in joining himself to a wife and in setting up a home with her as his partner, he does in conformity to a pattern set by God at creation, a pattern which because divinely ordained is in fact binding. A man's duty is to leave father and mother and to cleave to, and be one with his wife. The use made of these words by our Lord and by the apostle Paul (Matthew 19:5; Ephesians 5:31) shows that they remain mandatory for the Christian and, indeed, for all mankind.

Reverenced as God's gift

First-century life was dominated by Greek philosophy which had a strong belief that the body was intrinsically evil. Those, therefore, who wanted the 'higher life' were encouraged to avoid marriage, which inevitably involved a physical relationship. The Greeks thought that giving in to desires for physical union did damage to the life of pure contemplation to which the Sophists and others aspired. It was this kind of influence that led Paul to warn Timothy about liars whose consciences were seared and who, among other things, forbad marriage. His inspired comment shows the place of marriage in the creative providence of God: 'Everything God created is good, and nothing is to be rejected if it is received with thanksgiving, because it is consecrated by the word of God and prayer' (1 Timothy 4: 3–5).

Marriage, like food, is to be received with thanksgiving to God and, in the case of the Christian, sanctified or made explicitly holy and valid through the Word of God and prayer. Here, surely, is biblical warrant for a Christian marriage service at which the Word of God is declared and prayer offered.

The writer to the Hebrews similarly maintains the propriety of marriage for the Christian. 'Marriage should be honoured by all, and the marriage bed be kept pure' (Hebrews 13:4, AV 'Marriage is honourable in all and the bed undefiled'). Whether this is a command or a statement of fact, the supreme worth of marriage as God's gift to mankind is affirmed. It is to be held in reverence and kept free from pollution.

Since marriage was ordained by God its position could not be otherwise. Its intimacies are legitimate and morally pure and its violation by fornication or adultery is sin.

The analogy between God's relationship to his people and marriage occurs frequently in Scripture. In the Old Testament the Lord appears as Israel's husband, Israel being, as we have seen, an unfaithful, a spiritually adulterous wife. In the New Testament Christ is the Bridegroom and the church his bride, and husbands are urged to love their wives as he 'loved the church and gave himself up for her' (Ephesians 5:25). That the human relationships of husband to wife and wife to husband can be a parable of the relation between God and his people surely asserts the total propriety of marriage and gives it added sanctity as that which God has ordained for mankind.

Cemented by love

Marriage involves, and always has involved, a contract which binds the parties to each other. Whatever the procedure that leads up to it (engagement, betrothal, etc.), there comes a point where the families concerned, or the societies to which they belong, recognize this bond and make cohabitation legal. This is important, but of itself cannot make a marriage successful, cannot ensure that the two really become 'one'. Something else is necessary and that something can be summarized in one word, 'love'.

Love is one of the most debased words in the modern world. For some it connotes little more than erotic sensations and sex indulgence. For others it is sheer sentimentality, a soft giving in to the whims, the desires, the aspirations and even the tantrums of individuals or of groups. For the Christian love is something higher and richer than either of these things. It is an expression, however weak, of something that predominates in the character of God. When human beings love in the biblical sense they are reflecting or imitating him who is love. Says John, 'Let us love one another, for love comes from God. Everyone who loves has been born of God and knows God. Whoever does not love does not know God, because God is love' (1 John 4:7–8).

The New Testament has a special word for love, *agapē* (verb *agapaō*). This is rarely found in secular Greek literature and denotes esteem or respect for another person and concern and caring action for his well-being. It is an all-out, all-or-nothing love that respects, honours, esteems the one loved and that holds back nothing in seeking to benefit that one. It is this kind of *love* that is needed in, and that creates a true union in marriage.

The New Testament passages which deal with marriage all emphasize the need for husband and wife to give proper *personal esteem* to each other as persons. Paul urges the Christian wives of Ephesus to submit to their husbands in the same way as the church submits to Christ (Ephesians 5:22–24). There can be no doubt that he is referring to a submission based on respect or esteem for the husband. 'The wife must respect [fear] her husband' (Ephesians 5:33). Peter has a similar message: 'Wives . . . be submissive to your husbands, so that, if any of them do not believe the word, they may be won over without talk by the behaviour of their wives, when they see the purity and reverence of your lives' (1 Peter 3:1—2).

Both apostles show that personal esteem in a marriage is not to be thought of as one-way traffic; husbands are to respect and honour their wives. Says Peter, 'Husbands, in the same way,' (that is, in a way similar to that just demanded of wives) 'be considerate as you live with your wives, and treat them with respect as the weaker partner' (1 Peter 3:7). There is recognition here of the original ordinance that brought man male and man female together in mutual respect to become one flesh, man complete. Paul writing to Corinth instructs that husband and wife each give conjugal rights to the other, yielding control of the body and of its sexual desires to the other. 'The wife's body,' he says, 'does not belong to her alone but also to her husband. In the same way, the husband's body does not belong to him alone but also to his wife' (1 Corinthians 7:4). Each rules the other and neither is to refuse the other; the two are one in a relationship which could only work where there is complete mutual respect and trust.

Love also involves a *concern* for the needs and for the good of another, and proceeds to turn that concern into *caring action*. Love in the New Testament is a volitional thing, something which moves the will and which can, therefore, be commanded and willed. In relation to the marriage bond the clearest statement is in Ephesians 5:25—29 where Paul says, 'Husbands, *love* your wives, just as Christ loved the church and gave himself up for her to make her holy . . . and to present her to himself, as a radiant church, without stain or wrinkle or any other blemish, but holy and blameless. In the same way, husbands ought to *love* their wives as their own bodies. He who *loves* his wife loves himself. After all, no one ever hated his own body, but feeds and cares for it, just as Christ does the church . . .'

This passage has two important analogies. Firstly, a husband is to love his wife as Christ loved the church, that is, to the absolute extremity of being willing, as was Christ, to give up his own life for the sake of his partner. It was by loving that Christ secured the sanctification of the church — its separation for his own exclusive fellowship — and it is by

loving his wife with the totality of his being that a husband
wins her loyalty and secures her for his exclusive fellowship.
Secondly, a husband is to love his wife as he loves and cares
for his own body, a thing which most men do fairly well! He
is to nourish and cherish his wife as himself because in fact
she is himself — the two are one (v. 31).

We do not find wives being instructed to love their husbands in the same direct way, but the obligation clearly
exists. Paul told Titus to instruct older women to train the
younger women 'to *love* their husbands and children, to be
self-controlled and pure, to be busy at home, to be kind, and
to be subject to their husbands' so that the Word of God
should not be discredited (Titus 2:4—5). We can further
regard all the injunctions about wifely submission as implying
loving care for husbands, because respect and caring action
are simply two sides of the one coin, which the New Testament calls 'love'.

Love is thus the vital cement of a marriage, the one thing
which creates a lasting bond between two persons, each
complementary to and completing the other. This kind of
love is the great antidote to adultery. As a general rule a
woman who is loved is content to stay with her husband and
to be his alone, and similarly a man who gets the full
affection of his wife will keep himself for her alone.

Subordinated to Christ

All through the Bible the emphasis is on man's responsibility
to his Maker. His first duty is to love the Lord his God with
all his heart, with all his soul, with all his mind and with all
his strength. This is an absolute priority and must apply to
the realm of marriage and the family as much as to any other.
A marriage which does not give priority to the vertical God-
ward relationship is a marriage lacking in spiritual dimension
and, to the extent that this is so, is falling short of God's
ideal.

In Luke 14:26 we have rather startling words spoken by
our Lord: 'If anyone comes to me and does not hate his
father and mother, his wife and children, his brothers and
sisters — yes, even his own life — he cannot be my disciple.'
At first sight we might think that our Lord was telling every
disciple, actual or   would-be, that family ties must be

repudiated totally, but this is not the case. The Greek verb *'miseō'* can and often does mean 'to hate' in a malicious sense (e.g. Luke 6:22, 27; 19:14; 21:17) but it can also connote mere disregard for something or for someone while something else or someone else is given priority. That this is the force of our Lord's words becomes clear when we examine Matthew's account where our Lord is recorded as saying, 'Anyone who loves his father or mother *more* than me is not worthy of me.' The point is that God must be given priority over the family or, to put it the other way round, the family, important as it is, is not to have first place in our lives.

Paul's suggestion that husband and wife might forego sexual relations for a short period by agreement to devote themselves to prayer (1 Corinthians 7:5) shows how husband and wife are both expected to engage in this exercise. Peter's assertion that they function as joint heirs of the grace of life is followed by a statement of spiritual purpose: 'So that nothing will hinder your prayers' (1 Peter 3:7).

For Christians, then, the relation of both partners, husband and wife, to Christ takes, and must take, precedence over their relationships to each other. When each is rightly related to the Lord, the two together will live for his glory and their marriage will become part of the shining forth of that glory to the world. When the couple put God first they are in a position to call on and to appropriate whatever grace may be needed for happy married life. In the ups and downs, the joys and trials, that are inevitably part of the human condition, they will not be overwhelmed and their marriages will be stable because their ultimate and sufficient resource is not in themselves but in God.

The religious dimension is very important in the choice of a partner for life. It is always difficult for a marriage to grow and mature where complete harmony of outlook on the meaning and on the goals of life is absent. A marriage of a Hindu to a Muslim or a Jew to a Buddhist would inevitably involve far more personal adaptation and adjustment than one between two members of the one religion. For Christians the truth is the same — a mixed marriage will be a much more hazardous adventure than one between two people who share a similar faith in Christ.

In the Old Testament there was provision for incorporation into Israelite life of women from certain tribes who might be taken prisoner and married off to Israel, but these women in effect were to become Israelites. In the case of ordinary marriages a strong line was taken against contaminating 'the holy seed' by marriages with pagans. This practice was always regarded as leading to moral and spiritual degeneration. 'Foreign women', for example, made Solomon commit sin (Nehemiah 13:26).

In the New Testament we have Paul's insistence that believers should not become yoked together with unbelievers: 'Do not be yoked together with unbelievers. For what do righteousness and wickedness have in common? Or what fellowship can light have with darkness? What harmony is there between Christ and Belial? What does a believer have in common with an unbeliever? . . .' (2 Corinthians 6:14ff). No doubt this injunction has wider implications, but its relevance to the contracting of a marriage is unquestionable. A believer who deliberately enters marriage with an unbeliever is in grave danger of compromising his or her relationship to the Lord.

Subordination of one's life to Christ means that if a choice of a partner in life has to be made the one chosen will be a fellow believer, one with a similar philosophy of life and a similar dedication to the cause of Christ. It also means that within marriage the things of God will be given proper priority. Only so will there be true fulfilment and true happiness for a Christian and the stability of the maturing relationship will become a secure bastion against every enticement to immorality.

The biblical pattern for marriage does work and it is a sure antidote to adultery. Says Paul, 'Since there is so much immorality, each man should have his own wife, and each woman her own husband.'

Continence outside marriage
All through the Bible sexual relationships are presented as legitimate only within the context of a recognized marriage. The command, 'You shall not commit adultery,' contributes considerably to the establishment of this position in that it prohibits an extra-marital union between a married person

and anyone else, married or single. Interpreted strictly, it might seem to allow such a union between two uncommitted persons, but in fact such relationships were subject to the overall opprobrium of divine revelation. They were also excluded by ancient social structures in which a female was always under the guardianship of a male relative, father, uncle, brother or husband, and could only legitimately be joined with a man when the guardian sanctioned her marriage. At the same time prostitution was prohibited (Leviticus 19:29; Deuteronomy 22:21, where a girl found on marriage to have had pre-marital sex was to be treated as a prostitute and put to death, cf. 1 Corinthians 6:12—20).

Clearly Scripture saw marriage as the normal estate in which men and women are to live, but at the same time it recognized that there were, and always would be single or unmarried persons. There were the young unmarried men and women, many of whom were, however, betrothed at an early age and therefore set apart, consecrated and absolutely reserved for a fiancé or fiancée. There were widows and widowers, who were free to be remarried, and there were divorced persons who, like the widowed, were free to con- tract another marriage (Deuteronomy 24:1—4). For all such the biblical provision was marriage and the rule was continence (that is, abstension from sexual relations) until marriage became a reality. Pre-marital sex was always an offence.

In Paul's discussion of whether or not single people should marry, the criterion for remaining single is the possession of a gift enabling the person concerned to exercise self-control. Those who cannot exercise such control, who burn with sexual passion, are to gain the right to express and satisfy those passions by contracting a proper marriage: 'If they cannot control themselves, they should marry, for it is better to marry than to burn with passion' (1 Corinthians 7:9). Similarly, a wife who wrongfully separates from her husband has an obligation to remain single (1 Corinthians 7:11). Sexual indulgence in any form is not an option for the unmarried Christian. Sex is for marriage — always.

The celibate life
For some Christians a God-given vocation means acceptance

of an unmarried life. Such a life was frowned on in Jewish circles, in which every man was expected to marry. It did, however, have advocates in some of the monastic Essene communities which existed in the time of our Lord. He himself recognized the possibility when he spoke of those who renounce marriage because of the kingdom of heaven (Matthew 19:12). He was not for one moment, however, suggesting that celibacy was spiritually superior to marriage, but simply noting that there are some for whom marriage is impossible because of a demanding spiritual vocation.

His words have traditionally been taken as referring to lifelong bachelorhood, and with those of Paul in 1 Corinthians 7:32—35 form the biblical basis of Roman Catholic insistence on the celibacy of priests and nuns. In fact, neither our Lord nor Paul insisted on abstinence from marriage for those engaged in the Christian ministry, and Paul actually included those who forbad marriage among those who 'abandon the faith and follow deceiving spirits and things taught by demons', and as 'liars whose consciences have been seared' (1 Timothy 4:1, 2). The renunciation of marriage because of the kingdom spoken of by our Lord was entirely a voluntary matter. Renouncing marriage (Matthew 19:12) is literally 'eunuchizing themselves' and refers not to church legislation, but to deliberate personal choice. Any pressure to be celibate in the ministry of the gospel, whether by way of church laws, or by teaching that it is a spiritually superior way to live, would seem totally out of harmony with the spirit of Christ and of the whole New Testament.

Equally there is nothing in the words of our Lord or in the teaching of Paul to suggest that those whose vocation calls for an unmarried state in order to accomplish God-given tasks should not at a later stage in life become married. The appropriate celibacy could be of shorter or longer duration, temporary, semi-permanent or permanent. The choice is for the individual in the light of his or her 'own gift from God' (1 Corinthians 7:7).

Conclusion

The seventh commandment sets marriage and the family

second in importance to the preservation and integrity of life itself. It invests every human being with the right to a stable family in which to live or in which to be born and brought up. It precludes the intrusion of a second partner into the marriage and sets up the standard of sexual relationships only within marriage. It requires complete fidelity within marriage and implies complete sexual continence outside it.

'You shall not commit adultery.'

[1] *porneia* = fornication, but also any form of illicit sexual intercourse, including the unfaithfulness of a married woman (Arndt-Gingrich, *A Greek-English Lexicon of the New Testament*, pp. 699–700). I accept this as correct but am aware of the alternative interpretations: (i) that pre-marital fornication is in view; (ii) that marriage within the forbidden degrees is in view and that its discovery had rendered the husband and wife guilty of sin which would be put right by divorce.

10. The sanctity of person and possessions
The Eighth Commandment

'You shall not steal.'

Kidnapping or theft — or both?

The second table of the decalogue has five commands, each of which deals with an aspect of personal man-to-man relationships. At the same time each enshrines a basic human right.

The sixth commandment prohibits murder and affirms the right to life. The seventh prohibits adultery and affirms the right to a stable marriage and a stable home life. The eighth appears to prohibit all acts of theft and so to safeguard the right to own property. The ninth forbids false witness and asserts man's right to justice. The tenth appears to prohibit desires which might or might not result in stealing and so seems to affirm the same right as does the eighth, the right to own property.

Traditionally Christians have been happy to accept the interpretation which takes the eighth command as concerned with outward or overt acts and the tenth as focusing on the inward attitudes of covetousness which lie behind such acts. The New Testament seems to have understood the commands in this way, but the Hebrew verbs used in them suggest that the original instruction may not have been quite so clear.

Some scholars think that the eighth commandment was originally concerned with the prevention of one particular form of theft — the kidnapping of a fellow Israelite. They believe that it, therefore, confers on the individual not the right to own property but the right to have personal freedom. The tenth commandment is then seen as relating to every other type of theft, from the stealing of a man's wife to the stealing of his chattels.

On the basis of such an understanding, the second, or man-ward group of commandments, with the rights they confer, can be tabulated neatly as follows:

Commandment	Prohibition	Right
Sixth	Murder	Life
Seventh	Adultery	Marriage
Eighth	Kidnapping	Freedom
Ninth	False witness	Justice
Tenth	Theft	Possessions

This interpretation has obvious attractions. It harmonizes well with the fact that in the laws of Israel kidnapping, like murder or adultery, carried the death penalty (Exodus 21:16; Deuteronomy 24:7). It separates that crime, that very serious crime, from other forms of stealing, which carried lesser penalties and which could be corrected by prescribed or agreed acts of restitution or reparation. At the same time it eliminates the apparent overlap between the eighth and tenth commandments, which seems strange in a table of five key laws given by God to govern man's relationships to his fellows. Had there been fifty, or even twenty laws, we would expect some overlap, but somehow since God chose to give only five it seems natural to think that he wanted each to affirm something different from the others.

In the eighth command the significant idea is enshrined in the Hebrew verb *'ganab'* meaning 'to steal', or 'to steal away'. It had a wide range of meaning which included, but was by no means restricted to kidnapping. It occurs thirty-two times in the Old Testament and was used of stealing animals (Genesis 30:33; Exodus 22:1), of stealing images (Genesis 31:19, 30, 32), of stealing items devoted to God (Joshua 7:11) or of words spoken by him (Jeremiah 23:30). It was also used of stealing men's allegiance — their hearts (2 Samuel 15:6). On two occasions it specifically refers to kidnapping of the kind for which the ancient world was famous and by which a man was deprived of his freedom and sold off into slavery: 'Anyone who kidnaps (*ganab*) another . . . must be put to death' (Exodus 21:16; Deuteronomy 24:7). Clearly, then, this verb was not restricted to kidnapping but was widely used of other kinds of theft.

When the Pentateuch was translated into Greek at Alexandria in the third century before Christ the command was rendered by the verb *kleptō*, meaning 'to steal'. This is a word carrying the same broad spectrum of meaning as *ganab* did in Hebrew. When in the Gospels we read of the Lord and the apostles mentioning this command, the same verb, *kleptō*, is used and, as we will see, the prohibition was understood as relating to all forms of stealing and not just to the theft of persons. Clearly our commandment had come to be regarded as having this wider connotation. This is reflected in a number of Israelite civil laws which forbid the stealing both of persons and of possessions.

Regulations against kidnapping

Kidnapping was a crime against the person. It deprived the one concerned of freedom, much as murder deprived him of life. It also deprived his family of a father or a mother, a brother, a sister, a son or a daughter.

In the ordinances which follow the giving of the decalogue at Sinai the first, and apparently the most important, reference to stealing concerns kidnapping: 'Anyone who kidnaps another and either sells him or still has him when he is caught must be put to death' (Exodus 21:16). This, as we have seen already, puts kidnapping on a par with murder and adultery as a crime worthy of the death penalty. This provision was expanded somewhat in the Deuteronomic legislation where we read, 'If a man is caught kidnapping one of his brother Israelites and treats him as a slave or sells him, the kidnapper must die. You must purge the evil from among you' (Deuteronomy 24:7).

In both passages the focus is on the stealing by an Israelite of another member of the covenant people. The abduction and sale of foreigners was not proscribed, nor was the sale as slaves of prisoners taken in war. The one exception relating to the latter practice was in the case of female captives who became married to Israelites and who by that fact had become actual, or virtual Israelites. Because of the new status conferred on such a woman by her marriage to an Israelite man, she had to be given freedom in the same way as was the case with a naturally born Israelite wife if, or when, she became the victim of a husband's dislike. The protection given to captive wives clearly suggests that freeborn Israelite women, as members of the covenant community, were similarly protected. They could not be sold off into slavery even by their husbands. Much less could they be illegally kidnapped with a view to such sale. Clearly the commandment applied to women as well as to men.

Regulations against theft

In Israel stealing property was a different kind of offence from kidnapping. It was a civil wrong, a tort, actionable by the victim, whereas kidnapping was a crime against the person, for which the community was required to impose the death penalty. The stealing of property was put right by the offender restoring to the victim what he had stolen or making an equivalent restitution, and also by compensating him for the inconvenience and distress he had suffered by some additional payment. Kidnapping, on the other hand, was like murder, an ultimate crime for which the offender could make no restitution; he must pay the penalty of forfeiting his own life.

(i) *The book of the covenant*

A group of regulations relating to stealing is found in Exodus 22:1–15. The main emphasis is on the restitution to be made by the thief to his victim. In the first instance a man who had stolen and then either eaten or sold someone else's ox was to pay five oxen. A man stealing and then killing or selling a sheep was to pay four sheep. These penalties are heavier than the more usual 'double' restitution and would seem to recognize that by killing or selling an animal belonging to someone else a man made his theft absolute and irrevocable. He had deliberately taken the animal as his own and was not merely harbouring a stray. In either case, if such a thief did not have the necessary resources to make restitution, he was himself to be sold into slavery so that the money, cattle or sheep needed to pay the prescribed compensation would become available. This shows that a very serious view was taken of stealing and of the need to compensate its victims. Indeed, the making of restitution was

so important that in certain cases a thief would have to forfeit his freedom in order to make it.

If, however, a stolen animal was found alive in the
possession of the thief the compensation required was less:
'He must pay back double' (Exodus 22:4). In this event the
actual animal could be restored and presumably with it
another of more or less equal value. Restitution by paying
'double' seems in fact to have been the usual requirement —
a thief found guilty of stealing goods in the care of an
owner's neighbour was required to pay 'double'. Similarly
in a case of dispute (v. 9), where someone by saying, 'This
is mine' claimed as his own any animal or object and thereby
accused the man holding it of theft, the offender, if condemned by God, had to 'pay back double to his neighbour'.

In the same passage (Exodus 22:11—15) there are references to a number of other possible offences. One is the case
of animals grazing in a neighbour's field or vineyard, and
thus doing damage to the crops of the proprietor. The owner
of the animals then had to make restitution;he could not get
away with the theft of another man's crops. Similarly, if
someone lit a fire which caused the destruction of another
person's crops he was to make full restitution. The same rule
applied to borrowed animals which were hurt, killed or stolen
when their owner was not present. The borrower then had to
make full restitution. These regulations emphasized the
responsibility of the individual Israelite to respect the
property of others and where he became the cause of someone else being deprived of his property to make proper
restitution. The record does not, however, specify anything
more than exact or full restoration of what was lost.

(ii) *The Levitical code*
In the Levitical laws the question of restitution is still very
prominent but the requirement is full restoration plus one-
fifth and is coupled with an appropriate guilt or trespass
offering to be made in the sanctuary. 'If anyone sins and is
unfaithful to the Lord by deceiving his neighbour about
something entrusted to him or left in his care or stolen, or if
he cheats him, or if he finds lost property and lies about it,
or if he swears falsely . . . he must return what he has stolen
or taken by extortion, or what was entrusted to him, or the

lost property he found, or whatever it was he swore falsely about. He must make restitution in full, add a fifth of the value to it and give it all to the owner on the day he presents his guilt offering. And as a penalty he must bring to the priest, that is, to the Lord, his guilt offering, a ram from the flock . . . In this way the priest will make atonement for him before the Lord . . .' (Leviticus 6:1–7; cf. Numbers 5:5–8).

The offences listed here all relate to the deprivation of a neighbour by direct or indirect theft, but the emphasis is on the fact that they involve unfaithfulness to the Lord (v. 2). Israel was in a unique covenant relationship with God and had to live under the terms of that covenant, that is, in accordance with the law given by God as a code of conduct appropriate to his redeemed covenant people. To break the law by stealing was then a breach of faith against God as well as an offence against a fellow human being. It would interrupt an Israelite's right to have fellowship with God at tabernacle or temple and so, in addition to the making of restitution, required the presentation of a guilt offering. Again the seriousness of theft is clearly apparent.

The difference in the amount of restitution required in the Exodus and Leviticus passages is not precisely explained. The latter is in a context dealing with the guilt or trespass offering, discussion of which begins at Leviticus 5:14. This particular offering applied 'when a person . . . sins unintentionally in regard to any of the Lord's holy things' (5:15). Indeed the passage goes on to assert the principle that anyone who violated one of God's commandments was regarded as 'guilty', even if he did not know about the offence. It was precisely as an expression of mercy for such that God provided this offering. It is almost certain then that the stealing and the related offences mentioned in the subsequent paragraph (6:1–7) are also to be understood as sins committed unwittingly. The mention of false swearing and of lying (v. 3) would normally suggest deliberate deceit, but in this context while words that deceived are in view, they were apparently spoken without the intention to deceive. In that event this passage is speaking about offences in which there was the mitigating circumstance of ignorance, or of some measure of ignorance, and in the case of the thefts a less severe penalty was imposed than where full knowledgeability obtained. The payment of full restitution plus one fifth would ensure that the property owner suffered no permanent loss and that there was an element of deterrence to any who might be disposed to take chances based on ignorance.

The Old Testament regulations about theft consistently display a strong sense of fair play. The thief had to pay dearly for his offence and the victim had to be compensated for his loss. There was in fact a careful balance between the punishment of the criminal and the compensation by him of the victim — a principle of justice which modern states would do well to emulate. So often today the criminal gets off with a spell in prison at state expense, and the victim's compensation, if he receives any at all, is either from state funds or from an insurance company on the basis of premiums which he himself has paid. Either way the thief makes no personal restitution to his victim and in the long run stealing is probably encouraged rather than discouraged.

In the history of Israel's occupation of the land of Canaan there are not many recorded instances of theft, but there are plenty of references repudiating the actions and the attitudes of those who indulged in stealing. These passages would imply that theft was quite common and also that there was always an affirmation or reaffirmation by the prophets and by other faithful men of the commandment, 'You shall not steal.'

Repudiations of kidnapping

No specific case of an Israelite kidnapping an Israelite is recorded. Two passages may, however, suggest that it did occur in the eighth and seventh centuries before Christ. In the first, Hosea 4:2, written around 750 B.C., that is mid-eighth century, sins are listed which had brought Israel into a situation of controversy with God. 'Stealing' is mentioned between murder and adultery, implying that all three sins were crimes against the person and thus that kidnapping, or the stealing of persons, is in view. In the second, Jeremiah 7:9, written some 130 to 150 years later, a similar juxtaposition occurs in the question addressed to Judah: 'Will you steal and murder, commit adultery . . .?' Again a crime against the person — that is, kidnapping, seems to be in view.

The paucity of references to kidnapping might suggest that the crime was not very significant in Israel and might argue against the idea that it is the primary reference of the eighth commandment. On the other hand it could suggest the reverse, that the commandment was so clear and so effective that the crime was not committed except, perhaps, in the troubled days of degeneracy preceding the demise of Israel, 722 B.C., and the captivity of Judah which followed it some 120–140 years later.

Repudiations of theft

By seizure
About the end of the eighth century B.C., the prophet Micah delivered a devastating oracle against those in Israel who, from positions of privilege or of power, were able to rob other members of society:

> 'Woe to those who plan iniquity,
>   to those who plot evil on their beds!
> At morning's light they carry it out
>   because it is in their power to do it.
> They covet fields and *seize* them,
>   and houses, and *take them*.
> They defraud a man of his home,
>   a fellow man of his inheritance.
> Therefore, the Lord says:
>   "I am planning disaster against this people,
>   from which you cannot save yourselves.
> You will no longer walk proudly,
>   for it will be a time of calamity . . ."'

(Micah 2:1–3).

Micah was singling out those who held in their hands power over other people and was pronouncing 'woe' on the way in which such power was being abused to rob the poor of their farms and of their homes. This was a social injustice abhorrent to the Lord and evoking his anger. Indeed things were so bad that Judah was threatened with a deportation like that inflicted on the Northern Kingdom by the Assyrians in 721 B.C. It was only the reformation of Hezekiah, shallow and short-lived as it may have been, which deferred this fate for a time.

A century and a half later, when many of the Jews were captive in Babylon, Ezekiel gave them God's reasons for their plight: 'The people of the land practise extortion and commit *robbery*; they oppress the poor and needy and ill-treat the alien, denying them justice' (Ezekiel 22:29). Clearly, stealing of one kind or another was one of the major sins of the ordinary people.

Against this stands the divine law: 'You shall not steal,' and the constant affirmation of it by God's true servants. Isaiah, declaring the word of God, says 'I, the Lord, love justice; I hate robbery and iniquity' (Isaiah 61:8a). One of the psalmists says, 'Do not trust in extortion or take pride in stolen goods' (Psalm 62:10). The same kind of emphasis appears in the book of Proverbs: 'Do not', says the sage, 'exploit the poor because they are poor' (22:22). With specific reference to one's parents we find this statement: 'He who robs his father or his mother and says, "It's not wrong" — he is partner to him who destroys' (28:24). Clearly, God was against robbery and anyone who tried to make himself rich by stealing had no hope of divine favour.

By fraud

The great prophets unite to condemn theft by fraudulent retention or deprivation. Amos, who was perhaps the earliest of the prophets to write, delivered a threatening oracle against those who *oppressed* the poor and *crushed* the needy (Amos 4:1ff). Hosea about the same time likened Ephraim to a merchant who used dishonest scales and who loved to *defraud* (Hosea 12:7). Later on Jeremiah, addressing Judah, the then surviving Israelite kingdom, asserted that God would allow the people to remain in their land if, and only if, they changed their ways: 'If you do not *oppress* the alien, the fatherless or the widow . . .' (Jeremiah 7:6). Indeed, Jeremiah went further and called on the king to defend and deliver the victims of injustice: 'O house of David, this is what the Lord says: "Administer justice every morning; rescue from the hand of his *oppressor* the one who has been *robbed*" ' (Jeremiah 21:12). In the very last book of the Old Testament God promised to judge among others 'those who *defraud* labourers of their wages, who oppress the widows and the fatherless' (Malachi 3:5).

In each of the passages which have just been cited, the oppressor (Hebrew *'osheq*) is a fraudulent person and oppression is an act of fraudulently pressing down on another. The prophets unite to condemn such behaviour and seem to present it as a violation of our commandment. Wherever the poor or the underprivileged were exploited by those in positions of economic or political power, there was an offence not just against the victims but against God. Deceitful overcharging, the retention of wages due for work done, or any act of exploitation against an Israelite or a stranger was an oppression unacceptable to God.

Similar opposition to the fraudulent acquisition of what was rightfully the property of others emerges in the psalms. We have a prayer for the deliverance of the afflicted and the needy by the crushing of the *oppressor* in Psalm 72:4, and the prayer of a godly man that he be not left to the devices of his *oppressors* in Psalm 119:121. The sages also saw that fraudulent oppression was sheer folly, that the *oppressor* insulted God and would be the ultimate loser: 'He who *oppresses* the poor to increase his wealth . . . [will] come to poverty' (Proverbs 22:16).

One apparently common form of fraudulent deprivation resulted from the giving and the accepting of bribes. The giver of a bribe acquired for himself something which by the laws of strict justice should not be his. It might be freedom from the penalty of a law he had broken; it might be a position, a privilege or a property. Whatever it was, it was fraudulently obtained; the briber was a thief who violated the eighth commandment. Those who received bribes and who were influenced by them were also guilty of injustice. Such were the sons of Samuel who 'accepted bribes and perverted justice' (1 Samuel 8:3).

By inter-racial plunderings

There was an abundance of intertribal and international brigandage in Old Testament times. The Israelites were often on the receiving end — sometimes, indeed, as divine punishment for their own sin. Thus, when in the period of the judges they adopted some of the paganism of their

Canaanite neighbours, they were given into the hand of a
series of enemies — the Moabites, the Midianites and the
Philistines. These tribes plundered the land and stole Israel's
livelihood by force. In the same period a dispute arose
between the men of Shechem and Abimelech, the usurper
son of Gideon. The Shechemites set ambushes against Abimelech and robbed all who passed by (Judges 9:25).

In the heyday of Assyria's power the prophet Isaiah
pronounced the impending doom of that nation. He quoted
an Assyrian boast: 'I removed the boundaries of nations,
I plundered their treasures; . . . As one reaches into a nest,
so my hand reached for the wealth of the nations; as men
gather abandoned eggs, so I gathered all the countries'
(Isaiah 10:13—14). This had been no empty boast, for the
Assyrians had indeed plundered the earth and had incurred
in the process a reputation for terrible cruelty. The main
burden of the prophecy of Nahum is directed against their
ruthless militarism and their unmitigated greed. Like the
European nations in the eighteenth, nineteenth and twentieth
centuries A.D., they followed their military victories with
intrepid trading — trading that exploited the riches of the
conquered nations and that became in effect a means of
exploitation and *oppression.* It was theft by fraud! Thus
Nahum could charge, 'You have increased the number of
your merchants until they are more than the stars of the
sky' (Nahum 3:16). Little wonder he could say of Nineveh,
the Assyrian capital, 'The supply is endless, the wealth from
all its treasures' (Nahum 2:9). Perhaps the same charges
could be laid against Britain, France, Germany and the other
nineteenth-century colonial powers. Perhaps, indeed, the
Western world with its present economic difficulties is reaping the due reward of its exploitation of the countries it
once controlled!

By depriving God of his due

The story of Israel's defeat at Ai (Joshua 7) focuses our
attention on a very special kind of theft. Achan, we read,
took some of 'the devoted things' (v. 1). Jericho with its
people and their possessions had been put under a sacred
ban: 'The city and all that is in it are to be devoted to the
Lord' (Joshua 6:17). This meant that everything belonged

to God and was to become his through destruction and that
anyone who took or harboured what was so devoted to God
would himself come under the provisions of the ban. This is
precisely what Achan did. He coveted, he took and he hid in
his tent valuables that belonged to God. He stole what was
the Lord's and the ban of devotion to God became operative.
He and his family were destroyed. We read, 'All Israel stoned
him, and after they had stoned the rest, they burned them'
(Joshua 7:25).

Similar principles were involved when King Saul did not
completely destroy the Amalekites. 'Saul and the army
spared Agag [the Amalekite king], and the best of the sheep
and cattle, the fat calves and lambs — everything that was
good. They were unwilling to destroy them completely'
(1 Samuel 15:9). The result was a confrontation with Samuel
and the rejection of Saul as king of Israel: 'Because you have
rejected the word of the Lord, he has rejected you as king'
(1 Samuel 15:23b). For some reason Saul did not die on the
spot, but his rejection by God certainly led to the disintegra-
tion of his personality and ultimately to his destruction.

Another way in which an Israelite could steal what
belonged to God was by withholding tithes and offerings.
This, no doubt, was a common offence! It comes into sharp
focus in the post-exilic prophet Malachi who answered the
rhetorical question: 'Will man rob God?' by the firm pronouncement that the Jews of the day were doing just that!
When they asked how they were doing so the answer came
loud and clear: 'In tithes and offerings. You are under a
curse — the whole nation of you — because you are robbing
me' (Malachi 3:8—9). Clearly those concerned were negligent
in the duty of rendering of their substance to God and did
not realize that in so doing, that by using for themselves
what properly belonged to God, they were in fact robbing
him.

New Testament endorsement

When the eighth commandment was quoted or alluded to by
our Lord or by the apostles the authority of Sinai was in the
background. God had said, 'You shall not steal,' and there
was, or could be no room for argument. Stealing was sin.

Repudiation of theft

Our Lord is only recorded as quoting the eighth commandment on one occasion, his conversation with the rich young
ruler (Matthew 19:16—22; Mark 10:17—22; Luke 18:
18—25). The fact that he presented it as an essential of the
perfection sought by the young man shows that he fully
endorsed its absolute and abiding validity. In line with this,
however, is his condemnation of the Pharisees for the empty
outwardness of their morality: 'Woe to you, teachers of the
law and Pharisees, you hypocrites! You clean the outside of
the cup and dish, but inside they are full of *greed* and self-
indulgence' (Matthew 23:25). The Greek word translated
'greed' is *harpage* and means 'violent robbery', 'plunder' or
'pillage'. The tragedy was that, with all their outward
religious ceremony, the Pharisees were perverted and corrupt
in heart. They were self-seeking and self-gratifying sinners
who were prepared to get what they wanted, whether food or
other things, by less than worthy means, by extortion, by
plunder, by breaking the eighth commandment. Our Lord
would have none of it. For him the command was irrevocable:
'You shall not steal.'

In more general terms, our Lord frequently referred in
disparaging tones to those who steal, endorsing again the
'no-stealing' ethic of our commandment. In doing so he
used two common Greek words, *kleptēs,* a thief, and *lestēs,*
a robber. The first, *kleptēs,* normally refers to one who
steals by cunning deceit, by fraud or embezzlement or by
any secret underhand method. The second, *lestēs,* points to
the brigand who plunders openly and who unashamedly
resorts to violence in order to secure his loot. Both words
occur in John 10:8: 'All who ever came before me were
thieves and *robbers.*' In addition, we are told by the Gospel
writers that Judas was a thief (*kleptēs* John 12:6) and that
the criminals crucified with our Lord were robbers (Matthew
27:38, 44).

In the writings of the apostles, stealing continues to be
presented as sinful. The commandment is quoted along with
the sixth, seventh and tenth in Romans 13:9, where Paul
sums up those commands that deal with man-to-man relationships in the one sentence: 'Love your neighbour as yourself.'
He is backing up the injunction of verse 8: 'Let no debt

remain outstanding, except the continuing debt to love one another,' and clearly seems to imply that those who accumulate debts are, in fact, guilty of theft. Stealing is a way of being unloving to a neighbour and thus of running counter to the fundamental pattern of behaviour required of a Christian.

There is an important injunction in the Ephesian Epistle: 'He who has been stealing must steal no longer, but must work, doing something useful with his own hands, that he may have something to share with those in need' (4:28). In the context Paul is arguing that the new life in Christ is to be marked by a complete conversion. Thus the thief, who acquired his wealth, or some of it, by dishonest means, is to stop stealing and is to give himself to honest productive effort so as to earn not just enough to meet his own needs, but sufficient to enable him to help others. Dishonest acquisition of goods and of property is to be replaced by honest work and generous beneficence.

A similar emphasis appears in Titus 2:10 where Paul instructs his younger colleague, Titus, to teach Christian slaves, or indeed any Christians who owed service to a master, that they should not pilfer. The Greek word is *nosphizō* and implies setting something apart, or secreting it for oneself. It is the word used in the Septuagint for Achan's act of *taking* devoted things for himself (Joshua 7:1), and clearly implies a form of theft. Christian servants are to be different from those who purloin or pilfer the property of their masters. They are rather to adorn the doctrine of God by whole-hearted fidelity.

The apostle Peter was also forthright in his endorsement of the commandment and thus in ruling theft out of the Christian life. 'If any of you suffer,' he wrote, 'it should not be as a murderer or thief [*kleptēs*] or any other kind of criminal . . .' (1 Peter 4:15). So, too, was James in his condemnation of rich men who fraudulently held back wages from those who had worked for them: 'Look! The wages you failed to pay the workmen who mowed your fields are crying out against you. The cries of the harvesters have reached the ears of the Lord Almighty' (James 5:4). Whether the fraud involved inadequate payment or delayed payment, it was an offence, a sin, which God could not ignore.

On several occasions Paul declared himself and his colleagues innocent of stealing in relation to the Corinthian church in which, presumably, an accusation of some kind had been made against him. 'Make room for us in your hearts,' he wrote, '. . . we have exploited (literally, *defrauded*) no one' (2 Corinthians 7:2). Later he asked, 'Did I exploit [*defraud*] you through any of the men I sent you? . . . Titus did not exploit [*defraud*] you, did he?' These are rhetorical questions to which Paul knew his readers must give a negative answer. He was affirming his innocence and in the process endorsing the eighth commandment.

By contrast, in the first letter to the Corinthians Paul had found it necessary to rebuke his readers, or some of them, for practising fraud on each other! The details are not very clear but the result had been the unseemly spectacle of Christians washing their dirty linen in a heathen court. Paul was appalled and urged restraint and a readiness to suffer wrong and even to be cheated rather than bring disrepute to the name of Christ. The real tragedy was that his readers were guilty of breaking the eighth commandment, 'You yourselves *cheat* and do wrong, and you do this to your brothers' (1 Corinthians 6:8). It was in this context that the apostle solemnly listed *'swindlers'* among those who have no inheritance in the kingdom of heaven (1 Corinthians 6:9–10).

Repudiation of kidnapping
It will be remembered that in our discussion of the original theme of this commandment we saw that it seems to have been greatly, if not primarily, concerned with the stealing of human beings. While there is no discussion of kidnapping in the New Testament, there is one direct reference to those who practise it. This is in 1 Timothy 1:10 where Paul is explaining that the purpose of the law is the restraint of the lawless and the disobedient. He then goes through a list of such persons, covering effectively the whole gamut of the decalogue: 'the ungodly and sinful, the unholy and irreligious' (first four commandments relating to God and to religious piety), 'for those who kill' (or perhaps 'smite') 'their fathers and mothers' and 'murderers' (fifth and sixth commandments), 'adulterers and perverts' (seventh

commandment), 'slave traders' ('kidnappers', RSV — eighth commandment), 'liars' and 'perjurers' (ninth commandment) 'and whatever else is contrary to the sound doctrine'. The mention of 'slave traders', or 'kidnappers', apart from the stealing of goods and chattels in a list based on the decalogue would suggest that the early Old Testament emphasis on man-stealing had not been forgotten and that for Paul it was the most serious theft of all, the one ultimately in view in the eighth commandment.

The word used by Paul here (*andrapodistai*) points to those who made slaves by kidnapping and to those who subsequently trafficked in human lives either as slave-dealers or slave-stealers. They were those who deprived men of their basic right of liberty and would not, of course, include those who received into their service people who willingly and deliberately wished to be their slave servants, a position clearly recognized in the Old Testament.

In the ancient world and, in particular, within the Roman Empire of Paul's day, a slave was a valuable asset whose economic worth depended on his skills and on his health. A slave could be kidnapped not just initially to the loss of his freedom, but subsequently to the deprivation of his master. Paul is clearly proscribing all such kidnapping and again endorsing the prohibition of the commandment: 'You shall not steal.'

Repudiation of tax-evasion

In affirming the duty of Christians to submit to, rather than resist rulers, Paul asserts that the latter are God's servants enforcing law and order for the good of the citizen. The Christian as a citizen is to do what is good so as to have the approval rather than the wrath of his ruler. But he is also to be subject 'because of conscience', that is to say, as a matter of inward moral, rather than of merely external legal constraint. The Christian who resists would, in Paul's thinking, be violating the dictates of a biblically enlightened conscience.

Paul goes on, however, to make a special case of the Christian's responsibility to pay taxes. Because the authorities act as God's ministers and because the conscience instructed in the law of God endorses the meeting of one's obligations to the state, Christians do, and must, pay their taxes. 'Give everyone what you owe him: If you owe taxes, pay taxes, if revenue, then revenue . . .' (Romans 13:7) is the apostle's clear instruction. The words which follow, 'Let no debt remain outstanding', may be of more general application but in the context must include the owing of tax to the various authorities of central or local government to which it was due.

One incident in the ministry of our Lord clearly confirms this teaching. Peter was asked by the tax-collectors of Capernaum if his master paid tax. Peter responded positively: 'Yes', indicating an awareness of the fact that our Lord was accustomed to making the appropriate payment. Later he asked Jesus about the matter and was sent to the sea-shore to cast a hook and catch a fish, in the mouth of which he would find a shekel which would be sufficient to pay the tax due by Peter and himself. Jesus said to Peter, 'So that we may not offend them, go . . .' (Matthew 17:27). He had a conscience on the matter. He would not dodge or evade his responsibility nor allow Peter to do so. The tax would have to be paid. There would be no offence, no stealing of state tax.

The right to freedom and the problem of slavery

When we began an examination of this commandment we discovered that its primary thrust was probably in terms of prohibiting kidnapping. Even if it had, or soon acquired, a wider application to possessions, the prohibition on kidnapping is clear, and with it the affirmation that the individual had the right to be free. No Israelite was entitled to abduct another Israelite and to use him or sell him against his will. Each had an inalienable right to freedom.

This right to personal freedom raises the important issue of slavery, its incidence in Old Testament times and its treatment in the New Testament and by Christian thinkers.

Slavery in Old Testament Israel
The prohibition of kidnapping did not prevent Israelite society from having two forms of slavery — one involuntary

and involving foreigners, the other voluntary and for Israelites in special circumstances.

The involuntary enslavement of foreigners

An Israelite was permitted to acquire foreigners as slaves, either as a result of their capture in battle, or by purchase from other slave-owners or from slave-traders (Leviticus 25: 44—46; Deuteronomy 20:14; 21:10—14).

Such slaves tended to become part of the Israelite family and often had considerable intimacy with their masters. They could have privileges which were withheld from wage-earning staff or visitors. They could become circumcised and thereafter share in worship with the family (Exodus 12:44; Deuteronomy 12:12; 16:11). The possibility of a wise slave sharing in his master's inheritance is even envisaged (Proverbs 17:2; cf. Genesis 15:3). At least one slave, an Egyptian named Jarha, was given the privilege of marrying the daughter of a master who had no sons (1 Chronicles 2: 34—35).

In the case of females, a master would normally arrange marriage, either to himself, to one of his sons or to a servant or slave attached to his household. It would appear that by marriage or concubinage to an Israelite man such a woman was given a status above that of a slave. She became a virtual Israelite and so, if at a later stage her master decided to divorce her, he had to give her the same freedom as would have been the right of a free-born Israelite woman. He could not sell her as a slave (Deuteronomy 21:10—14).

In Israel, as elsewhere in the ancient world, a slave was his master's property. But this did not mean that he could be abused or treated as a mere chattel. If the master should so abuse as to kill instantly his slave the master was to be punished (Exodus 21:20). If the slave survived for several days and then died there was to be no punishment, it apparently being considered that the death was not directly due to the master's abuse and that, even if indirectly attributable to that abuse, the loss of the slave was in itself adequate punishment. If a slave were struck and lost an eye or even a tooth, he had the right to immediate freedom (Exodus 21:26—27), in which case the master suffered punishment by losing the services of the slave and the capital invested in his purchase.

An interesting provision prohibited the handing over of a runaway slave to his master: 'Let him live among you wherever he likes . . .' (Deuteronomy 23:15—16). This put a duty on an Israelite to provide asylum for slaves who had escaped from oppressive masters. It is possible, perhaps probable, that, since freedom to settle where he pleased was to be given, runaway slaves belonging to foreign masters rather than to Israelite masters were in view. At any event, the humanitarian, the unique humanitarian emphasis, of Israelite law is in focus.

We have no way of knowing how many foreigners were enslaved in Israel at any point in the Old Testament era. Indeed, much of the evidence points not to the personal possession of slaves but to something more like a corps of slaves serving the nation in matters civil, religious or military. Thus Joshua made the Gibeonites 'woodcutters and water carriers for the community and for the altar of the Lord' (Joshua 9:27) and Solomon used forced labour for his great building projects (1 Kings 9:15—21). We also read of David conquering Rabbah and consigning its people and other Amalekites 'to labour with saws and with iron picks and axes' and 'to work at brickmaking' (2 Samuel 12:31; cf. the AV rendering 'put them under saws', which suggests torture or massacre and is a less likely, though possible rendering).

The lists of those who returned from the Babylonian exile include 7,337 slaves who accompanied 42,360 free-born persons (Ezra 2:64—65; Nehemiah 7:66—67). This is about one in seven but we have no way of knowing how many of those concerned were owned by individuals or by the community as a whole.

The voluntary indenture of labour
While an Israelite was absolutely prohibited from forcibly depriving another Israelite of personal freedom, he could accept such a person into his household in a special relationship that was sometimes regarded as that of *a slave*. It was, however, distinguished from slavery of the type discussed above and was, in fact, little more than a contract of service. The master bought, and thereafter owned not the person, but the labour of the servant. He was, as we would say 'bonded' to his master, but he was not totally a bondman. He was

committed to some years of service but he had personal free-doms. He could bring his wife with him or be given a wife by his master and he had the prospect of release in the seventh year and of then taking with him not only his wife and family, but a golden handshake from his master (Exodus 21: 1–6; Leviticus 25:39–43; Deuteronomy 15:12–18). There was, however, provision for such an arrangement to become permanent, in which event the initiative had to come volun-tarily from the servant: 'But if the servant declares, "I love my master . . . and do not want to go free . . ." ' The master could then have the arrangement ratified by a ceremony involving the piercing of an ear (Exodus 21:6; Deuteronomy 15:16–17).

Those who indentured their labour in this way became long-term hired servants and it seems probable that the master undertook to pay or underwrite debts which they had incurred. In any event, wages seem to have been paid at half the normal rate (Deuteronomy 15:18), a fact which was to be taken into account when a servant was released from his bond, at which point the golden handshake was to be commensurate with services rendered and, presumably, adequate to enable the servant to resume independent living as a viable economic unit.

In these provisions there is a consistent protection of the integrity of the servant's person. He could not be bludgeoned or treated harshly (Leviticus 25:43). He could not be forced into a permanent bondage but must himself make and com-municate the decision to remain in his master's service. Up to the very last minute the master was warned to put no pressure on a servant entitled to release: 'Do not consider it a hardship to set your servant free' (Deuteronomy 15:18).

It is probably safe to conclude that such a provision was essential in Israelite life as a way of helping those who found the going hard, who could not survive in an economically competitive world and who needed the security provided by an established and ongoing family business, much as a build-ing under construction needs scaffolding. God was seeing to it that such were given a viable means of survival without being exploited.

In the records relating to the involuntary enslavement of foreigners and to the voluntary indenturing of Israelites, the

Old Testament is remarkable for humanitarian safeguards which far outshone those of contemporary society — and, indeed, those of later Greek and Roman times, when slaves were often treated with great harshness. Among the covenant people the healthier, the more humane attitude derived from a recognition that master and slave or servant were alike God's creatures. Hence the words of Job:

> 'If I have denied justice to my menservants and maid-
>   servants
>   when they had a grievance against me,
> what will I do when God confronts me?
>   What will I answer when called to account?
> Did not he who made me in the womb make them?
>   Did not the same One form us both within our
>   mothers?'
>   (Job 31:13—15.)

Slavery in New Testament thought

The New Testament word for slave, *doulos,* carries the idea of subjection to a lord or master. It is used of anyone in a serving role with responsibility to a master and can only be interpreted as definitely referring to a slave when the context sets it in opposition to a free person.

The main references to slaves occur in Paul's Epistles. They seem to accept the fact that slavery existed and to encourage those believers who were slaves to be content with their situation. 'Were you a slave when you were called?' asks Paul. Then 'Don't let it trouble you' is his inspired comment (1 Corinthians 7:21). Naturally, however, if an opportunity to become free presented itself a slave was advised to avail himself of it, but this can in no way be construed as an encouragement to feelings of discontent or of an attempt to break free from the control of a master.

The ground of Paul's plea for contentment is the fact that in Christ a man had acceptance with God, whether he was a free man or a slave. 'Don't let it trouble you . . . For he who was a slave when he was called is the Lord's freed man; similarly, he who was a free man when he was called is Christ's slave' (1 Corinthians 7:22). Difference of social status was now of no significance in the calling of God to

salvation and to Christian fellowship: 'For we were all baptized by one Spirit into one body – whether Jews or Greeks,
slave or free – and we were all given the one Spirit to drink'
(1 Corinthians 12:13; cf. Galatians 3:28; Colossians 3:11). In
Paul's mind God makes no difference between the slave and
the free man: 'The Lord will reward everyone for whatever
good he does, whether he is slave or free' (Ephesians 6:8).

The Epistle to Philemon gives a concrete illustration of the
outworking of Paul's principles. In it the apostle asks his
friend Philemon to receive back one, Onesimus, who had
evidently become a Christian through Paul's ministry. This
Onesimus had belonged to Philemon and had through deser-
tion, and possibly other misdemeanours, turned out quite
useless to his master. Now, however, he had become useful
and Paul sent him back to his master with this letter of
commendation, in which he asked Philemon to welcome him
back not as a mere slave but as 'better than a slave, as a dear
brother' (v. 16).

There is no specific instruction that Onesimus be declared
a free man and no record of how Philemon reacted to Paul's
request. Certainly if he heeded what Paul wrote he would
have exercised a very benign control over Onesimus and
might indeed have given him freedom or virtual freedom. At
any event, Paul's request was that Philemon receive Onesimus
as he would receive Paul himself, that is, as a friend and
brother in the Lord. Such a request demanded a new understanding of the master/slave relationship and was in the long
run an important factor in the emergence of a Christian
conscience against slavery. How, after all, could a human
being be treated as a brother 'in Christ' and be deprived of
personal freedom?

At the same time, on a number of occasions Paul strongly
exhorted servants to be submissive and obedient to their
masters: 'Slaves [servants] obey your earthly masters in
everything . . . Whatever you do, work at it with all your
heart, as working for the Lord, not for men' (Colossians
3:22–23; cf. Ephesians 6:5–6; 1 Timothy 6:1; Titus 2:
9–10). Such statements put an obligation on Christian
slaves to live out the Christian ethic in their servitude,
honouring their masters and fostering the good of those
masters rather than cheating them.

The New Testament seems, then, to accept the fact of slavery but, while not condemning it as such, introduces into it qualities of Christian charity and integrity which would transform the attitudes both of masters and of servants. History has shown that it took nearly eighteen centuries before the full impact of these principles gripped the followers of Christ and caused them to campaign for the ending of slavery in their various countries.

The New Testament is sometimes criticized for its failure clearly to reject slavery and because it accepts, or tacitly accepts, the social order of its times and apparently leaves succeeding generations to do the same. In a sense those who make such criticism are correct in their analysis. The gospel does not make a frontal attack on the existing social order, but requires the believer to live by God's standards in the society of which he is a part. If he is a free man he is to respect a believing slave as a brother in Christ. If he is a slave he is to give proper respect to those who are free, and in particular faithful and whole-hearted service to his own master. Across the board the dignity of the human person is recognized: the faith is not to be held with partiality. 'If you show favouritism, you sin' (James 2:9); 'There is neither . . . slave nor free' (Galatians 3:28).

The gospel could, and did, change men in a society that tolerated slavery. It so transformed them that they became better slaves or better slave-owners. It is thus a message that is relevant in every kind of society. It still changes men, bond and free, even if technically most today are free. Its principles uphold the right of the individual, unless under judicial condemnation of some kind, to personal freedom. Since the ten commandments are part of the gospel — what heaven has bound and what the Christian evangelist is to bind — the prohibition on kidnapping stands as the all-important safeguard. You shall not steal your neighbour; you shall not deprive him of his freedom.

The right to property

In prohibiting theft the eighth commandment asserts the right of the individual to acquire and to own property. That there is such an offence as stealing shows the legitimacy of being able to say of this or of that, 'It is mine.' This is the right to own property.

All through Scripture property is presented as a stewardship held in trust from God, but at no point is the fact of owning it, or even of owning a great deal of it, condemned. Thus when there was a spontaneous sharing of possessions in the early days of the church there was no compulsion. Peter did not rebuke Ananias for owning a property, but for the deceit of pretending that the offering he presented was the whole product of the sale he had made. Indeed, Peter's words affirmed the right to own property inherent in the eighth commandment: 'Didn't it belong to you before it was sold? And after it was sold, wasn't the money at your disposal?' (Acts 5:4.)

The burden of Scripture is not, however, to emphasize man's right to own property but to call him to have a proper and a responsible attitude to it.

The acquisition of property

The eighth commandment shows — and the New Testament affirms — that there is a wrong way to obtain possessions, namely, by stealing. The biblical view is that possessions are rightly acquired in one of two ways: by gift or inheritance, and by personal effort or work. When God created man he gave him clear instructions that he was to support himself by the use of both brain and brawn. In the book of Proverbs one of the most condemned characters is the sluggard or lazy person, the one who dislikes and declines work. Paul is equally strong: 'If a man will not work, he shall not eat' (2 Thessalonians 3:10).

All too often modern life seems to provide men with excuses for failing to work. Sometimes they can easily live by breaking the eighth commandment — they steal from one another, from employers and from the state, and seem able to do so with an incredible lack of conscience. Goods, materials, stationery and time are stolen from shops and factories. Wages are claimed where no work has been done. Money is embezzled. Tax payments are fiddled or avoided. Expense accounts are inflated. Telephone calls are made for personal reasons and no payments are made for the service. Stealing is indeed one of the premier malaises of our day.

Those of us who are Christians must set an example to those who are not. We will sometimes be disadvantaged by individuals and by groups who ruthlessly pursue gain but we must never be tempted into following their example. As followers of Christ we are bound by the law of God and we can only glorify him and enjoy his blessing as we do his will. The command is clear, 'You shall not steal.'

The use of property
The property we 'own' is ours, not for selfish ends but to use for him to whom ultimately all belongs. Each of us will have to give an account of his stewardship. How then should a Christian use his property, his wealth? At least four answers have to be given.

1. *To maintain himself and his family.* To fail to do this is to abandon any semblance of Christianity: 'If anyone does not provide for his relatives, and especially for his immediate family, he has denied the faith and is worse than an unbeliever' (1 Timothy 5:8).

2. *To help the needy and the underprivileged.* In ancient Israel there were laws requiring generosity in the treatment of the poor and of strangers. Our Lord, dissenting totally from the eye-catching alms-giving of the Pharisees, insisted that his followers give alms secretly. He commended those who gave even a drink of cold water to the needy and condemned those who declined to do so. Later on, the apostles put his teaching into practice, as those who had plenty shared with those who had little and as a series of collections were made for famine-stricken saints in Judea. The clear teaching is that wealth is to be used for the Lord in helping those of his creatures who are in need.

3. *To maintain the state.* The Christian, like everyone else, is duty-bound to pay whatever taxes may be levied for the maintenance of state enterprises. In Israel of old there was a system of tithing which supported the various activities of the theocratic state — the administration of justice and of local affairs as well as the upkeep of religion. The tithe had to maintain those who did some of the things now done for

us by civil servants. The people of God maintained the local and national administrations of the day and their successors today have a similar responsibility. Our Lord said, 'Give to Caesar what is Caesar's.' Paul said, 'Give everyone [the authorities] what you owe him: if you owe taxes, pay taxes; if revenue, then revenue . . .' (Romans 13:7).

4. *To support the Lord's work and the Lord's servants.* The apostle Paul argued very strongly for the right of those who serve the Lord in a teaching or missionary ministry to be supported by those to whom they ministered: 'The Lord has commanded that those who preach the gospel should receive their living from [or through] the gospel' (1 Corinthians 9:14). That Paul had not claimed such support did not invalidate the principle. As the ox that treads the corn is not muzzled, but can eat some of the corn, so God's servants are entitled to proper remuneration for the work they do — remuneration incidentally at a level sufficient to allow them to maintain not just themselves but their families. 'Don't we have the right to food and drink? Don't we have the right to take a believing wife along with us, as do the other apostles . . .? Or is it only I and Barnabas who must work for a living?' The argument continues, 'If we have sown spiritual seed among you, is it too much if we reap a material harvest from you? If others have this right of support from you, shouldn't we have it all the more?' (1 Corinthians 9:4–12.) The questions are rhetorical but their aim is clear. Paul is demonstrating the right of gospel preachers to be supported and affirming the responsibility of believers who benefit from their preaching to give that support.

It is the great privilege of the Christian to use his wealth for the work of God, and in particular for the support of those engaged in that work. The Lord loves the cheerful giver and he expects that his people honour him by setting aside regularly, as he prospers them, a portion of their income to be given for his use.

The need to subordinate property
From what we have been saying it is surely clear that while man has the right to own property he is not to be mastered

by it. The Bible always puts material possessions in a secondary place. They are not of ultimate worth and not to be
compared with heavenly treasure which cannot be stolen
and which is not subject to decay.

The Lord Jesus urges us to seek first, not earthly treasure,
but the kingdom of God and his righteousness (Matthew
6:33). He often brought out into relief the folly of those
who made a god of their property. There was the rich fool
who thought he was set fair for a long and comfortable retire-
ment. There was the rich young ruler who declined to put
God before his property and who went away crestfallen and
sad. Such provided vivid and urgent warnings to his hearers
of the danger of making a god of one's property. They bear
the same warning to us. Those who give first place to their
possessions or to the acquisition of additional property show
that God the Lord is not really their God and surely call in
question the reality of any claim they make to be followers
of Christ. Property is to be used, not worshipped. It must
be in a subordinate position in the affections of the heart.
Said the Lord Jesus, 'You cannot serve both God and
Money.' The Christian must, then, put property in every
shape or form — money, chattels, land, houses or business —
in a secondary place in his affections. He must learn to keep
his life free from the love of, and the service of money and
to be content with what he has (Hebrews 13:5).

Conclusion

Like the other man-ward commandments, the eighth has
wide implications for human behaviour. It proscribes stealing
of every kind. It confers the right to own property, but on a
responsible rather than on an absolute basis.

The prophet Samuel was a unique character in Israelite
life. His claim to honesty is one of the most tremendous
and telling testimonies to be found anywhere. He was the
epitome of integrity, as his people readily recognized when
they accepted the challenge he put to them about himself: ' "Here I stand. Testify against me in the presence
of the Lord and his anointed. Whose ox have I *taken*? Whose
donkey have I *taken*? Whom have I *cheated*? Whom have

I *oppressed*? From whose hand have I *accepted a bribe* to make me shut my eyes? If I have done any of these, I will make it right." "You have not cheated or oppressed us," they replied. "You have not *taken anything* from anyone's hand." Samuel said to them, "The Lord is witness against you, and also his anointed is witness this day, that you have not found anything in my hand." "He is witness," they said' (1 Samuel 12:3–5).

Samuel has set the pattern for us and for all time.

'You shall not steal.'

11. Safeguarding justice and truth
The Ninth Commandment

'You shall not give false testimony against your neighbour.'

The ninth commandment has come down to us in two slightly different forms. In Exodus it reads, 'You shall not give false testimony against your neighbour' or more literally, 'You shall not answer your neighbour as a lying witness' (Exodus 20:16). In Deuteronomy the literal rendering would be 'You shall not answer your neighbour as a witness of emptiness' (Deuteronomy 5:20).

The difference is not brought out in our versions because the Hebrew words have an overlap of meaning and are, therefore, to a degree synonymous. Nevertheless the distinction in emphasis is probably of some importance, the words in Exodus (Hebrew *'ed sheqer*) stressing deceit and lying, while those in Deuteronomy (Hebrew *'ed shaw*) focus on the groundlessness, the emptiness, the vanity of a testimony which lacks substance.

In both forms the command is primarily concerned with the testimony of those involved in judicial hearings. The word translated witness (*'ed*) is derived from a verb meaning 'to answer'. It is frequently used of giving answer at the bar of law in a court hearing. The 'lying witness' or the 'witness of emptiness' mentioned in the commandment is then in the first instance the person who publicly accused another by *answering* with a false testimony before the judges in court. The false witness would destroy, or attempt to destroy, the other person's reputation by having him condemned for an offence of which he was not in fact guilty.

It is sometimes thought that this commandment is directed

against what we know as perjury, that is, the giving of false evidence under oath. There is no proof, however, that Israelites accusing or witnessing in court were normally expected to do so under oath. The provision made, as we have seen previously, for swearing by the name of the Lord, seems to have been less a judicial than a religious matter, having to do with single-minded devotion to the Lord. Where something approaching an oath did come into legal matters it was in the right given to judges or to priests acting in a judicial role to put members of the public under an adjuration in order to force a testimony or a defence from them (Leviticus 5:1; Numbers 5:19; cf. Matthew 26:63). If in such circumstances a false witness was borne there would be an offence approximating in some ways to what we know as perjury. Since the primary reference of the command is to testimony given in court, it must be understood as proscribing all deceptive witness, including that given under oath. While it is not directed specifically at perjury, the prohibition of that particular offence is certainly included in it.

The root sin of a false witness is his deception, his lie. He could not be a false witness without perpetrating a lie. If the primary reference of our commandment was to accusations made in court, it certainly follows that its application extends outside the courts and into the whole fabric of Israelite life. There was an obligation resting on all to speak truthfully of neighbours: 'You shall not give false testimony against your neighbour.'

In the light of these considerations it becomes necessary to examine this commandment in two stages, seeing it firstly as *safeguarding justice* and secondly as *protecting truth*. We will trace each theme through both the Old and New Testaments and try to focus on their implications for modern times.

Safeguarding justice

This commandment was obviously designed to prevent the miscarriage of justice which takes place, or tends to take place, wherever 'false accusations' are given a hearing. It was concerned that every Israelite have a fundamental right to a just reputation and to be punished at the bar of the law only when he had actually committed an offence worthy of penalty. It enshrined in Israelite law, and thus in the moral law, what we today would call 'the right to justice'.

The Israelites, like the rest of mankind, were the victims of the Fall and it is not surprising, therefore, that the concern of the commandment for justice was not always maintained. The classic case in the Old Testament is perhaps that of Naboth, who refused to sell or barter his vineyard to King Ahab. Jezebel, the infamous wife of the king, made arrangements to have Naboth brought before the elders and nobles (i.e., the judges) of his town and accused by two false witnesses, base fellows, of cursing both God and the king. At the mouth of the two witnesses the charge was accepted, Naboth was condemned and taken out of the city to be stoned to death (1 Kings 21:1—14). He suffered the death penalty on the basis of a groundless, a lying accusation, and his death was thus officially authorized or judicial murder rather than an expression of retributive justice.

Old Testament regulations

It is fairly clear that in the ancient Near East an accused person was often considered guilty until he demonstrated himself innocent. The onus of proof was on the defendant rather than on the accuser. In Israel, however, the position was rather that an accusation created a dispute between the accuser (or adversary — *the satan*) and the defendant, in which each were witnesses and each could call other witnesses. The judge's role was to settle the matter justly by giving a verdict of guilty or innocent.

Fair play for all
The ordinances or judgements recorded in Exodus 21—23, which expound the implications of the ten commandments, include two very strong endorsements of the ninth. The first reads, 'Do not spread false reports. Do not help a wicked man by being a malicious witness. Do not follow the crowd in doing wrong. When you give testimony in a lawsuit, do not pervert justice by siding with the crowd, and do not show favouritism to a poor man in his lawsuit' (Exodus

23:1—3). The malicious witness is literally 'a witness of (or
in a charge of) violence', a witness whose testimony could
cause the community to end the life of the accused by
violent means. The warning against going with, and saying
the same things as the crowd is important. Public justice is
often gross injustice, when the crowd is roused to such a
pitch of emotion that all rationality disappears. Important,
too, is the requirement that justice be fair and without
partiality, not discriminating against or favouring the poor
man because he is poor, and equally not discriminating
against the rich and the powerful because sometimes some
such men are unscrupulous, nor favouring them because of
what they are.

The second passage, a few verses further on, emphasizes
the need to ensure that, where the death penalty could be
applied, the poor and the righteous get fair play: 'Do not
deny justice to your poor people in their lawsuits. Have
nothing to do with a false charge, and do not put an innocent or honest person to death, for I will not acquit the
guilty . . .' (Exodus 23:6—8). The fact that God cannot
ignore such wickedness or acquit such false accusers is
presented as a deterrent to any who might be tempted to
injure or destroy someone else by accusing him falsely of a
criminal offence.

The Levitical code also emphasized fair play and justice.
The people of God were required to be holy in this matter
because he is holy. They were to be like him. One passage
which expounds these implications of the ninth commandment is Leviticus 19:15—16: 'Do not pervert justice; do
not show partiality to the poor or favouritism to the great,
but judge your neighbour fairly. Do not go about spreading
slander (Hebrew, as a *rakil*, a talebearer) among your people.
Do not do anything that endangers your neighbour's life.
I am the Lord.' The upholding of legal justice was clearly
prominent but equally clearly the wider implications of the
command were in view. Malicious talebearing, or any effort
to destroy a neighbour by saying things about him, presumably from an unloving motive (cf. v. 18), was to break
the law of God.

The obligation to disclose evidence

The provision of Leviticus 5:1, that someone who had first-hand knowledge of a matter could be put on oath to make a true 'answer' before the judge or judges sitting in court, is another measure aimed at safeguarding justice. No Israelite in possession of knowledge material to the guilt or innocence of another, and material, therefore, to the purity of life in the community, had the right to maintain silence. He must give his evidence and if he failed to do so guilt attached to him; he would bear his iniquity. Such a man could only re-establish himself in the community by presenting an appropriate guilt offering (Leviticus 5:6). This law, that a man put on oath must bear witness to what he knows, lies behind the suggestion of Proverbs 29:24 that a man who hears the adjuration (the call to answer an oath at law) and discloses nothing is partner with a thief and a hater of his own life! It was also this law which Caiaphas, the high priest, invoked at the time of our Lord's trial. In face of our Lord's deliberate silence he said, 'I charge you under oath by the living God: Tell us if you are the Christ, the Son of God' (Matthew 26:63). In due obedience to the law our Lord broke his silence and became a witness confirming the charges that had been made against him. Thus, while false witness was prohibited, the bearing of a true witness was required and could be insisted upon by those in positions of judicial responsibility.

The requirement for two or three witnesses

Alongside the other provisions is a firm insistence that before anyone was condemned the accusation had to be established on the testimony of more than one witness. We read, 'One witness is not enough to convict a man accused of any crime or offence he may have committed. A matter must be established by the testimony of two or three witnesses' (Deuteronomy 19:15). In Numbers 35:30 and Deuteronomy 17:6 the same principle is enunciated with specific reference to the death penalty: 'No one is to be put to death on the testimony of only one witness.' Again the good name, and in some cases the life, of the citizen was being safeguarded by laws which put the brakes on hasty, on malicious, on ill-informed or on groundless accusation.

It is probable that to some degree the two or three witnesses necessary to secure a conviction had to be independent of each other. Collusion or conspiracy would have to be excluded if justice was to be safeguarded. This is not, however, spelled out clearly in the Old Testament but the rabbinic records of later times show that the Jews of our Lord's time and subsequently interpreted the situation in this way. They insisted that the witnesses be examined independently and that any discrepancy in their testimony render their accusation void (*Mishnah,* Sanhedran 5:2). This requirement was conveniently side-stepped at the trial of our Lord (Mark 14:56—64). In addition the rabbis required that an accuser or an accusing witness testify to what he himself had personally seen the accused do. Secondhand or hearsay evidence was inadmissible (*Mishnah,* Sanhedran 3:6).

Punishment appropriate to the false accuser
The regulations in Deuteronomy include a very firm law specifying that anyone found guilty of false witness should himself suffer the precise penalty which the victim of his charge would have borne if convicted: '. . . If the witness proves to be a liar, giving false testimony against his brother, then do to him as he intended to do to his brother. You must purge the evil from among you. The rest of the people will hear of this and be afraid, and never again will such an evil thing be done among you' (Deuteronomy 19:18—20). There could hardly be a stronger and yet a fairer deterrent against false witness and false accusation.

Bribery proscribed
The bringing of false accusations was sometimes accompanied by some kind of interference with the independence of judges. Often this took the form of a gift or promise of a gift, in return for which favour the judge would be expected to decide for the giver. Bribery, to give this kind of 'giving' its proper name in current English, is consistently condemned in Scripture because it perverts the thing that our ninth commandment seeks to protect, namely justice. In Moses' instruction for the appointment of judges the principle is set out with great clarity: 'Appoint judges and officials for each

of your tribes in every town . . . and they shall judge the people fairly. Do not pervert justice or show partiality. Do not accept a bribe, for a bribe blinds the eyes of the wise and twists the words of the righteous. Follow justice and justice alone . . .' (Deuteronomy 16:18–20; cf. Exodus 23:8).

The point is that a judge is prejudiced if he takes a bribe; his eyes are blinded and his mind becomes partial so that he does not see where justice lies. The cause of the righteous, the innocent accused, is subverted. This is precisely what happened when the sons of Samuel, Joel and Abijah, were made judges when Samuel became old. They failed to walk in Samuel's ways and used their position to get gain for themselves. 'They accepted bribes and perverted justice' (1 Samuel 8:3).

The laws of Israel were, then, formulated to deter every false or baseless accusation, to safeguard at law the reputation of the innocent and to preserve a high standard of justice in the whole community. The right to justice was kept in focus. The thrust of the ninth commandment and of the associated legislation is that justice was to be safeguarded and done at all times and in all circumstances. While the individual had the right, and in some cases the duty, to initiate or corroborate an accusation at law, he must never stoop to the wickedness of a false accusation. The Lord said through Moses, 'Have nothing to do with a false charge' (Exodus 23:7). Avoid it like you would avoid a plague! *'You shall not give false testimony against your neighbour.'*

New Testament endorsement

The New Testament has a number of fairly clear references to the ninth commandment. John the Baptist cited it when he told his hearers not to extort money or accuse people falsely (Luke 3:14). The Lord Jesus, speaking of evils which come out from a man's heart and defile his character, included *'false testimony'* and *'slander'* (Matthew 15:19), and the apostle Paul in a list of those who break the commandments mentioned *'liars'* and *'perjurers'* (1 Timothy

1:10). Clearly God's requirement still stood, and still stands: 'You shall not give false testimony against your neighbour.'

The teaching of the New Testament on justice is mainly concerned with relationships between believers, either as individuals each to the other, or as a group to an individual or to other groups. There is no proclamation of civil law. Under the new covenant God was calling to himself a spiritual community, a kingdom not of this world, but made up of believing men and women drawn from all nations, men and women who would be, who are expected to display justice, whatever the laws of the states in which they happen to live.

The New Testament, like the Old, builds its insistence on justice on the character of God. He is truly just. With him there is no partiality, no respect of persons. He judges each one impartially according to his deeds (1 Peter 1:17). He shows no partiality in the matter of national identity, accepting in every nation anyone who fears him and does what is right (Acts 10:34). In the heavenly song of Revelation 15:3 praise is ascribed to him, the King of the ages, who is *'just* and true' in all his ways.

Requirement for two or three witnesses

The requirement that no one be condemned except on the word of two or three witnesses comes over into the New Testament as a principle of some importance. It is probable that the then current Jewish tradition requiring that there be no collusion between the witnesses was also regarded as important.

When our Lord taught his disciples how to deal with an offending brother, the second stage in the procedure involved taking others along so that every word might be confirmed by the evidence of two or three witnesses (Matthew 18:16). The point was that if the matter could not then be settled but had to be taken to the church for decision there would be more than one witness to what had been said. He also cited this law in a slightly different form in a discussion with some of his opponents. 'In your law,' he said, 'it is written that the testimony of two men is valid' (John 8:17).

Paul's second letter to the church at Corinth contains much stern rebuke and indicates that he planned a third

visit to it on which he would have to deal with people who
had not repented of impurity, sexual sin and debauchery
(2 Corinthians 12:21). He seems to have been angry about
the situation, but even so he wanted to be absolutely just
in his treatment of the offenders: 'Every matter must be
established by the testimony of two or three witnesses'
(2 Corinthians 13:1).

A similar emphasis emerges in connection with the
disciplining of sinning elders. 'Do not entertain,' wrote Paul
to Timothy, then caring pastorally for the church   at
Ephesus, 'an accusation against an elder unless it is brought
by two or three witnesses' (1 Timothy 5:19). In other
words, there was to be no question of discipline on the basis
of a charge raised by one witness. At the same time, Timothy
was to see that there was no partiality shown in favour of the
elder who persisted in sin. He was to be treated in exactly
the same way as those who did not hold pastoral office:
'Those who sin are to be rebuked publicly . . . keep these
instructions without partiality, and to do nothing out of
favouritism' (1 Timothy 5:20–21). Thus insistence on more
than one witness was applied to safeguard justice where
charges arose that could result in church discipline.

Partiality excluded

As God is without partiality, just in all his ways, so his
children are to avoid partiality and to be just in their judgement of, and dealings with their fellows.

The apostle James focuses on a danger that constantly
arises in church life, that of showing partiality to the rich
or to the influential. 'My brothers,' he writes, 'as believers
in our glorious Lord Jesus Christ, don't show favouritism'
(James 2:1). He then cites a case in point, the giving of more
attention and a more prominent place to the man who
appeared in fine clothing than to the one who came in
shabbily dressed. Making such a distinction dishonoured
the poor man and was an injustice to him, a denial of the
royal law of Scripture which says, 'Love your neighbour
as yourself.' To show partiality is a sin, just as is murder
or adultery. It is strenuously to be avoided because one day
all of us are ourselves to be judged (James 2:1–12).

Another area where partiality shows its ugly head is in the

judgements we tend to make of each other. We do not, we cannot, see people exactly as they are because we are limited in our perception and warped and prejudiced in our thinking. It is, therefore, dangerous and terribly unwise to condemn other people, even when we think we have evidence to prove them in error. Paul knew the danger all too well and urged, 'Judge nothing before the appointed time; wait till the Lord comes. He will bring to light what is hidden in darkness and will expose the motives of men's hearts.' Then, and only then, he concluded, will every man receive a truly objective evaluation of his life and of his motives: 'Each will receive his praise from God' (1 Corinthians 4:5).

It was unjust or partial judgements that were the focus of our Lord's instruction: 'Do not judge, or you too will be judged' (Matthew 7:1). He illustrated his point by speaking of those who thought they could remove a speck of dust in a brother's eye, but who, as they tried to do so, were blinded by a veritable log or plank which was blocking their own vision. For him it was sheer hypocrisy to criticize someone else's speck without first getting one's own vision cleared. What we all need is to be rid of our prejudices, but because we are part of a fallen race this is never completely possible. We must therefore recognize that every judgement we make is imperfect and to some degree partial, for or against those we judge. Before we judge or criticize anyone we need to remember that in the end God will judge us all impartially: 'In the same way [we] judge others, [we] will be judged.' God will be just towards us. It is our responsibility to be just to one another.

Slander excluded

One of the easiest ways to deprive others of justice is to speak of them in such a way that their reputation is falsely damaged, their character is unjustly defamed. In our modern world such a report in spoken form is known as *'slander'* and in published form (books, press, radio, television) is known as *'libel'*. In the New Testament this distinction was not made but there are a number of words which refer to the general area of slanderous speech and which are always in contexts showing that it is to be regarded as an obnoxious sin to be excluded from the Christian life.

The word 'devil' (Greek *diabolos*, meaning 'an accuser') is widely used of one whose accusations are false. Satan, the arch-enemy of God and of men, is called 'the devil' and was described by our Lord as having 'no truth in him . . . a liar and the father of lies' (John 8:44). But men can take on the same malicious role. Those listening to our Lord were told that they belonged to 'their father, the devil', their will being to do their father's desires. Like the devil, they were guilty of making accusations that were untrue and they were, therefore, violating the canon of justice enshrined in the ninth commandment.

In the Pastoral Epistles Paul twice insists that Christian women must not be slanderers (*diabolōus*). In the first instance (1 Timothy 3:11) the reference is almost certainly to women serving in the church as 'deacons' (not 'wives of deacons' as rendered in AV and NIV) while in the second (Titus 2:3) it is to 'older women'. In both instances a good testimony was specially important, and slanderous conversation would have had the reverse effect.

Another Greek word, *blasphēmia,* meaning slanderous, irreverent speech, points to the same sin. It was, of course, used frequently of gross impiety in speech concerning God, but its implications are basically the same for speech directed to a fellow human. Blasphemy gives expression to malice. It involves words spoken in order to damage the reputation of another and so to deprive him of what is justly his. Hence Paul's injunction: 'Get rid of all bitterness, rage and anger, brawling and slander (*blasphēmia*), along with every form of malice' (Ephesians 4:31; cf. Colossians 3:8; 1 Timothy 6:4).

The abiding priority of justice

Every human being is neighbour to other human beings. The ninth commandment sets up a most important guidepost for the attitudes and the actions of the individual in relation to his neighbours. It makes justice an abiding priority.

A right to be accorded
By proscribing false accusation God conferred on mankind the right to a just verdict at the bar of law and to a just

reputation in the community at large. Where false accusations are not made no one is likely to be condemned unjustly or to have his reputation tarnished.

Ancient Israel was, of course, marked by many departures from the ideal of justice but the ideal persisted and was upheld by prophets and sages. Micah's words epitomize it as well as any:

> 'He has showed you, O man, what is good.
>   And what does the Lord require of you?
> To act *justly* and to love mercy
>   and to walk humbly with your God' (Micah 6:8.)

This ideal was endorsed by the New Testament so that the followers of Christ are also committed to justice. Each is prohibited from bearing false witness against his neighbour and is required to recognize the right of that neighbour to justice. He has to care as much about giving justice to others as about getting it for himself, because his underlying obligation is to love his neighbour as he loves himself.

The Christian, then, has to practise and not just talk about justice, and has to do so in relation to his neighbour, whether or not the society in which he lives operates on just principles. His obligation is to keep God's law: 'You shall not give false testimony.'

When, as sometimes happens, the Christian is called upon to give testimony in a court of law, or for that matter in any court where issues concerning a neighbour are being heard, he must seek to follow the biblical ideal and avoid partiality. He will not show bias for his relatives or friends and against a stranger. He will not lean towards the rich or the influential, nor against them and in favour of the poor and the insignificant. He will be, he must be, a man of integrity, a man of justice who will not be bought over by favours or bribes. He will tell the truth as he knows it and will take the utmost care to ensure that he makes no false accusation against anyone.

Whether the role is the raising of an accusation or the giving of testimony relevant to an accusation raised by someone else, the Christian has to act in love towards all his neighbours. He should not, therefore, be motivated by

desires to score points over, or gain an advantage over an
opponent. His concern must rather be that justice be done.

Equally when the Christian sees someone overtaken in a
fault and finds himself in the position of having to comment,
he must be concerned to be absolutely fair and just in what
he says. He must be concerned for the temporal and spiritual
well-being of the other and must act in great humility,
remembering that he, too, is frail and subject to failure, like
the one on whom he is passing judgement. He must
remember that in ultimate terms judgement belongs to the
Lord.

While Christians must ever strive for justice, they must
acknowledge their inability fully to achieve it. The judgements we pass on others are inevitably less than perfectly
just. When we speak about them to some degree we deprive
them of justice. Hence Paul's advice: 'Judge nothing before
the appointed time; wait till the Lord comes. He will bring
to light what is hidden in darkness and will expose the
motives of men's hearts. At that time each will receive his
praise from God' (1 Corinthians 4:5).

The biblical principle that an accusation be received only
at the mouth of two or three witnesses may not always be
adhered to in the complicated world of today. The obligation
to corroborate evidence is not, of course, one that rests on
the individual, but on those receiving an accusation and
hearing the case. The Christian may have to urge his community to adopt better rules of evidence but when he himself is called to act as a witness his duty is clear. He must
not give false testimony; he must speak the truth. His con-
tribution to the picture should be one that helps the court
to come to a verdict that will give justice to the accused.

A cause to be espoused

If the ninth commandment bestows the right to justice, it
must surely also require that society structure itself to
maintain that right. The Christian, committed as he is to
God's standards, must advocate and work for justice in
society. It will not do to leave matters to people who are
not committed to Christian principles, as so often has
happened as Christians withdraw into a shell and worldly
parties gain control. Christians should rather exert an

influence for good and for righteousness. They should be the salt of the earth and the light of the world, countering corrupting influences with purifying and illuminating ones. They should, with equal or greater expertise than that of the propagandists of the world, present the standards of Holy Writ and the demands of a holy God. The tragedy, alas, is that the world is cleverer and more successful than God's people and often the case simply goes by default. Standards below those set in Scripture carry the day. Jesus still has to lament, 'The people of this world are more shrewd in dealing with their own kind than are the people of the light' (Luke 16:8).

Christians must then be found on the side of justice, even when it means going against the popular outlook of the time. They should support every effort to introduce high standards of justice into society and to maintain such standards. Those with ability to communicate should preach and teach. They should write about justice and talk about it on radio and television. The Christian presence and the Christian stance should be proclaimed and exemplified. Society should hear a constant clamour for justice, for just laws and just procedures, from those who are believers within it. This is not to say that the church should control society or be linked with the state. It is simply to say that every Christian, and all Christians taken together, have a responsibility to work for the highest standards of justice. The ninth commandment and the subsidiary related teachings of the Bible commit them to this task. They have no right to opt out.

Resort to court action to be restrained
In addition to careful avoidance of false accusation in the interests of justice, the biblical ethic places restraint on the initiation of litigation against a neighbour. The warning of the ancient sage remains valid:

> 'What you have seen with your eyes
>   do not bring hastily to court,
> for what will you do in the end
>   if your neighbour puts you to shame?'
>
> (Proverbs 25:7—8.)

The point was that accusations can boomerang or back-fire, ending in the shame, not of the accused, but of the accuser. It was no light thing to make a formal accusation in ancient Israel and our Lord clearly had a similar attitude. Thus when a group of scribes and Pharisees brought a woman 'caught in the act of adultery' asking him to pass judgement on her — 'Now what do you say?' — he said, 'If any one of you is without sin, let him be the first to throw a stone at her' (John 8:7). A Jewish law required an accuser to cast the first stone at a criminal condemned to death, that is, to take full responsibility for the outcome of his accusation. Jesus put the matter rather differently but with great effectiveness. He showed those concerned that they had been too ready to accuse a neighbour even if, as appears to have been the case, the accusation was true.

There seem to have been a number of Christians in the church at Corinth who were similarly hasty in making accusations at court. The tragedy was that the accusations were made against fellow believers in a pagan court. Paul was disgusted with their antics. 'The very fact that you have law-suits among you means that you have been completely defeated already. Why not rather be wronged? Why not rather be cheated?' (1 Corinthians 6:7.) They were too selfish, too quick to try to gain advantage over others by accusations at court. Their attitudes were quite unchristian and, to Paul, totally to be deplored. Again resort to accusation of a neighbour at court is discouraged.

There is therefore a sound biblical basis for restraint. The Christian should not easily or hastily resort to litigation, particularly if the defendant happens also to be a believer. This is not to say that he will never go to court. He may have to do so for a declarative judgement or to gain relief from an unfaithful marriage or business partner. He may be forced into court action to maintain his own or his family's rights, but when this happens he must ensure that he does not act in malice against any defendant. He shares the same rights as his neighbour and must never seek to advance his interest unfairly to the disadvantage of others. He is to love his neighbour as he loves himself and he has to remember the words of the Lord Jesus, 'Love your enemies.' The Christian is to have a caring concern for the well-being of his opponents.

This is a difficult ethic, if ever there was one, but a proper motivation by love — *agape* or caring concern and caring action — is what our Lord demands. Nothing less will do, and this each of us must work out in his own situation and in the context of the legal system under which he lives.

Safeguarding truth

When we speak of 'truth' we usually mean the opposite of falsity, the opposite of what is baseless, empty or deceptive. In the Bible, however, truth is often not so much a matter of factual accuracy as of personal reliability. The emphasis is on the integrity, the fidelity, of a person. It points to the constancy of a parent bringing up, nursing his or her child and evoking over a long period the trust of the child.

Old Testament emphasis

The truthfulness of God
The Lord is presented as the faithful God 'who remains faithful (AV, 'keepeth truth'; Hebrew, *'emeth*) for ever' (Psalm 146:6). Because truthfulness is the hallmark of his character, he always acts in truth and can be trusted to send forth his love and his faithfulness (His *'emeth* — AV, truth — Psalm 57:3). The point is that in God an integrity of character, an internal reliability itself called 'truth', is that which ensures factual accuracy in his communications with others. Because he is true, he can be relied upon at all times. Even a dubious character like Balaam had to acknowledge this: 'God is not a man, that he should lie' (Numbers 23:19).

The prophet Samuel spoke of God as the Glory of Israel and said, 'The Glory of Israel does not lie or change his mind' (1 Samuel 15:29). One of the psalmists, Ethan, quotes the Lord as saying, 'Once for all, I have sworn by my holiness — and I will not lie to David' (Psalm 89:35). So God is presented as one who speaks the truth, who does not lie, and as one who keeps the truth he has spoken, who does what he says. In other words, he is thoroughly genuine, thoroughly reliable; the truth that is his nature shines through in words and deeds that are wholly consonant. Truth, in short, is an attribute of God. There is no contradiction or lie in him and what he is sets the standard for what men ought to be. The Old Testament bases its teaching on truth and falsehood on the character of God.

Against this background we can proceed to look at the way in which the Old Testament seeks to safeguard truth by the constant affirmation that lying and deceit are contrary to the will of God for his creatures.

The denunciation of lying

Lying normally belongs to interpersonal human relationships. It is in their dealings with each other that men cheat and falsify and manipulate facts to misrepresent and deceive. Two proverbs will serve to epitomize the Old Testament's abhorrence: 'A false witness will not go unpunished, and he who pours out lies will perish' (Proverbs 19:8). 'Do not testify against your neighbour without cause, or use your lips to deceive' (Proverbs 24:28). In both proverbs we have the parallelism of Hebrew poetry, the second line repeating in different words and with some expansion the thought of the first. Thus the liar or deceiver is equated with the bearer of a false or groundless witness at court.

The same wisdom pervades the Psalms. In several instances God charges the wicked with harnessing their tongues to deceit (Psalm 50:19). He says the mouth of the wicked is full of curses and lies and threats (Psalm 10:7). He himself is revolted by lying deceits and reacts against them. He does not want in his house those who lift up their souls to idols or swear by what is false (Psalm 24:4). A psalm, attributed to David, has a prayer invoking divine wrath on such people:

> 'For the sins of their mouths
>   for the words of their lips,
>   let them be caught in their pride.
> For the curses and lies they utter,
>   consume them in wrath,
>   consume them till they are no more'
>
> (Psalm 59:12–13.)

The writings of the prophets also emphatically denounce lying. Isaiah rebukes the men of Judah as 'deceitful children' (Isaiah 30:9) and Hosea lists lying with murder, stealing and adultery as marks of a society which has become unfaithful to God (Hosea 4:2). His contemporary, Amos, is particularly hard on the deceitful traders of the day who falsified balances and exploited the poor by giving them less than proper value for their money, 'skimping the measure, boosting the price and cheating with dishonest scales' (Amos 8:5; cf. Micah 6:11; Proverbs 11:1). The exploitation of the poor by deceit of one kind or another also troubled Isaiah, who wrote of scoundrels making up wicked schemes 'to destroy the poor with lies' (Isaiah 32:7). Jeremiah got to the root of the matter when he pronounced the human heart 'deceitful above all things and beyond cure' (Jeremiah 17:9). Because there is an inward defect, a perversion of character, which twists and defies truth, men deceive one another. As the same prophet puts it,

> 'Friend deceives friend,
>   and no one speaks the truth.
> They have taught their tongues to lie . . .
> Their tongue is a deadly arrow;
>   it speaks with deceit.
> With his mouth each speaks cordially to his neighbour,
>   but in his heart he sets a trap for him'
>
> (Jeremiah 9:5, 8).

The evil of lying finds focus in another area of speech — the making of promises. God, as we have already noticed, is absolutely faithful to his word: 'Not one word has failed of the good promises he gave . . .' (1 Kings 8:56). Often, however, men fail to keep their promises, thus making those promises into veritable lies. Hence the words of the sage about promises or vows to God: 'It is better not to vow than to make a vow and not fulfil it' (Ecclesiastes 5:5). Equally, the Old Testament expects the man of God to honour his promises to men at all times. We can sense deep feelings of scorn against false or baseless promises in the proverb: 'Like clouds and wind without rain is a man who boasts of gifts he does not give' (Proverbs 25:14). The man who promises something and fails to deliver the goods is guilty of falsity like that of clouds and winds which raise hope in a time of drought, but which fail to produce the rain that is desperately needed. Such words are lies and utterly unworthy of a man of God.

One of the most despised forms of lying was that which misrepresented God, or which deceived men about ultimate reality and the things of the spirit. In the context in which occult and spiritist practices were proscribed, God warned the Israelites against prophets who would presume to speak in his name words which he had not commanded (Deuteronomy 18:20). Again and again, we find the lying utterances of such prophets pronounced false. A passage in Jeremiah does this in a very striking way. The Lord says, ' "I have heard what the prophets say who prophesy lies in my name. They say, 'I had a dream! I had a dream!' How long will this continue in the hearts of these lying prophets, who prophesy the delusions of their own minds? . . . For what has straw to do with grain?" declares the Lord . . . "Therefore," declares the Lord, I am against the prophets who wag their own tongues and yet declare, 'The Lord declares.' Indeed, I am against those who prophesy false dreams . . . They tell them and lead my people astray with their reckless lies, yet I did not send or appoint them" ' (Jeremiah 23:25–32).

The simple fact is that Israel seems to have been riddled with dreamers, men and women who imagined that their own thoughts and visions were revelations of the divine mind, and who by propounding their falsities were deceiving others as well as themselves. Even worse was the fact that such false prophecies were often proclaimed in God's name and introduced by 'The Lord declares'. Such deceit God just could not countenance. To lie about human affairs was bad enough; to lie about God was to invite his strong opposition: 'My hand will be against the prophets who see false visions and utter lying divinations' (Ezekiel 13:9).

The problem of the deceits of the saints

Honesty demands that we take note of, and in some way try to account for, a number of instances of untruth spoken or practised by the saints of Old Testament times and recorded as having the benediction of the civil and religious leaders, or even of God himself. We think, for example, of Abraham's affirmations to the Egyptians and to Abimelech that Sarah was his sister (Genesis 12:11–19; 20:1–18), of Isaac's similar behaviour (Genesis 26:7–11) and of Jacob's pretence to be Esau in order to acquire for himself his brother's inheritance (Genesis 27:18–19, 24). Other examples are the reply of the Israelite midwives to Pharaoh's enquiry as to why they had not destroyed Israelite infants (Exodus 1:19–20) and Elisha's fending off of the Syrian army which had come to Dothan to arrest him (2 Kings 6:19).

The first thing to be said is that Scripture faithfully records what men did and does not seek to present its heroes as paragons of perfection. It is, therefore, to be expected that among the deeds of some, who are otherwise commended as good and righteous, there would be instances of verbal dishonesty. When, perhaps at a later stage, the person concerned is commended as righteous, we need not think that he or she was without moral flaw or that his or her every action is being endorsed. For example, the references in Hebrews 11:31 and James 2:25 to Rahab the prostitute do not specifically endorse the immorality of her life or the untruths spoken by her.

Another point to be noticed is that Scripture teaches that truth sometimes has to be concealed: 'A gossip betrays a confidence, but a trustworthy man keeps a secret' (Proverbs 11:13). Not everyone is entitled to know all that is known by another. Israelite tactics in war were based on this principle. Joshua's ambush before Ai (Joshua 8:3–29) seems to have been a matter of such concealment. When the Israelites – or a section of their forces – retreated on divine instructions (Joshua 8:18) their intention of leading the men of Ai into a trap was concealed and the men of Ai were deceived. Similarly, the Israelite midwives by speaking a part of the truth and leaving the rest unsaid concealed the full truth of the situation from Pharaoh. Samuel, by declaring a genuine intention to sacrifice at Bethlehem, concealed for the moment his additional intention of anointing the Lord's chosen successor for Saul.

When, however, we find a record showing divine initiation

or endorsement of such things explanation becomes more difficult. Clearly God's instructions were behind the deceptive retreat of some of Joshua's men from Ai (Joshua 8:1–29). The failure of the men of Ai to discern the Israelite ambushes may imply that they had misread the situation and lay some of the blame for defeat at their own door, but the clear implication is that God intended them to be deceived. Our highest wisdom is to accept the facts as presented to us in Scripture in the knowledge that God, whose character we know to be perfect, was working out his purposes in ways that were righteous and that in no way violated his own commands. He is faithful, ever keeping truth: he always acts in truth; he is not a man that he should lie. That the explanation of some of his ways is beyond us is not an adequate reason for doubting his integrity or his truth.

New Testament application

In the New Testament 'truth' (Greek, *alethēia*) again has two aspects. It carries an objective sense relating to the real facts of a situation or the valid content of a teaching. Truth is thus what *is* real, rather than what a human mind may think to be real. The second sense is subjective and has to do with the integrity of a person, with qualities like truthfulness, reliability and faithfulness. Truth in this sense is a positive quality of character, something which makes a man's life genuine. He wears no masks; he makes no pretences; he acts in accordance with reality. It is this second or subjective aspect which mainly concerns us as we consider the New Testament application of the ninth commandment.

The New Testament, like the Old, grounds its teaching on truth in the character of God. Truth is important in human life because it is an essential attribute of God's character. He is truth, the Truth. We begin, therefore, with a consideration of truth as a divine attribute.

Truth – a divine attribute
Our Lord sometimes spoke of God the Father, the one who had sent him, as one who was 'true' (John 7:28; 8:26). In the first of these passages he used the adjective *alēthinos*, a form

in which the ending (*inos*) points to the essential nature of the person or thing described as 'true'. God, it is affirmed, is by nature true. He is really genuine in his inner or essential life. Truth is an attribute of the divine nature and to receive the testimony of Jesus to God is to accept this fact: 'The man who has accepted [Jesus' testimony]has certified that God is truthful' (John 3:33).

Subsequently the apostolic writers presented God in similar terms. He is 'the living and true God' (1 Thessalonians 1:9 − *alēthinos* again). He acts according to truth; words spoken on his instigation are 'trustworthy and true' (Revelation 22:6). His judgements are 'based on truth' (Romans 2:2, Greek *kata alēthecan*). In the visions of the book of the Revelation he is addressed as 'Sovereign Lord, holy and *true*' (6:10), and as the Lord God Almighty, who is just and true in his ways and in his judgements (15:3; 16:7; 19:2).

Truth is also an attribute of the Lord Jesus Christ. The prologue to John's Gospel describes him as 'the true light' (John 1:9). The same Gospel records his own saying: 'I am the true vine,' the vine that is real by nature (*alēthinē*, John 15:1). He claimed the same quality of truth for his own judgements as he postulated of his Father's judgements: 'If I do judge, my decisions are right' (John 8:16). He even identified himself in terms of absolute and ultimate truth: 'I am the way and *the truth* (*he alētheia*), and the life' (John 14:6). It was as such, indeed, that the writer of the fourth Gospel had come to know him: 'The Word became flesh and lived for a while among us. We have seen his glory . . . full of grace and truth' (John 1:14). The glory of Christ seen by his disciples involved 'grace and truth'.

Similarly truth is attributed to the third Person of the Trinity. He is 'the Spirit of truth', whose function is to declare the things of Christ to the disciples (John 14:17; 15:26; 16:13−15). Like the Lord Jesus, he is said to be 'the truth' (*hē alētheia*): 'The Spirit is the truth' (1 John 5:7).

Clearly then, the Triune God, Father, Son and Holy Spirit, is true in his essential being. There is no disharmony due to error or inconsistency in his character. There is no danger of his misleading us by inadequate, inarticulate or erroneous guidance. He never lies (Titus 1:2) because falsity would be totally out of keeping with his nature (Hebrews 6:18; cf. 2 Timothy 2:13).

The character of God as truth is the basis of the obligation resting on Christians to be men and women of truth, men and women who eschew falsehood in every shape or form. Peter puts the matter clearly: 'Just as he who called you is holy, so be holy in all you do; for it is written, "Be holy, because I am holy"' (1 Peter 1:15–16). As God, all-holy, is true, so his people must be holy and, in being such, like him they will be true.

Truth – a Christian duty
The presentation of Christian duty comes positively in injunctions to espouse and do the truth, and negatively in prohibitions of its opposite, falsehood.

(i) *Among our fellows*
Truth in its objective sense is that which God has revealed for our learning, something which man can know. Indeed, God desires that all men should 'come to a knowledge of the truth' (1 Timothy 2:4). Some, of course, fail to gain this knowledge. They turn away from listening to it (2 Timothy 4:4); they never arrive at it (2 Timothy 3:7). Others receive it and come to know and love it. Those who truly espouse it do more than receive facts to store up in the mind. They show that they know the truth by doing it, by living consistently with it, by walking in it. 'The elder' who penned the second and third Epistles of John rejoiced in those who walked in the truth (2 John 4; 3 John 4). Peter, thinking along the same lines, wrote of those who had purified their souls by obeying the truth (1 Peter 1:22). Paul urged the Ephesian Christians to gird their loins with truth, thus making it a vital part of their armour in the Christian warfare.

The thrust of these statements is that truth is not merely something a man knows in his mind, but something he is or ought to be. Truth is a quality of character to be espoused and maintained; truth is something to be done. The constant danger is of failing to live according to the truth or, more literally in John's words, that 'we do not do the truth' (1 John 1:6). When this happens falsehood to some degree takes over and the ninth commandment is broken.

The Pharisees introduced a host of oaths aimed at

enabling their followers to affirm that they were really speaking the truth. A man could swear by heaven or by earth, or even by his own head, but not by the name of the Lord, lest he incur divine wrath for some element of falsity in the oath. Our Lord rejected the practice, telling his followers to be men of their word, men known for honesty apart from any oath, men whose 'Yes' meant 'Yes' and whose 'No' meant 'No' (Matthew 5:37). Paul endorsed this emphasis on honest speech, and thus on the ninth commandment, when he told the Ephesian believers to put off falsehood and speak truthfully among themselves (Ephesians 4:25). He was equally straightforward with the Colossians: 'Do not lie to each other . . .' (Colossians 3:9).

Paul was able to affirm on a number of occasions that his own preaching and writing had been marked by complete honesty. Regarding his early contacts with the other apostles he told the Galatians, 'I assure you before God that what I am writing you is no lie' (Galatians 1:20.) To the Corinthians he said, 'The God and Father of the Lord Jesus, who is to be praised for ever, knows that I am not lying' (2 Corinthians 11:31). In Romans 9:1 and 1 Timothy 2:7 he asserted that what he was writing was 'truth' and not lies. Writing to Thessalonica (1 Thessalonians 2:5) he affirmed that he had never used words of flattery, that is, words which would have made his readers think falsely that he thought well of them, or better of them than was actually the case.

Dishonesty in our relationships with other people can take many forms. We can lie by words or acts that are intentionally deceptive. We can lie by suggestion, as often happens in advertising where a product is boosted beyond its real properties. We can lie in our Christian propaganda if we mislead those we seek to win or lead! How many converts or potential converts have been told that if they believe in Christ thier problems of health, or wealth, or love and hate will all be solved overnight? We can lie by failing to discover the truth of things about which we talk, by presenting only part of the story or by failing to speak what we know. The New Testament position is that we are to be men and women of truth. Exaggeration. understatement and every other form of false witness are prohibited.

The New Testament, like the Old, has no time for those

who present their fellow men with a false picture of God.
Our Lord warned against false prophets who appear in
sheep's clothing — mild, attractive, smooth, persuasive — but
who are inwardly like ferocious wolves, bent on destroying
those who become their prey (Matthew 7:15). Later on he
spoke of 'false Christs and false prophets' who would 'appear
and perform great signs and miracles, to deceive even the
elect — if that were possible' (Matthew 24:24). Such are not
to be believed.

The trouble is, of course, that finite and fallible men all
too easily believe a lie. They are limited in mental capacity
and can never grasp the whole of reality or even of a particular event: 'we know in part'. In addition they are perverted
and twist and falsify the parts they do grasp. At no point
are men more prone to believe error than in relation to
God, whose infinity puts him beyond their complete ken.
In talking about him then, it is easy to pass on a partial or a
warped view and thus to communicate error. Even the most
alert and the most sincere can be found 'lying about God'.

Paul was acutely aware of this danger and was specially
careful of his own teachings. He was also strong in condemnation of those whose teachings were contrary to divine
revelation and who therefore lied about God. Thus he
designated as *bewitching* those who tried to lead the Gentile
Galatian believers into acceptance of circumcision and the
yoke of Judaism (Galatians 3:1). He said that those upsetting
things in Colossae were taking the believers captive 'through
hollow and deceptive philosophy' (Colossians 2:8). Timothy,
then representing the apostle in Ephesus, was warned about
some who follow the teachings of 'hypocritical *liars*' and
who would 'forbid people to marry and order them to
abstain from certain foods . . .' (1 Timothy 4:2–3). Such
teachings were to be countered by the truth and rejected by
the brethren. 'Have nothing to do with godless and old
wives' tales' is Paul's clear instruction (1 Timothy 4:7).

(ii) *In our dealings with God*
Lying to an omniscient God is ultimately impossible. Men
cannot deceive him who knows everything. Yet they often
make the attempt, as did the Pharisee in our Lord's parable
who told, or rather thought he told, the Lord how good he

was: 'God, I thank you that I am not like all other men — robbers, evildoers, adulterers — or even like this tax collector. I fast twice a week and give a tenth of all I get' (Luke 18:11). Full of self-righteous pride, he was lying to God, or trying to do so. In fact his words did not rise above the ceiling. He was simply praying 'about (literally 'to' or 'with') himself'. He was deceiving himself, but he was not deceiving God.

The story of Ananias and Sapphira highlights the folly of dishonesty or attempted dishonesty before God. At a time when the believers in Jerusalem were sharing their possessions, these two sold a property and brought part of the price to the apostles for distribution. Clearly Ananias gave the impression that he was presenting the whole proceeds and it was this deceit, and not the amount brought, which constituted his sin. As Peter said, 'Didn't it belong to you before it was sold? And after it was sold, wasn't the money at your disposal?' (Acts 5:4.) Ananias had been under no obligation to sell his property and under no obligation to present its entire value to the church, but he was under obligation to be truthful. Instead he bore a false witness and Peter's rebuke was clear: 'You have not lied to men but to God.'

In the New Testament, then, lying is presented as contrary to the will of God. It is listed among the sins marking those who are excluded from the ultimate bliss of the eternal kingdom. 'Nothing impure will ever enter it, nor will anyone who *does* what is shameful or *deceitful* . . .' 'Outside are the dogs, those who practise magic arts, the sexually immoral, the murderers, the idolaters and *everyone who loves and practises falsehood*' (Revelation 21:27; 22:15).

On one occasion the Lord Jesus put the matter very strikingly in the course of a discussion with a group of Pharisees. They had contended for direct descent from Abraham but Jesus pointed out that if they had been Abraham's children, as they thought they were, they would do what Abraham did. Rather they were doing what they had heard and learned from another father (John 8:38, 41). That father was in fact the devil: 'You belong to your father, the devil, and you want to carry out your father's desire' (John 8:44). Our Lord was not suggesting biological descent from Satan but simply stating that by doing the kind of things the devil did, by taking their cue from him rather than from God, they had made themselves his children.

The aspect of the devil's character most in view and clearly being followed by those to whom our Lord spoke was his deceitfulness: '. . . not holding to the truth, for there is no truth in him. When he lies, he speaks his native language, for he is a liar and the father of lies' (John 8:44). Clearly those who deceive by telling lies do the devil's work and make themselves his children.

Lying is a serious sin and Christians are as obligated to avoid it, as were the Israelites of old. They are to be men and women of truth, lying neither to one another nor to God, neither about God nor to themselves: 'You shall not give false testimony.'

The priority of truth

The believer today is obligated by the teaching of Scripture that truth is a Christian duty. He is to be a man of his word, whose 'yes' means 'yes' and whose 'no' means 'no', and not the other way round. In simple fact, he is to be a man of complete honesty, acting and speaking the truth in every relationship of life.

In communications about neighbours
The biblical duty to be truthful when speaking to neighbours has already been expounded in some detail. Again the obligation comes down the centuries and cannot be evaded today. Paul's words epitomize it: 'Therefore each of you must put off falsehood and speak truthfully to his neighbour' (Ephesians 4:25). Each one of us has to be a man of truth. No lesser standard can ever be acceptable to a follower of him who is 'the truth'. If this is not true of our day-to-day communications with or about our neighbours, then it is time we confessed our sin, time we put right our wrong-doings, time we sought God's forgiveness and his power to amend our ways.

The Christian should stand out for the reliability of his word. He should not make dogmatic statements on the basis of partial evidence or his own subjective impressions. He will take time to research the truth of what he proposes to say and even then recognize that his view of the matter may be incomplete and biased. His concern for the well-being of others, be they friendly or unfriendly towards him, will keep him from stances that could prejudice their position unfairly. He will never put them under blackmailing threat or in any way deprive, or try to deprive them of their rights. His integrity will govern his entire life and sustain him in any injustice he may suffer as a result. He is, he will be, a man of truth.

The problem of concealment

In the course of our examination of the Old Testament protection of truth we noted that there were times when the truth, or some part of the truth was concealed and that this was apparently quite legitimate.

There are, however, many situations in life when concealment becomes a perplexing problem. For example, terminal, or possible terminal illness often poses a difficulty. Should patients always be told, or only if they ask, or never at all? While some people rise to the occasion when they learn the truth and make the best of their remaining days and maybe prepare for the next life, others lose the will to live and quickly degenerate, possibly losing unnecessarily, or with unnecessary speed, a reasonable quality of life.

The issues can be highly complex and it would be foolish to adopt a dogmatic stance to be taken in every situation. That there are biblical examples of the withholding of information from those who might misuse it or be hurt by it, seems to assert the moral acceptability of doing so. In a sense the withholding of information may in a negative way deceive the other party, but this is hardly the same as a deliberate act of false witness.

Withholding information will not be a breach of the ninth commandment if the motive is love for the one from whom information is withheld, that is to say, if the withholding is done not to cheat or deprive, but to increase the well-being of the person concerned. The great commandment is that we love our neighbours as ourselves. Fulfilling that, we will do all in our power to avoid doing them hurt. If the disclosure of some aspect of the truth would harm or hurt a neighbour the right course will probably be to withhold it.

In one's own soul
Self-deception is a strange anomaly. In a way the very idea
is a contradiction in terms, for if a man deceives himself he
knows what he is doing and he is not deceived! Yet human
perversity is such that people seem somehow able to kid
themselves that something true is false or that something
false is true. Indeed they seem able so to deceive themselves
that sometimes at least they really believe the lies, the
delusions, they foist on themselves!

While, at first sight, lying to oneself might appear less
serious than lying to other people, it does in fact do considerable damage to the inner self and is often at the root
of the emotional stresses which are such a feature of modern
life. Men's sins find them out in strange ways and not least in
the inner tensions which their lack of inward honesty breeds.

The apostle John focuses on self-deception when he writes,
'If we claim to have fellowship with him [God] yet walk
in the darkness [i.e., in ways not harmonious with God's
will] we lie and do not live by the truth . . . If we claim to
be without sin, we deceive ourselves, and the truth is not in
us' (1 John 1:6, 8). The deception he had in mind is mainly
moral, involving the acceptance as good of practices which
by God's standards are morally evil. His call to his readers to
walk in the light as he [God] is in the light is a call to
absolute honesty with oneself and ultimately with God, to
whom the sin is to be confessed and before whom the folly
of self-deception is to be ended.

It is the task of psychologists to explain how men deceive
themselves. They have indeed done much to elucidate the
devices used to avoid or escape from facing up to reality. We
do 'kid' ourselves! The biblical requirement is that we
become honest with ourselves and thus with God. David
acknowledged this in a time of deep contrition: 'You desire
truth (Hebrew, *emeth*) in the inner parts' (Psalm 51:6). For
him, as for all of us, the way to peace with God and with
himself and to a happy and well-ordered life was the way of
complete honesty, the way of inward truthfulness.

The Lord Jesus put the challenge of inner truthfulness to
the Samaritan woman at Sychar's well. He had already
brought her face to face with reality: 'You have had five
husbands, and the man you now have is not your husband'

(John 4:18). When she turned the subject to the place of Mount Gerizim he kept up the pressure: 'The true worshippers will worship the Father in spirit and *truth*, for they are the kind of worshippers the Father seeks. God is spirit, and his worshippers must worship in spirit and in truth' (John 4:23—24). Worship is not, and never can be, an external thing, a matter of the right place or the right rituals. It is rather a matter of honestly and without pretence — in truth— lifting the heart and soul to God in adoration and humble obedience. Inward truthfulness is the essential without which worship and a right relation to God are impossible.

The Fall brought man into the devil's kingdom and into the thraldom and falsity of the devil's ways. Man is by nature, therefore, less than honest — he is deceitful — with his fellows, with God and with himself. He belongs, as Jesus put it, to his father, the devil.

God is truth and the ground of all truth. His requirement is that men model their lives on what he is, and not on the devil. To this Jesus, who presented himself as the very incarnation of the truth, calls us. Discipleship involves, then, an inward change, with truth and honesty taking the place of falsity and deceit. God desires truth in the inward parts.

The ninth commandment protects truth and makes it an abiding obligation not to be evaded.

'You shall not give false testimony.'

12. Searchlight on motives
The Tenth Commandment

*'You shall not covet your neighbour's house.
You shall not covet your neighbour's wife, or
his manservant or maidservant, his ox or
donkey, or anything that belongs to your
neighbour.'*

The tenth commandment focuses on the attitudes of heart,
the motives, the desires which underlie our actions. It makes
God's demands deeply inward and reminds us that he
searches the heart and examines the mind (Jeremiah 17:10).

As we study this commandment, we will do well to confess with the psalmist that the Lord has searched and known
us. We will do well to pray as the psalmist prayed,

'Search me, O God, and know my heart;
   Test me and know my anxious thoughts.
See if there is any offensive way in me,
   and lead me in the way everlasting'
                              (Psalm 139:23–24; cf. v. 1).

Old Testament presentation

Two versions
There are several differences between the wording of this
commandment as recorded in Exodus and in Deuteronomy.
The Exodus reading is 'You shall not covet (Hebrew,
chamad) your neighbour's house. You shall not covet
(*chamad*) your neighbour's wife, or his manservant or maidservant, his ox or donkey, or anything that belongs to your
neighbour' (Exodus 20:17). The Deuteronomic version is
'You shall not covet (*chamad*) your neighbour's wife. You shall

not set your desire (*'avah*) on your neighbour's house or land, his manservant or maidservant, his ox or donkey, or anything that belongs to your neighbour' (Deuteronomy 5:21).

In the first instance, the Hebrew verb *chamad* is used for both prohibitions in Exodus, but only for the first in Deuteronomy, where another word, *'avah*, occurs in the second. The difference between them does not, however, seem to be very significant. Both are used of desires which could be good, bad or indifferent. *Chamad* occurs in Isaiah 53:2, 'nothing in his appearance that we should *desire* him,' and *'avah* in Psalm 132:13–14 of God *desiring* Zion for a habitation. In neither case is there any suggestion of illegitimacy in the desires. In the context of the tenth commandment it is quite certain, however, that both words refer to desires for the acquisition of things to which the desirer has no entitlement of any kind. Desires directed to wrong objects, to what belongs to another, are prohibited.

In the second place, the form found in Exodus puts the primary emphasis on the neighbour's house and the secondary on his wife, while that in Deuteronomy turns it the other way round – wife first and house second. A common explanation for this is that in Exodus the word 'house' is used comprehensively for a man's 'household' and that the whole of the second part of the command expounds its meaning, first place being accorded to the wife. This theory asserts that in Deuteronomy the word 'house' is more restricted and refers not to the household but to a possession less important than a wife. Many scholars are not satisfied with this and argue that the Deuteronomic version reflects a later and an improved view of womanhood, which required that a man's wife be mentioned before the house in which he lived, or the household of which both he and she were a part. That the book of Deuteronomy deals sensitively with the concerns and rights of women is without question, but it is by no means certain that Exodus does not assume what Deuteronomy makes explicit, or that the apparent difference in the view of womanhood in the two books explains the different order they have for the two main imperatives in the tenth commandment.

Another difference is that Deuteronomy adds the neighbour's 'land' to the list of items not to be coveted. This reflects, no doubt, the fact that Deuteronomy presents divine law in terms meaningful not to desert wanderings, but to settled life in the land of Canaan, and the fact that there an Israelite could have personal title to a plot of land.

Illegitimate gain prohibited — both as desire and as deed

In our study of the eighth commandment we indicated a somewhat tentative acceptance of the traditional Christian understanding of this commandment. This is that it goes right to the inner source of action, to the desires that motivate the will, and prohibits every desire to gain for oneself position or possession to which one is not legitimately entitled. At the same time we noted that while the two Hebrew verbs used in the command, *chamad* and *'avah,* refer primarily to inner thoughts and desires, to covetings, they often extend their meaning to include the actions men undertake to gain their goals. Thus this command, by prohibiting covetous desires, also prohibits actual acts of theft and so to some degree overlaps with the eighth.

It is sometimes argued that since the decalogue was Israel's code of criminal law it could not contain a law in which the primary emphasis is on inner thought and motivation, matters that would be beyond the powers of any magistrate or court to judge. This commandment must therefore, it is held, refer to acts of theft which can be subject to litigation and, if proven, to the appropriate penalties. However, it is hardly necessary to regard the decalogue in terms of strict criminal law and better, surely, to think of it as a collection of ten enactments, spiritual and moral, which set the tone for and was, therefore, basic to, Israel's criminal law. As such, the inclusion of a law requiring a worthy attitude of mind is entirely appropriate and, indeed, entirely necessary. Its absence would be a very serious omission that would leave the commandments capable of a purely outward or formal interpretation.

The Old Testament does not present us with a great deal of information about the subsequent interpretation or application of this commandment. Achan's confession provides one concrete example: 'When I saw in the plunder a beautiful robe from Babylonia, two hundred shekels of silver and a wedge of gold . . . , I *coveted* (Hebrew: *chamad*) them, and took them' (Joshua 7:21). Achan desired and took what he had no right to take and did so, no doubt, with the motive of enriching himself. What he took was, of course, under a ban of destruction to the Lord, and by taking it Achan put himself under the same ban. What he did was a violation of the tenth commandment: 'You shall not covet,' as well as of the eighth: 'You shall not steal.' He had obtained gain illegitimately, first by desiring it and then by taking it. So, too, had those condemned for wicked injustice in Micah 2:2: 'They covet (Hebrew, *chamad*) fields and seize them . . .'

In addition there are a number of passages in which those who desire or hold illegitimate gain are roundly condemned. These use a Hebrew word *betsa'*, which is not in the tenth commandment and which is not directly related to *chamad* or *'avah*. In general its emphasis is on dishonest or illicit gain or profit. The Authorized Version usually translated it by 'covetousness' but more modern versions tend to render it as 'gain' and to add an adjective like 'dishonest', 'unjust' or 'evil', to show that it relates to wealth wrongfully obtained rather than to the underlying desires. Nevertheless it is not unreasonable to regard the condemnation of 'unjust gain' as being a condemnation of covetousness. Indeed the prophets so regarded it. Jeremiah, for example, denounced those who were 'greedy for gain' (Jeremiah 6:13) and those whose 'eyes and heart [were] set only on dishonest gain' (Jeremiah 22:17). Habakkuk pronounced a woe on him who 'builds his realm by unjust gain' (Habakkuk 2:9).

Clearly, 'gain' to which a man had no personal right was totally out of harmony with the spirit of Old Testament religion. It was to be a qualification of those appointed to help Moses judge lesser disputes among his people that they 'hate *dishonest gain*' (*betsa'*, AV 'covetousness', Exodus 18:21). Sadly, men of the opposite ilk were all too soon in positions of judicial authority, to the great detriment of community life. We read, for example, of the sons of Samuel who turned aside after gain, who 'accepted bribes and perverted justice' (1 Samuel 8:3). Like Achan they were in breach of God's command: 'You shall not covet.'

To desire, to seek, to acquire or to hold unjust or dishonest gain is sin. It involves an attitude which displaces the Lord from first place in a man's affections and in effect causes him to be contemptuous of things divine. In addition his family suffers. Says the sage, 'A greedy man brings trouble to his family' (Proverbs 15:27). Better far to eschew covetousness — the sage again: 'He who hates ill-gotten gain will enjoy a long life' (Proverbs 28:16).

Community justice protected

It is possible, perhaps probable, that the tenth commandment also sought to protect the position of a man as head of a household. In ancient Israel this seems to have carried with it the status of eldership and the duty of sitting in the gate to take responsibility with other family heads for the administration of justice in the local community. If a man was deprived of this headship by the seizure of his household or of some vital element in it — his wife, his house, his farm etc. — the administration of justice on the democratic or semi-democratic principle of each family playing a part through its head or elder would have been jeopardized.

The institution of a community eldership seems to have functioned throughout Israel's history. It probably began when Moses accepted the advice of Jethro, his father-in-law (Exodus 18:13—27). It is clearly part of the administrative structure presented in Deuteronomy and was restored by those who returned from exile in Babylon after the decree of Cyrus in 539 B.C. (Deuteronomy 19:12; 21:2—4; 22: 15—21; 25:7—9; Ezra 10:8, 14). It would thus seem to have been a highly important aspect of community life and its protection by the tenth commandment could follow naturally from the law against false evidence in the ninth. In any case the tenth has a strong reference to those areas of life in which a family head had personal authority — his house. his family, his business. It thus asserted the right to have a household of one's own and to exercise the rights of family headship not just in one's own interests, but by taking one's place as an elder in the interests of the larger community to which one belonged.

Ancient Israel can hardly be described as a democracy in the modern 'one man one vote' sense of the term, but the judicial system involving family heads in service as elders, to handle local and less serious legal matters, was a provision of a democratic nature. It assured that responsibility was shared among all the families making up the community, that an accused person would have a representative of his own family among the judges and that no single person of ill disposition could secure the condemnation of a brother Israelite. While the ninth commandment insisted on true evidence and so protected the individual from false accusation, the tenth went on to insist that his case be heard in a setting which allowed for an expression of opinion by every party interested in the matter, that is, by every family making up the community concerned.

The revolt of Absalom against his father David provides some illustration of the breaching of this side of the command, but since David was king and supreme judge in the land his position was not truly parallel to that of an ordinary family head who sat with others of similar status as an elder in the town or village council. Yet Absalom coveted his father's position and, by deliberately stealing the hearts of the people through offering them judicial pronouncements, sought to deprive him of it (2 Samuel 15:1—6). Absalom's covetousness in this area of the life of the nation was at the highest level possible in the land but was essentially of the same kind as any covetousness which intruded into and so sought to disrupt the normal and proper administration of justice, an administration protected to some degree at least by the tenth commandment: 'You shall not covet your neighbour's house.'

New Testament endorsement

When the New Testament alludes to the tenth commandment it normally uses words which refer to coveting as an activity of the mind. This shows that in the time of our Lord and of the apostles the command itself was seen as dealing primarily with a man's inner desires rather than with his outward acts.

There is an exception to this pattern in Mark's account of our Lord's interview with the rich young ruler in which six commandments, the sixth, seventh, eighth, ninth, tenth and fifth, were used to challenge him (Mark 10:19). In citing the tenth our Lord used the very strong Greek word '*apostereo*' which means not an inward coveting, but a definite act of depriving someone of his or her rights by robbery or theft. The NIV renders his words into English by 'Do not

244 The Ten Commandments

defraud'. In the parallel passages in Matthew 19:18 and Luke 18:20 there is no mention at all of the tenth commandment and some Greek manuscripts of Mark, including *Codex Vaticanus* in its primary text, omit the words: 'Do not defraud.' The majority of Mark manuscripts do, however, have these words and scholars therefore accept them as authentic.

This would seem to imply that for our Lord this command related both to inward lustful desires and to the actions men take to achieve them. In that case it overlapped to some degree with what has traditionally been regarded as the requirements of the eighth commandment. Since Mark 10:19 is a single occurrence among a considerable number of references which stress inner attitudes, we will regard its emphasis on outward acts of fraud as having been dealt with in our study of the eighth commandment. This leaves us free to examine the New Testament teaching on covetousness.

In the main, two groups of Greek words are used but there are also three or four forms which occur only occasionally. The first group involves the verb *epithumeō* and the noun *epithumia* which together occur more than fifty times. They focus on strong inward urges and are rendered into English by words like 'covet', 'desire', 'lust' or 'concupiscence'. The second group is made up of a verb, *pleonekteō*, meaning 'to desire a gain or an advantage' and two nouns *pleonexia* meaning 'covetousness' or 'greed' and *pleonektēs* meaning 'a covetous person'. They occur some twenty times in all.

The other words are *orgeo* meaning to 'covet' or 'desire', *orexis* meaning 'lust', *philarguria* meaning 'love of money', *philargurios* meaning 'a lover of money' and *zēloō* meaning 'to be zealous for' or 'to desire to have'. Between them these words occur on some eight occasions.

In our Lord's teaching

General endorsements
Several passages highlight our Lord's endorsement of our commandment by focusing on the inner motives that lie behind sinful acts and by calling for an inward purity of heart as the quality essential to a good, a righteous life.

One of these passages is in the parable of the sower, where the thorns which grew up and choked the Word of God, rendering it unfruitful, are interpreted as the worries of this life, the deceitfulness of wealth and the *desires* (*epithumia*) for other things (Mark 4:19). When a hearer of the Word allows these things to dominate his life the solemn fact is that the Word he receives becomes quickly overgrown and choked; it bears no fruit; there is no blessing in his life. Covetousness, the desire for gain, can so master a man, that even the Word of God becomes ineffective within him. The sad words of Jesus are 'making it unfruitful'. To some of us it probably seems strange, perhaps even unacceptable, that the sovereign Word of God should not be effective in any life to which it is directed. Does not Scripture say that God's Word will not return to him void? Yet here is the Lord Jesus implying that in some cases it would be voided, and voided by the covetous wills of men. But he it was who said this, and his teaching we must receive, even if it is in paradox, or apparent paradox, with other Scriptures. Covetousness, lust, call it what we will, damages the soul. It involves a grasping after gain, material worldly gain. Often the desired gain turns out to be a mere mirage because it dims the mind to the truth and makes it insensitive to values that are real and eternally lasting. Covetousness chokes God's Word, the Word that brings us salvation. It gives, or may give us, things *now*, but it denies us the real thing, both *now* and in the *hereafter*.

Another passage is that which records teaching our Lord gave after a clash with the Pharisees about the empty and outward formality of their religion. He pointed out that what a man eats or drinks goes through his digestive system without having any effect on his spiritual or moral condition, as the Pharisees thought it had — what goes in from without cannot defile a man. Rather it is that which comes out from a man's heart, a part of his being distinct from his stomach, that defiles him. His evil thoughts, sexual immorality, theft, murder, adultery, *greed,* malice, deceit, lewdness, envy, slander, arrogance and folly — 'All these evils', said Jesus, 'come from inside and make a man unclean' (Mark 7:14–21). The list mixes inner attitudes, evil thoughts — *greed,* envy, pride, folly — with outward acts — sexual immorality, theft, murder etc., but clearly attributes every defiling thing to the heart, the soul, within the man. It is what goes on there, coveting included, and coveting especially, which really damages and defiles him.

What our Lord is saying is that a man's primary responsibility is to be pure in heart, to have honest, clean, unselfish thoughts and to avoid desires that make him grasp after personal gain or that breed sinful acts. His words elaborate the proverb: 'Above all else, guard your heart, for it is the wellspring of life' (Proverbs 4:23). He himself said, 'Blessed are the pure in heart,' a beatitude much more easily verbalized than put into practice.

About coveting material possessions
In the sermon on the mount and in several similar records of our Lord's teaching, great emphasis is laid on the responsibility of the disciple to be without worry, without anxiety, knowing that even more richly than an earthly father gives good gifts to his children, God will give good things to those who ask him. He is to seek first God's kingdom, to set his affections supremely on God's righteousness, leaving his material needs to God's gracious provision.

Covetousness for material gain was the soul-destroying vice of the man who came to Jesus asking help to obtain a share of an inheritance. 'Teacher,' he said, 'tell my brother to divide the inheritance with me.' Our Lord declined to become involved in the family dispute but he instantly pinpointed the real problem within the heart of the enquirer, focusing on that and not on the brother the man was so obviously blaming. 'Watch out!' said our Lord to the man and to all who were listening, 'Be on your guard against all kinds of *greed* (*pleonexias*); a man's life does not consist in the abundance of his possessions' (Luke 12:13–15). Clearly the man before him was as full of greed as the proverbial egg is full of meat. Love of possessions, sheer coveting of what his brother held, was the dominant motive of his heart and this meant that more important things, the things of the spirit and of eternity, had little or no place there. The cares of this world, the deceitfulness of riches and the desire for other things had choked whatever awareness of God he may have had.

To ram home the point, our Lord told a parable about a

rich man who found himself with a plentiful harvest and no
adequate storage barns for its fruits (Luke 12:16–21). The
man was not condemned for being rich or for having a good
harvest, but for an attachment to his possessions which
excluded all thought of God or of eternity, and which
betrayed a covetous spirit. He lived for the enjoyment of the
present, for the making and conserving of gain for his own
pleasure. Covetousness had taken over and he looked forward
only to the comfort, the ease, the happiness he thought his
gain would bring to him. He said to himself, 'You have
plenty of good things laid up for many years. Take life easy;
eat, drink and be merry.' He had no God-ward dimension to
his life; he did not even think of the hereafter! He was a fool,
and God in his sovereign summons told him so: 'You fool!
This very night your life will be demanded from you.' It is
folly, utter and complete folly, to live solely for possessions,
to allow motives of gaining possessions to control life. Man
does not and cannot live by bread alone; eternal life is not
obtained by gaining possessions. As Jesus said, 'This is how
it will be' (like the rich fool) 'with anyone who stores up
things for himself but is not rich toward God.'

The point is, of course, that when men live for material
things they make a god of their possessions. Covetousness, or
the desire for possessions, becomes a kind of worship, a
religion, and when that happens the true God is dethroned.
Paul called covetousness 'idolatry'. It is a sin which makes
worship of God impossible. This is why our Lord said, 'You
cannot serve both God and Money' (Luke 16:13). One or the
other must dominate. If we allow the desire for possessions
to have first place in our lives we are *not* worshippers of God,
however much we profess to be so.

Luke tells us that the Pharisees objected to this teaching of
Jesus and actually scoffed at him for it, because they 'loved
money' (*philarguroi*, Luke 16:14). The Pharisees were, of
course, the professed champions of orthodoxy: they were
pernickety in the extreme, imposing petty religious restrictions which they asserted were essential to righteousness.
They argued about dress, about hand-washing, about sabbath
observance, and they imposed intolerable burdens on
ordinary folk. Yet despite their religiosity they 'loved
money', they were covetous men who wanted riches for

themselves. Little wonder our Lord responded with the story of the rich man and Lazarus, depicting the intolerable torment reserved for those who live solely for self-enrichment. Let modern Christians who put money-making high on their list of priorities and who, like the Pharisees, sometimes impose petty restrictions on others, take note.

About coveting other persons
The seventh commandment proscribes adultery or the possession of someone else's spouse. The eighth proscribes kidnapping or the wrongful depriving of someone of his or her freedom. The tenth hits at the underlying motivation that leads to both offences.

There is a very clear and challenging statement designating sexual covetousness as adultery. 'I tell you that anyone who looks at a woman lustfully' (literally, to desire — *epithumeo*) 'has already committed adultery with her in his heart' (Matthew 5:28). For our Lord adultery is not merely a matter of a wrongful physical union of male and female, but also of the desires for such a relationship, whether these are fulfilled or not. The man who has such a thought, who looks lustfully after a woman who is not his wife, has by that very thought committed a sin inwardly and that sin in God's sight is called adultery even if no physical union occurs.

Our Lord's emphasis is on the thoughts behind the look. He does not say that a man who looks at a woman has committed adultery. It is the man who looks lustfully, with a desire to possess a woman to whom he has no right, who sins. Since in other Scriptures women are given the same responsibilities as men in relation to marriage, it follows that a woman who lustfully looks at or entices a man is equally guilty before God. We need to avoid behaviour that produces a strong psychological/emotional dependence of male on female or female on male other than within marriage, because this so easily passes over into a situation where lustful desires arise. Such desires are covetous and are in themselves adulterous and can easily lead on to outward and physical adultery.

In the teaching of our Lord there is no obvious reference to the kind of coveting which leads to kidnapping and so to breach of that aspect of the eighth commandment.

Nevertheless, anything which would tend to prevent others from realizing their potential in freedom as persons would seem to be out of harmony with his teaching. The possessiveness that deprives a child of education in order to have his labour at home, in business or on the farm can be a form of exploitation based on selfish covetousness. Similarly, any pressure to prevent a son or daughter from contracting marriage imposes a bondage on that person and is really a selfish coveting of the child for the parent's own benefit.

About coveting power and prestige

The accumulation of wealth always brings with it a measure of power and prestige for the owner. Money talks; money gets things done. The man who pays the piper can call the tune and in the process others recognize his power and so give him the appropriate prestige. Desires for personal power or prestige are as dangerous as, and often underlie, those for possessions.

Clearly our Lord's disciples were desirous of power and prestige. It is recorded that on several occasions they discussed or argued about their position in the kingdom. Once Jesus, knowing the topic of their conversation, asked them what they had discussed as they journeyed. He got a response of silence, simply because they had been debating which of them was the greatest (Mark 9:34). On another occasion he had James and John asking him for the privilege of seats on his right hand and on his left hand in the glory of his kingdom (Mark 10:35–37). One wanted to be Prime Minister, the other Chancellor of the Exchequer! Both wanted position, power, prestige.

Our Lord's response to this kind of desire was kindly but firm. He reiterated and elaborated on earlier teaching that discipleship involved not self-aggrandizement but self-denial. 'If anyone would come after me, he must deny himself and take up his cross and follow me. For whoever wants to save his life will lose it, but whoever loses his life for me and for the gospel will save it. What good is it for a man to gain the whole world, yet forfeit his soul?' (Mark 8:34–36; cf. Matthew 10:38; Luke 14:27). Faced with the argument about who would be greatest, Jesus said, 'If anyone wants to be first, he must [shall] be the very last, and the servant of all' (Mark 9:35). What he meant was that ultimately God would bring down those who covet and who grasp after personal position. They would be like Lucifer who had covetously said, 'I will ascend to heaven; I will raise my throne above the stars of God . . . I will make myself like the Most High,' and whose fate was to be 'brought down to the grave, to the depths of the pit' (Isaiah 14:13—15).

In the case of James and John, our Lord asked if they were prepared to share his baptism of suffering, a question which drew from them the rather glib answer: 'We can' (Mark 10:39). With the hope of high office in their minds, they would be prepared to suffer a bit on the way! Jesus had not finished with them, however. They would indeed have their share of suffering but the promise of places at his right and his left hand he did not and could not make (vv. 39—40).

The other disciples quite naturally became angry with James and John. Presumably they felt that the two sons of Zebedee were trying to steal a march on them by obtaining a promise of position which would put them further down the promotion scale and in lower-ranking jobs. This showed that the others also coveted position and Jesus, sensing their anger, called the whole group together to teach them all that while grasping for position was the way of the world, it was not to be the way of his kingdom. 'You know', he said, 'that those who are regarded as rulers of the Gentiles lord it over them, and their high officials exercise authority over them. Not so with you. Instead, whoever wants to be great among you must be your servant, and whoever wants to be first must be slave of all' (Mark 10:42—44).

In all this Jesus himself was and is the supreme example of self-denial. He did not covet position. His remarks following the request of James and John concluded with the famous saying: 'For even the Son of man did not come to be served, but to serve, and to give his life as a ransom for many' (Mark 10:45). That was it. He did not come to be fussed around as one holding the centre of a power ring. He did not come to be served in the way potentates of earth are served. Rather he came deliberately to serve others and supremely to do so by giving his life for the redemption of men.

His washing of the disciples' feet was a case in point. He, the host, took the towel and basin provided in the upper room and proceeded to wash the disciples' feet. The disciples were no doubt embarrassed because they had neglected to obtain the services of a slave to perform the normal courtesies of such an occasion. Our Lord did what every one of them seems to have been unwilling to do: he put himself unhesitatingly in the position of the slave and gave himself in service that others would regard as menial and demeaning. Then he used the occasion to encourage similar attitudes in the disciples: 'Now that I, your Lord and Teacher, have washed your feet, you also should wash one another's feet. I have set you an example that you should do as I have done for you. I tell you the truth, no servant is greater than his master . . .' (John 13:14–16). The disciples evidently felt such a task was beneath the dignity they coveted for themselves. They were making themselves greater than their master, grasping position and power when they should have been giving themselves and their resources without reserve.

It is by serving others, by genuine unselfish service like that of the Lord, that men of the kingdom fulfil God's will. Self-giving, self-negation, rather than self-elevation is to be the dominant Christian motive.

About coveting through religion

Some people use religion, the Christian religion, evangelical Christian religion indeed, as a means by which to realize their covetous ambitions. They profess faith and go through the motions of serving God, but consciously or unconsciously, they seek to satisfy desires for possessions, prestige or power. The request of John and James for privileged positions in our Lord's kingdom would seem to indicate that to some degree they thought of discipleship as a means to get gain for themselves.

If we may go back to the Old Testament, we find that the book of Job deals with precisely this issue. The prologue (chapters 1 and 2) tells how in a mysterious council in heaven God permitted Satan to put Job's faith to the test. God had affirmed that Job was a man of excellent character and of genuine piety, but Satan retorted by asserting that

Job's faith and service were simply the expression of his covetousness. 'Does Job fear God for nothing?' was the question used to smear Job's reputation by implying that his devotion to God was not due to reverence, but to selfish desires to gain possessions and power. Let God remove Job's possessions and Job's faith would wilt and die, he would curse God to his face (Job 1:9—11).

God then permitted Satan to act against Job but not to touch his person (v. 12). In a series of calamities Job lost all that he possessed and his seven sons as well. Satan's ploy failed, however, for Job rather than cursing God fell down before him in worship (Job 1:20—21). Another round followed and as a result Job lost his health, being afflicted from head to foot with horrible sores. Again he refused to abandon his faith and showed convincingly that his religion was not a matter of coveting gain for himself. As he had received good at God's hand, he was now ready to receive adversity (Job 2:10).

A long dialogue ensued with a group of friends who came to comfort him but who, in a succession of speeches, did just the reverse, provoking him to say harsh things against themselves and against God. In the end Job met God in direct confrontation and had to confess the sin of the things he had been saying and pray for the friends with whom he had been so angry. Then God restored his fortunes and gave him twice as much as he had had originally (Job 42:10). This conformed to the Old Testament practice of restitution, under which a thief had to restore to his victim property double the value of what he had stolen (Exodus 22:4, 7). Job had been the victim of robbery and God in vindicating him ensured that he received the proper restitution of double what he had lost. That God so blessed Job means that in the long run Job became even more wealthy than he had been before, but it does not vitiate the thesis of the book that Job served God from a due and proper sense of reverence, and not because he was motivated by desires for personal gain.

The Lord Jesus came to the heart of this matter in the sermon on the mount when, as noted briefly earlier, he taught his disciples not to be anxious about the things of this life. Unbelieving Gentiles, he said, seek such things, but the believer knows that his heavenly Father knows his needs and can be relied upon to supply them. The Christian's duty, then, is to seek first God's kingdom and his righteousness. It is to put God and the things of God, his rule and his standards of right living, first and to desire those things that involve self-submission and self-negation rather than those that produce gain for himself. Our Lord followed this with a promise that the things his disciples need will in God's goodness be added to them: 'Seek first his kingdom and his righteousness, and all these things will be given to you as well' (Matthew 6:33).

While we can trust God to supply our needs, we are not to set our hearts on what he does supply or on earthly treasure of any kind. In the first instance such treasure is quite impermanent; it can decay or be stolen, whereas heavenly treasure is permanent and not subject to decay or theft. That treasure lasts not just for time but for eternity. In the second place the location of what a man treasures, of what he 'seeks first in life', in fact of what he desires or covets, settles the affection of his heart and the direction of his life: 'Where your treasure is, there your heart will be also' (Matthew 6:21).

The clear message of all this is that if we profess or practise religion with a view to obtaining personal gain, our treasure is on earth in that gain, and not in heaven as our religion or our religiosity would pretend. The heart of anyone who does so is fixed not on God, but on the things of earth. He serves not God but earthly gain. He cannot at one time serve both. Said Jesus, 'You cannot serve God and Money.' This highlights the close relationship of the tenth and first commandments. Covetousness for the things of earth, even if cloaked by religious profession, is an apostasy, an abandonment of the worship of God, a putting of another god before him.

What has just been said has an important implication for the preaching of the gospel, namely that it is no part of the preacher's business to tell people that faith in Christ will bring them earthly gain, whether that gain be presented in terms of health, wealth, power, prestige or whatever. Such preaching arouses and plays on motives for gain and, instead of drawing men to Christ, draws them after whatever kind of

gain is presented. It has disastrous results because those who
think that conversion will bring prosperity become dis-
illusioned, backslidden or apostate when they discover that
this is not the case.

Missionary work over the last two hundred years has
produced abundant evidence of the bane of a love of gain.
People in the under-developed world heard the gospel from
missionaries who appeared to be rich and well-equipped,
who had relatively advanced ways of living and considerable
technical know-how. Often the well-meaning missionaries
brought foreign funds and disbursed them as gifts or as
wages. It was the easiest thing in the world for their hearers
to think that if they espoused Christianity or added Christ
to their pantheon they would prosper like the white man
and soon possess some of his status symbols. The result was
a spate of what have been called 'rice Christians', people
responding to the gospel because of gain they hoped to
receive, because of things they coveted and thought the
new religion could provide. When they discovered that
prosperity was not automatic, many went back to paganism
and in many cases became opposed to the gospel.

In the writings of the apostles
Like our Lord, the apostolic writers of the New Testament
endorse the tenth commandment. They write to expose
and condemn covetousness and on a number of occasions
either cite or allude to the command itself.

The Epistle of James
James is one of the earlier books of the New Testament and
has been thought by some to have been the first to have
been written. It firmly attributes the troubles that beset
men to inordinate desires, lustings, covetings, which arise
inwardly, and which lead to both sin and stress.

Temptation to evil, James argues, comes not from God
but from a man's own desires: 'Each one is tempted when,
by his own evil desire, he is dragged away and enticed
(*epithumia*). Then, after desire (*epithumia* again) has conceived, it gives birth to sin; and sin, when it is full-grown,
gives birth to death' (James 1:14–15). He attributes
squabbling – 'fights and quarrels' – to desires occurring

within the readers. 'Don't they come', asks James, 'from your *desires* (*hedonōn* literally 'your pleasures') that battle within you?' Then he answers in the affirmative: 'You want something (*epithumeo*) but don't get it. You kill and covet (*zēloō*), but you cannot have what you want. You quarrel and fight' (James 4:1—2). We wonder if the early believers to whom James wrote actually descended to physical violence. Possibly he refers to heated disputes and divisions and exaggerates his words in order to make them see the seriousness of what they were doing. At any event, his main point is to pin down the source of the trouble in the wrong *desires* of those concerned. His reference earlier to an earthly wisdom involving selfish ambition (James 3:14—15) might indicate that covetous lust for position, power or prestige was one of their chief sins.

The testimony of Paul

Paul bears testimony in two distinct ways to the effect of this commandment in his own life. In the first place, he tells us that it had a part in his conversion, or at least in the processes of conviction associated with his conversion. The law of God, fairly clearly the ten commandments, was the one thing which had made him aware of sin, and to illustrate its force he cites the tenth: 'I would not have known what it was to covet if the law had not said, "Do not covet" ' (Romans 7:7—8). For Paul the law had been a tutor, a schoolmaster, showing him his need of Christ and as he looked back the command that came to his mind was the tenth. Perhaps as a pious Jew he could honestly claim to have kept the other laws at least to the letter, but here was one that he knew he had not kept, one before which he knew himself condemned, because it touched his inner motives in a deeper way than any other.

In the second place, Paul, as an apostle of Christ, claimed to have been free of covetousness in relation to his readers. He could tell the Thessalonians that when working among them he had not been putting on a mask to cover up greed. This was something they knew and of which God was witness. Neither had he been seeking praise from men, either from the Thessalonians or from others (1 Thessalonians 2:5—6). Similarly, in his farewell speech to the elders from Ephesus,

Paul could affirm inner integrity: 'I have not coveted anyone's silver or gold or clothing.' He could call his hearers as
witness that his actions were of the reverse order and that
his desires were to give to rather than to get from them
(Acts 20:33—34). He had toiled to support himself and to
help the weak, exemplifying an otherwise unrecorded saying
of Jesus: 'It is more blessed to give than to receive.' This
saying and Paul's reference to it tell us again that desires
for personal gain are at the wrong end of the scale for divine
approval. What God wants is the desire that gives possessions,
powers, position to others; not the desire that wants, that
covets these things for oneself.

The teachings of Paul
For Paul the keeping of this law was a matter of loving one's
neighbours. In affirming that Christians should love one
another he cites the seventh, the sixth, the eighth and the
tenth commandments, and says that they and any other
commandment are summed up in this sentence: 'Love your
neighbour as yourself.' 'Love' he goes on 'does no harm to
its neighbour' (Romans 13:9—10). True Christian love
(*agapē*) is not a selfish, not a getting, but a giving thing. It
gives concern and care to others and so will do them good
rather than harm. It excludes coveting after possessions,
persons or power. It cancels out anything that would harm
a neighbour. We cannot covet from those we love, for when
we covet we cease to love.

On a number of occasions Paul lists *greed* with the other
violations of the decalogue as marks of godless or unrighteous behaviour, and as excluding men from God's kingdom (Romans 1:29—32; 1 Corinthians 6:10; Ephesians
5:5). They are the baser earthly elements in human nature
that the Christian must put to death (Colossians 3:5—8).
Yet they can, and too often do, find a place in the life of a
professing Christian and may even call for the exercise of
spiritual discipline against him (1 Corinthians 5:11).

In one or two instances Paul makes more specific reference to the dangers of having a desire for money. He sees
the fact that men would be 'lovers of money' (*philarguros*
2 Timothy 3:2) as a mark of the apostasy he expected. He
urges that the only worthwhile gain for the Christian is a

godliness accompanied by real contentment of soul, an acceptance of God's provisions and a quiet trust in him to supply every need. He exposes the folly of the money-loving believer: 'People who want to get rich fall into temptation and a trap and into many foolish and harmful desires (*epithumia*) that plunge men into ruin and destruction' (1 Timothy 6: 9). For him any Christian who allows desires for wealth to dominate his life puts himself in the way of temptation and on a path that has taken, and is taking many others to destruction. This is because 'the love of money (*philarguria*) is a root of all kinds of evil', and because it is through eagerness (*oregō*) for money that some 'have wandered from the faith and pierced themselves with many griefs' (1 Timothy 6:10). Clearly Paul knew of some who had backslidden and whose inner lives were tortured by conflict as a result of allowing the desire for riches, the love of money, to have a prime place. Covetousness of this kind is ultimately destructive of faith. It puts wealth in the place of God; it is a form of idolatry, a violation of the first as well as of the tenth commandment.

The General Epistles
Two references call for notice. The first is in the Epistle to the Hebrews and is similar to Paul's advice to Timothy about the love of money: 'Keep your lives free from the love of money (be without *philarguria*) and be content with what you have, because God has said, "Never will I leave you; never will I forsake you"' (Hebrews 13:5). Again the point is that a proper faith in God renders the love or coveting of money unnecessary. The Christian is called to have other and better priorities than earthly possessions, prestige or power.

The second passage is 2 Peter 2:14–16 where the unrighteous are described as being 'experts in *greed*' (literally 'exercised or trained in greed – *pleonexia*) – by virtue of which they are designated 'an accursed brood'. Peter goes on: 'They have left the straight way and wandered off to follow the way of Balaam, son of Beor, who *loved the wages of wickedness.*' In other words, those who have hearts and minds exercised in covetousness, who are 'experts in greed', transgress before God as did

Balaam, whose story is recorded in Numbers 22–24. Peter
has no doubt about the seriousness of this sin. Balaam had
been specifically rebuked for his transgression, and by
implication those who are or who again become covetous
head for and deserve similar rebuke. They put themselves
among those who are under God's curse, 'an accursed
brood'.

The New Testament clearly, then, endorses the tenth
commandment. Indeed, it seems to lay more weight on it
than on any other, no doubt because it more than the others
focuses on man's inner motivation. It judges the desires of
the heart and shows that when men turn to other gods,
when they take God's name in vain or desecrate his day,
when they fail to honour their parents, when they murder,
commit adultery, steal or bear false witness, they do so
from an inward selfishness. They want gain of some kind
for themselves and so are putting self before God and before
their fellow men.

Our Lord and the apostles were not unconcerned with
outward acts of sin. Our study of the earlier commandments
has surely shown how thoroughly the breach of any of God's
laws was opposed. But in a very wonderful way, and with
more depth than the prophets and sages of old, Jesus emphasized the vital nature of inner motivation. The look, the
covetous look of lust is a sinful act of adultery, even if no
physical adultery occurs. Man's motivation, the group of
desires to which his acts give expression, comes under God's
judgement just as definitely as do those acts. Where the
motivation is a desire for gain of any kind – possessions,
prestige or power – in circumstances in which there is no
legal or moral entitlement, the tenth commandment is
broken and sin is committed. 'You shall not covet your
neighbour's house. You shall not covet your neighbour's
wife, or his manservant or maidservant, his ox or his donkey
or *anything* that belongs to your neighbour.'

The sin of our race

The tenth commandment focuses on the inner seat of

motivation in the human soul. It exposes the selfish desires for gain which lead to all manner of sins and which blight a man's relationship with God and with his fellows. Covetousness comes round full circle and stands alongside and virtually overlaps the first commandment. Covetousness, we are taught, is idolatry. It idolizes objects of desire and dethrones him whose right it is to rule and direct the life. It puts self and possessions before God. He who is covetous has another god than the Lord. He breaks the tenth and the first commandments.

Covetousness is very much with us. It is evident in every tribe and in every nation. It pervades every walk of life and all the strata of society. Few, if any, of us dare throw a stone at another, for covetousness is in all of us. We want possessions, houses and gadgets, cars and modern conveniences, and we are not content with what would be adequate for our needs. We want to keep up with, or outshine, the proverbial Joneses next door or along the street. We want position and feel hurt if friends or colleagues, bosses or those we supervise, do not give it to us. We want power and are jealous and envious of those who have it. In short, we covet. We lack that contentment, born of true godliness, which the Scriptures tell us is 'great gain'. We are not what we ought to be.

An incredible amount of theft takes place in industry and commerce. Materials and finished goods are purloined from factories and warehouses in small amounts or by the lorry load. Shops employ detectives and use detection devices, but cannot stop goods being removed by people who do not pay for them. Employees clock in or sign in on a job and proceed to fritter away time for which they get paid. In some cases they manipulate things so effectively that they get paid on occasions when they are not even present! Business telephones are used for unauthorized private calls for which no payment is made. Accounting records are fiddled by those in positions of trust and with the advent of computers large spoils are at stake. Expense accounts are blown up and tax returns dishonestly completed. Bribery to gain privileges or avoid penalties has become increasingly common. Social security benefits provided for the needy are abused to an alarming extent. There is cheating in examinations at school or college. There is cheating in sport and in the world of gambling that nowadays is so closely associated with it.

Gambling itself is a major industry. National and local governments run lotteries. Betting shops abound and will accept wagers on anything from horse racing to the result of an election. Casinos and other gaming facilities multiply. Men of business gamble on the purchase of stocks and shares or on the fluctuations of exchange rates between national currencies. Whatever the form, gambling is an attempt to gain wealth at the expense of others and without work. No service is rendered, no goods are exchanged, there is little serious use of the mind. Covetousness is its root.

The catalogue could be extended almost indefinitely. Our purpose, however, is to note that the practices we have listed, and a host of others, arise because man's heart is covetous. Men do these things because they have desires, lustful desires, for personal gain. They set themselves to acquire gain without ever having to expend effort or money. They want that to which they have no legal or moral entitlement, that which belongs to, or should belong to another, to a neighbour. They steal and they gamble because they first covet. This underlying coveting is simply selfishness working itself out in terms of desire and often also in terms of action. It is, in fact, man asserting himself over against his neighbours and over against God.

The materialism of the twentieth century provides an environment that fosters a covetous spirit. In no past age did people have the quantity of possessions they have today, yet they are rarely satisfied with what they have. Changes in design and style come so quickly that we constantly want to update and upgrade our possessions. Our living standards are rising and we feel we need a great deal of money to keep up with them. The more we have, the more we seem to want.

Conversations in homes and in cafes, in staff rooms and workshops often centre on possessions or the desire to obtain them. Society has structured itself in a pattern which enables groups of workers, a growing number of groups indeed, to hold a whole nation to ransom. The negotiation of wages on a national or regional basis and the amalgamation of smaller enterprises into large ones means that one dispute can spell paralysis and employers and government are virtually compelled to concede the claims of workers, if not in full, as nearly so as makes no difference. Power seems to reside with the workers, be they doctors or dockers, dentists or drivers, and they go out to get their wishes with little thought for the needs of other groups or of people who are in no way involved in their dispute. Indeed, often the emphasis is on differentials, one group of workers wanting to catch up on another and at the same time to keep ahead of those deemed to be of a lower grade.

An earlier chapter stressed the obligation resting on employers to pay fair and proper wages and to do so without delay. That responsibility is reiterated now. A covetous employer who holds back or keeps down wages for selfish gain is as much in breach of our commandment as anyone. But equally there is an obligation on employees, be they blue or white collar, to act responsibly and only to make wage demands commensurate with the value of work done and with the general level of wages at the time. So often the story is one of sheer greed and plain covetousness, with everybody reaping its ever-ripe fruit in terms of inflation and economic instability.

Plainly the great need is for a change of heart right across the board, for a new spirit of concern for the well-being of others, a willingness to tighten our belts and to deny ourselves some of the unnecessary luxuries in which we indulge. Human nature being what it is, it is hard to see such a change coming about without a mighty movement of the Spirit of God bringing multitudes into the kingdom and under the rule of Christ, and purifying those already in that kingdom of the covetousness that is still in them. With Isaiah we can, we must, pray, 'Oh, that you would rend the heavens and come down . . . to make your name known to your enemies, and cause the nations to quake before you!' (Isaiah 64:1—2).

The biblical answer to man's deep-seated malaise is twofold. First of all it urges a spirit of Christian contentment. The Lord Jesus put it negatively when he warned against anxiety for the things of this life: 'Do not worry, saying, "What shall we eat?" or "What shall we drink?" or "What shall we wear?" For the pagans run after all these things, and your heavenly Father knows that you need them. But seek first his kingdom and his righteousness and all these things will be given to you as well' (Matthew 6:31—33).

Jesus recognized that men have real needs, needs that must be met, but he was concerned lest his followers allow anxiety, even over legitimate needs, to dominate their lives. He wanted them to trust their heavenly Father totally and to be quietly confident in him. With such a confidence covetousness could have no place.

The apostle Paul was equally adamant in his first letter to Timothy: 'Godliness with contentment is great gain. For we brought nothing into the world, and we can take nothing out of it. But if we have food and clothing, we will be content with that. People who want to get rich fall into temptation and into a trap and into many foolish and harmful *desires* that plunge men into ruin and destruction. For the love of money is a root of all kinds of evil. Some people, eager for money, have wandered from the faith and pierced themselves with many griefs. But you, man of God, flee from all this [the love of money, the discontented desire for possessions], and pursue righteousness, godliness, faith, love, endurance and gentleness' (1 Timothy 6:6–11).

The point is that the Christian is to have a different set of values from those of his unregenerate past. He is to be primarily desirous, not of personal wealth, but of spiritual and moral qualities like righteousness and love. He is to aim at, to desire, these things and avoid the love, the coveting, of wealth. As the Lord Jesus put it, a choice has to be made between God and money. We can serve one or the other, but not both at the same time. God's requirement is that we serve him and desire his truths and his values and thus be content as his children.

Few of us seem to have and enjoy this contentment born of a trust which takes God at his word and believes he will not fail. Instead we are engulfed in the rat race, coveting bigger wage packets or attractive promotion. It is high time we allowed the Word of God, and in particular the tenth commandment, to stand in judgement over us.

Covetousness is idolatry, a challenge to the rightful sovereignty of the Lord. It dethrones him in the life of everyone who indulges in it. Let us, then, see to it that this vice is given no quarter in our hearts.

'You shall not covet . . .'